The Rites of the Catholic Church

as Revised by the

Second Vatican Ecumenical Council

Volume Two

The Roman Ritual and Pontifical
revised by
Decree of the Second Vatican Ecumenical Council
and published by authority of Pope Paul VI
and Pope John Paul II

THE RITES

OF THE

CATHOLIC CHURCH

VOLUME TWO

Prepared by the
International Commission on English in the Liturgy
A Joint Commission of Catholic Bishops' Conferences

Approved for use in the
Dioceses of the United States of America by the
National Conference of Catholic Bishops
and confirmed
by the Apostolic See

STUDY EDITION

A PUEBLO BOOK

The Liturgical Press   Collegeville, Minnesota

1991

Concordat cum originali:
Ronald F. Krisman, Executive Director
Secretariat for the Liturgy
National Conference of Catholic Bishops

Published by authority of the Committee on the Liturgy,
National Conference of Catholic Bishops

All the liturgical texts in this volume have been approved by the
National Council of Catholic Bishops and confirmed by the
Apostolic See.

Design: Frank Kacmarcik

ISBN: 0-8146-6037-1

Printed in the United States of America.

CONTENTS

Blessing of Objects and Places 325

PREFACE

This volume is primarily a collection of the liturgical rites and texts which constitute a part of the Roman Pontifical as revised by mandate of the Second Vatican Council.[1] Additional rites have been added from the Roman Ritual to complete this collection. The individual rites were revised and published in Latin by Pope Paul VI and Pope John Paul II during the period from 1963 to 1984.

The English version of the Latin texts has been prepared by the International Commission on English in the Liturgy, a Joint Commission of Catholic Bishops' Conferences, established in 1964 for this purpose. This version has been approved by the various conferences of bishops and is published by authority of those conferences and is thus the official and authentic text for the dioceses of the respective territories.[2]

On October 25, 1973, Pope Paul VI reserved to himself the power to approve directly all the translations into the vernacular of the sacramental forms.[3] In the case of English and other major languages the approbation is given by the Congregation for Divine Worship and the Discipline of the Sacraments after consultation with the conferences of bishops. Thus, in this volume those parts of the sacramental form of orders (for the ordination of deacons, priests, and bishops) "which belong to the nature of the rite and are consequently required for validity"[4] have been directly approved by the Apostolic See (rather than being approved by the respective conferences of bishops and confirmed by the Apostolic See).[5]

ORDINATION OF DEACONS, PRIESTS, AND BISHOPS

With the suppression of the canonical institute of tonsure,[6] a new rite was created for admission to candidacy for ordination as deacons and priests, in accord with the apostolic letter of Paul VI, *Ad pascendum.*[7] This letter, which also provides for a rite of commitment to celibacy on the part of unmarried men who are candidates for the order of deacons, is printed in this volume before the rite of admission to candidacy.

The rite of admission was issued by decree of the Congregation for Divine Worship, dated December 3, 1972.[8] (The commitment

to celibacy for unmarried candidates for the diaconate, referred
to in the decree, has been incorporated into the rite of ordination
of deacons.)

Next, an English translation is given of the apostolic constitution
of Paul VI, *Pontificalis Romani,*[9] in which the new rites are approved and the essential forms and matter for the sacrament of
orders are determined for the Latin Church.

The Latin text of the several rites of ordination, prepared by the
Consilium for the Implementation of the Constitution on the Liturgy, was issued by decree of the Congregation of Rites, August
15, 1968.[10]

INSTITUTION OF MINISTERS AND BLESSING OF PERSONS

These ministries were established by Paul VI by the apostolic letter *Ministeria quaedam.*[11] The new ministries, which are now carried out by lay persons, replace the corresponding minor orders,
which were suppressed along with tonsure and subdiaconate;
the two ministries are also to be exercised by candidates for ordination, either before or after they are admitted to candidacy for
holy orders. (In the apostolic letter provision was also made for
the restoration or establishment of other lay ministries, in addition to the two ministries common to the Latin Church.)

The Latin text of the rites of institution or blessing of readers and
acolytes was issued by decree of the Congregation for Divine
Worship dated December 3, 1972.[12]

This section of the book also contains rites for the blessing of persons who are publicly consecrated to God.

The first series of blessing are taken from the American edition
of the *Book of Blessings* which was authorized for use in the
United States of America by decree of the National Conference
of Bishops on March 19, 1989. Blessings are provided for individ-
uals who exercise pastoral care in a parish or other community
or for those who have a special liturgical ministry in the community, that is, readers, altar servers, sacristans, musicians, ushers,
and extraordinary ministers of holy communion.

In addition to these blessings there are others that are concerned
with a particular state of life.

Among these rites is the traditional consecration of unmarried women to the life of religious virginity. The revision, which has been formally decreed by the Second Vatican Council,[13] was published by the decree of the Congregation for Divine Worship, May 31, 1970,[14] not only for nuns but also for individual consecrated women who do not live in religious communities.[15]

The decree of promulgation explains the development of the venerable rite in this way: "The rite for the consecration of virgins is one of the most treasured in the Roman liturgy. Consecrated virginity is among the most excellent gifts bequeathed by our Lord to his Bride, the Church. From apostolic times women have dedicated their virginity to God, so adding to the beauty of the mystical body of Christ and making it fruitful in grace. Even from the earliest times, as the Fathers of the Church bear witness, mother Church in her wisdom set her seal on this high vocation by her practice of consecrating those who followed it by means of a solemn prayer. This prayer, enriched in the course of time by other ritual elements to bring out more clearly the symbolism of virginity in relation to the Church, the Bride of Christ, was incorporated into the Roman Pontifical."

The commitment of men and women to the evangelical counsels and to a common life in a religious community has been an essential part of the Church's life. The *Rite of Religious Profession* was promulgated on February 2, 1970 as a portion of the revised Roman Ritual. This revision is a direct response to the mandate of the Second Vatican Council which requested "That a rite of religious profession and renewal of vows be drawn up that would contribute greater unity, simplicity, and dignity and that, apart from exceptions in particular law, it should be adopted by those who make their profession or renewal of vows within Mass (art. 80)."

Two other rites in this part of the volume are for the blessing of an abbot of a monastery of men and the blessing of an abbess of a monastery of women. In the decree of the Congregation for Divine Worship, dated November 9, 1970,[16] by which the Latin text was published, the following explanation of the rites is given: "The blessing, after canonical election, of an abbot or an abbess of a monastery is a traditional rite in the Church's liturgy. The whole religious community is then seen praying for God's grace to come upon the person they have chosen to lead them along the way to perfection. In the course of the centuries this rite took on different forms for different times and places. In our own day, therefore, it seems fitting that these traditional rites should be revised by removing from them what no longer suits our modern mentality so that they may express more clearly the spiritual responsibilities of the head of a religious family."

BLESSING OF OBJECTS AND PLACES

One of the most important blessings that annually occurs in the life of the Church is the blessing of the oil of the sick and the oil of catechumens and the consecration of chrism. The revised rite for these blessings was promulgated on December 3, 1970 by the Congregration for Divine Worship. Although the oil of the sick and oil of catechumens may be blessed by a priest, the consecration of the chrism, according to ancient tradition, is reserved to the bishop, who is assisted by his presbyters for this solemn rite.

On May 29, 1977, the Congregation for the Sacraments and Divine Worship published the revised rite of Dedication of a Church and an Altar. The decree notes that this "is properly considered among the most solemn liturgical services." The building where the community gathers to worship is an image of the Church itself, which is God's temple built from living stones. The first six chapters provide the community with rites to be celebrated at the time of the laying of a foundation stone or commencement of work on the building, the dedication of a church and altar, or the blessing of a church and altar. The seventh chapter presents the revised rite for the blessing of a chalice and paten. The rite clearly states that these vessels, intended solely and permanently for the celebration of the eucharist, are blessed and become sacred by their use.

The Congregation for the Sacraments and Divine Worship issued the final rite contained in this book, *The Order of Crowning and Image of the Blessed Virgin Mary,* on March 25, 1981. This rite is for use by the bishop when he wishes to honor images of the Blessed Virgin Mary which are the object of special veneration by the faithful of the diocese. The Order contains the rites for crowning an image of the Blessed Virgin Mary within Mass (Chapter 1), within Evening Prayer (Chapter 2), and within a celebration of the Word of God (Chapter 3).

In the several decrees referred to above, the day on which the respective rite was to have been put into effect (in the Latin version) is determined, either as a specified day or simply upon publication of the rite. The English and other vernacular versions are to be put into effect on the day determined by the respective conferences of bishops, after they have approved translations and received confirmation from the Apostolic See.

[1] Const. on the liturgy nos. 25, 71, 76, 80.

[2] See Const. on the liturgy, no. 36, 3-4.

[3] Congregation for Divine Worship, circular letter of the Secretary of State: *AAS* 66 (1974): 98-99.

[4] Paul VI, apostolic constitution *Pontificalis Romani*, June 18, 1968: *AAS* 60 (1968): 372-373.

[5] See Const. on the liturgy, no. 36, 3.

[6] Paul VI, motu proprio *Ministeria quaedam*, August 15, 1972: *AAS* 64 (1972): 529-534.

[7] Motu propio, August 15, 1972: *AAS* 64 (1972): 534-540.

[8] *AAS* 65 (1973): 274-275.

[9] June 18, 1968: *AAS* 60 (1968): 369-373.

[10] The text of the decree, which was not published in *AAS*, is found in the Latin edition of the rites, *De Ordinatione Diaconi, Presbyteri, et Episcopi.*

[11] Motu proprio, August 15, 1972: *AAS* 64 (1972): 529-534.

[12] *AAS* 65 (1973): 274-275.

[13] Const. on the liturgy, no. 80.

[14] *AAS* 62 (1970): 650.

[15] See introduction, no. 5.

[16] *AAS* 63 (1971): 710-711.

ORDINATION OF DEACONS,
PRIESTS, AND BISHOPS

ORDINATION OF DEACONS, PRIESTS, AND BISHOPS

CHAPTER III
ORDINATION OF A PRIEST

CHAPTER VI
TEXTS FOR USE IN ORDINATION

Readings

Litany of the Saints

APOSTOLIC LETTER

ISSUED *MOTU PROPRIO* LAYING DOWN CERTAIN NORMS REGARDING THE HOLY ORDER OF DEACONS

POPE PAUL VI

For the nurture and constant increase of the people of God, Christ the Lord instituted in the Church a variety of ministries that work for the good of the whole Body.[1]

Since the apostolic age itself the diaconate had had a distinctive and superior rank among these ministries and has always been held in great honor by the Church. Explicit testimony of this is given by the Apostle St. Paul both in his Letter to the Philippians, in which he sends his greetings not only to the bishops but also to the deacons,[2] and in his Letter to Timothy, in which he highlights the qualities and virtues that deacons must have in order to be proved worthy of their own ministry.[3]

Later, when the early writers of the Church acclaim the dignity of deacons, they do not fail to extol also the spiritual qualities and virtues required for the carrying out of that ministry, namely, fidelity to Christ, moral integrity, and obedience to the bishop.

St. Ignatius of Antioch declares that the office of the deacon is none other than "the ministry of Jesus Christ, who was with the Father before all ages and has been manifested in the final time."[4] He also remarks: "The deacons too, who are ministers of the mysteries of Jesus Christ, should please all in every way, for they are not servers of food and drink, but ministers of the Church of God."[5]

St. Polycarp of Smyrna exhorts deacons to be "disciplined in all things, merciful, diligent, walking according to the truth

---

[1]See LG no. 18: AAS 57 (1965) 21–22; ConstDecrDecl 124.
[2]See Phil 1:1.
[3]See 1 Tm 3:8–13.
[4]Ignatius of Antioch, *Ad Magnesios* 4, 1: Funk PA 1, 235.
[5]*Idem, Ad Trallianos* 2, 3: Funk PA 1, 245.

of the Lord, who became the servant of all."[6] The author of
the *Didascalia Apostolorum*, recalling the words of Christ,
"Anyone who wants to be great among you must be your
servant,"[7] addresses the following fraternal exhortation to
deacons: "Accordingly you deacons also should act in such a
way that, if there should be a need that calls on you even to
lay down your life for someone, you would do so. . . . If the
Lord of heaven and earth served us and suffered and sustained everything on our behalf, should we not do this all
the more for others, since we are imitators of him and have
been given the place of Christ?[8]

When moreover the writers of the first centuries give instruction on the importance of the diaconal ministry, they offer
many examples of the manifold important duties entrusted
to deacons and clearly show how much authority they pos-
sessed in the Christian communities and how great their
contribution was to the apostolate. The deacon is described
as "the ear, mouth, heart, and soul of the bishop."[9] The deacon is at the service of the bishop in order that the bishop
may serve the whole people of God and take care of the sick
and the poor;[10] he is correctly and rightly called "one who
shows love for orphans, for the devout and for the widowed,
one who is fervent in spirit, one who shows love for what is
good."[11] Furthermore, he is entrusted with the duty of taking the eucharist to the sick confined to their homes,[12] of
conferring baptism,[13] and of attending to preaching the word
of God in accordance with the will and intention of the
bishop.

Accordingly, the diaconate flourished in a wonderful way in
the Church and at the same time gave an outstanding witness of love for Christ and for neighbor through the perform-

[6]Polycarp of Smyrna, *Ep. ad Philippenses* 5, 2: Funk PA 1, 301–303.
[7]Mt 20:26–27.
[8]*Didascalia Apostolorum* 3, 13, 2–4: Funk DidConst 1, 214.
[9]Ibid. 2, 44, 4: Funk DidConst 1, 138.
[10]See *Traditio Apostolica* 39 and 34: B. Botte, ed., *La Tradition Apostolique de
Saint Hippolyte, Essai de reconstruction* (Münster, 1963) 87 and 81.
[11]*Testamentum D. N. Iesu Christi* 1, 38: I. E. Rahmani, ed. and tr. (Mainz,
1899) 93.
[12]See Justin Martyr, *Apologia* 1, 65, 5 and 67, 5: G. Rauschen, ed., *S. Iustini
Apologiae duae* (2nd ed., Bonn, 1911) 107 and 111.
[13]See Tertullian, *De Baptismo* 17, 1: CCL, *Tertulliani Opera*, Part 1 (1954) 291.

ance of works of charity,[14] the celebration of sacred rites,[15] and in pastoral service.[16]

Exercise of the office of deacon enabled those who were to become presbyters to give proof of themselves, to display the merit of their work, and to acquire preparation—all of which were requirements for receiving the dignity of the priesthood and the office of pastor.

As time went on, the discipline concerning this holy order was changed. The prohibition against conferring ordination without observing the established sequence of orders was strengthened, but there was a gradual decrease in the number of those who, instead of advancing to a higher order, preferred to remain deacons all their lives. As a consequence, the permanent diaconate almost entirely disappeared in the Latin Church. It is hardly necessary to mention what was decreed by the Council of Trent when it proposed to restore the sacred orders in accordance with their own nature as ancient functions within the Church.[17] But it was only much later that the idea matured of restoring this important order also as a truly permanent rank. Our predecessor Pius XII briefly alluded to this matter.[18] Finally, Vatican Council II supported the wishes and requests that, where this would lead to the good of souls, the permanent diaconate should be restored as an intermediate order between the higher ranks of the Church's hierarchy and the rest of the people of God. The permanent diaconate was meant to be an expression of the needs and desires of the Christian communities, a driving force for the Church's service or *diakonia* toward the local Christian communities, and a sign or sacrament of the Lord Christ himself, who "came not to be served but to serve."[19]

---

[14]See *Didascalia Apostolorum* 2, 31, 2: Funk DidConst 1, 112. See also *Testamentum D. N. Iesu Christi* 1, 31: I. E. Rahmani, ed. and tr. (Mainz, 1899) 75.
[15]See *Didascalia Apostolorum* 2, 57, 6 and 58, 1: Funk DidConst 1, 162, 166.
[16]See Cyprian, *Epistolae* 15 and 16: G. Hartel, ed. (Vienna, 1871) 513–520. See also Augustine, *De catechizandis rudibus* 1, cap. 1, 1: PL 40, 309–310.
[17]See Council of Trent, sess. 23, cap. 1–4: Mansi 33, 138–140.
[18]See Pius XII, Address to participants in the second meeting of Catholics from around the world, on the lay apostolate, Rome, 5 Oct. 1957: AAS 49 (1957) 925.
[19]Mt 20:28.

For this reason, at the third session of the Council, in October 1964, the Fathers ratified the principle of the restoration of the diaconate and in the following November the Dogmatic Constitution *Lumen gentium* was promulgated. In article 29 of this document a description is given of the principal characteristics proper to that state: "At a lower level of the hierarchy are deacons, who receive the laying on of hands 'not unto priesthood but only for a ministry of service.' Strengthened by sacramental grace, they have as their service for the people of God, in communion with the bishop and the presbyterate, the *diakonia* of liturgy, word, and charity."[20]

The same Constitution made the following declaration about permanency in the rank of deacon: "As the discipline of the Latin Church currently stands, these diaconal functions, supremely necessary to the Church's life, can be carried out in many places only with great difficulty. Henceforth, therefore, it will be permissible to restore the diaconate as a distinct and permanent rank of the hierarchy."[21]

This restoration of the permanent diaconate required however that the instructions of the Council be more profoundly examined and that there be mature deliberation concerning the juridical status of both the celibate and the married deacon. Similarly, it was necessary that matters connected with the diaconate of those who are to become priests should be adapted to contemporary conditions, so that the time of diaconate would furnish the proof of way of life, of maturity, and of aptitude for the priestly ministry that ancient discipline demanded from candidates for the presbyterate.

Thus on 18 June 1967, we issued the Motu Proprio *Sacrum Diaconatus Ordinem*, by which suitable canonical norms for the permanent diaconate were established.[22] On 17 June of the following year, through the Apostolic Constitution *Pontificalis Romani recognitio*,[23] we authorized the new rite for the conferring of the sacred orders of deacons, presbyters, and bishops and at the same time defined the matter and the form of the ordination itself.

Now that we are proceeding further as today we promulgate

[20]LG no. 29 [DOL 4 no. 149].
[21]LG no. 29 [DOL 4 no. 149].
[22]See DOL 309.
[23]See DOL 324 [dated, 18 June 1968].

the Motu Proprio *Ministeria quaedam,* we consider it advisable to issue certain norms concerning the diaconate. We also desire that candidates for the diaconate should know what ministries they are to exercise before ordination and when and under what considerations they are to take upon themselves the obligations of celibacy and liturgical prayer.

Since entrance into the clerical state is deferred until diaconate, there no longer exists the rite of first tonsure, by which a layman used to become a cleric. But a new rite is introduced by which one who aspires to ordination as deacon or presbyter publicly manifests his will to offer himself to God and the Church, so that he may exercise a sacred order. The Church in accepting this offering chooses and calls him to prepare himself to receive a sacred order. In this way he is properly admitted into the ranks of candidates for the diaconate or presbyterate.

There is a particular reason why the ministries of reader and acolyte should be entrusted to those who, as candidates for sacred orders, desire to devote themselves to God and to the Church in a special way. For the Church, which "never ceases to receive the bread of life from the table both of God's word and of Christ's body and to offer it to the faithful,"[24] considers it to be very advantageous that, both by study and by gradual exercise of the ministry of the word and of the altar, candidates for sacred orders should through intimate contact understand and reflect on the double aspect of the priestly office. The result is that the genuineness of ministry becomes especially striking: the candidates are to approach holy orders fully aware of their vocation, "fervent in spirit, serving the Lord . . . constant in prayer, and aware of the needs of the faithful."[25]

We have weighed every aspect of the question thoroughly, sought the opinion of experts, consulted with the conferences of bishops and taken their views into account; we have taken counsel with our esteemed brothers who are members of the sacred congregations competent in this matter. By our apostolic authority we therefore decree the following norms, amending, if and insofar as is necessary, the provisions of the Code of Canon Law now in force, and we promulgate them with this Motu Proprio.

[24]DV no. 21 [DOL 14 no. 224].
[25]Rom 12:11–13.

1. a) A rite is hereby introduced for the admission of candidates for ordination as deacons and presbyters. In order that this admission be properly made, the free petition of the aspirant, drawn up and signed by his own hand, is required, as well as the acceptance by the competent ecclesiastical superior given in writing, through which the election by the Church is effected.

Professed members of clerical religious institutes who are preparing for the priesthood are not bound to this rite.

b) The competent superior for this acceptance is the Ordinary (the bishop and, in clerical institutes of perfection, the major superior). Those can be accepted who give signs of an authentic vocation and, endowed with good moral qualities and free from mental and physical defects, wish to dedicate their lives to the service of the Church for the glory of God and the good of souls. It is necessary that those who aspire to the transitional diaconate already have completed at least their twentieth year and have begun their course of theological studies.

c) In virtue of being accepted, the candidate must care for his vocation in a special way and deepen it. He also acquires the right to the necessary spiritual assistance by which he can develop his vocation and submit unconditionally to the will of God.

2. Candidates for the permanent diaconate and for the transitional diaconate, as well as candidates for the presbyterate itself, are to receive the ministries of reader and acolyte, unless they have already done so, and are to exercise them for a suitable period, in order to be better disposed for the future service of the word and of the altar.

Dispensation from receiving these ministries on the part of such candidates is reserved to the Holy See.

3. The liturgical rites by which admission of candidates for ordination as deacons and presbyters takes place and by which the aforementioned ministries are conferred should be performed by the Ordinary of the aspirant (the bishop and, in clerical institutes of perfection, the major superior).

4. The intervals (interstices) established by the Holy See or by the conferences of bishops between the conferring, during the course of theological studies, of the ministry of readers and that of acolytes, and between the ministry of acolytes and the order of deacons, must be observed.

5. Before ordination candidates for the diaconate shall give to the Ordinary (the bishop and, in clerical institutes of perfection, the major superior) a declaration drawn up and signed in their own hand, by which they testify that they are about to receive the order freely and of their own accord.

6. The special consecration to celibacy observed for the sake of the kingdom of heaven and its obligation for candidates to the priesthood and for unmarried candidates to the diaconate are in truth connected with the diaconate. The public commitment to celibacy before God and the Church is to be celebrated, even by religious, in a special rite, which is to precede ordination to the diaconate. Celibacy taken on in this way is a diriment impediment to entering marriage.

In accordance with the traditional discipline of the Church, a married deacon who has lost his wife cannot (*inhabiles sunt*) enter a new marriage.[26]

7. a) Deacons called to the presbyterate are not to be ordained until they have completed the course of studies prescribed by the norms of the Apostolic See.
b) In regard to the course of theological studies to precede the ordination of permanent deacons, the conferences of bishops, with attention to the local situation, will issue the proper norms and submit them for the approval of the Congregation for Catholic Education.

8. In conformity with the General Instruction of the Liturgy of the Hours nos. 29–30:
a) Deacons called to the priesthood are obliged by reason of their ordination to celebrate the liturgy of the hours.
b) It is most fitting that permanent deacons should each day recite at least a part of the liturgy of the hours, to be determined by the conference of bishops.

[26]See Paul VI. Motu Proprio *Proprio Sacrum Diaconatus Ordinem* no. 16: AAS 59 (1967) 701.

9. Entrance into the clerical state and incardination into a diocese are brought about by ordination to the diaconate.

10. The rite of admission as candidates for ordination to the diaconate and priesthood and of the special consecration of celibacy will be published soon by the competent department of the Roman Curia.

Transitional Norms: Candidates for the sacrament of orders who have already received first tonsure before the promulgation of this Motu Proprio retain all the duties, rights, and privileges of clerics. Those who have been promoted to the order of subdiaconate are held to the obligations taken on in regard to both celibacy and the liturgy of the hours. But they must celebrate once again their public commitment to celibacy before God and the Church by the new special rite preceding ordination to the diaconate.

All the matters decreed by us in this Letter, issued *motu proprio*, we order to be confirmed and ratified, anything to the contrary notwithstanding. We also determine their effective date to be 1 January 1973.

Given in Rome, at St. Peter's, 15 August 1972, the Solemnity of the Assumption, the tenth year of our pontificate.

Paul VI

CHAPTER I

ADMISSION TO CANDIDACY FOR ORDINATION AS DEACONS AND PRIESTS

INTRODUCTION

1. The rite of admission to candidacy for ordination as deacons and priests is celebrated when there is clear evidence that the aspirants' properly formed intention has sufficiently matured.

Those who have made profession in a clerical religious institute are not bound to the celebration of this rite.

2. The aspirants must make a public expression of the intention to receive holy orders. The bishop, in turn, or the major superior of a clerical religious institute, gives the public acceptance of this intention.

3. The rite of admission may be celebrated on any day, but preferably on the greater feast days, in a church or other suitable place and either within Mass or at a celebration of the word of God. Because of its character this rite is never combined with ordinations or with the institution of readers or of acolytes.

LITURGY OF THE WORD

4. The readings are taken, in whole or in part, from the liturgy of the day or, alternatively, from the texts suggested below.

CELEBRATION OF ADMISSION

HOMILY

5. After the gospel, the bishop, wearing his miter, sits, and gives the homily, which he concludes with these or similar words:

Dear brethren in Christ, our brothers stand here today in the presence of the Church, recommended to us and to you for admission among the candidates for holy orders.

Christ gave this command: "Ask the Lord of the harvest to send laborers into his harvest." Our brothers know the Lord's concern for his flock, they see the needs of the Church, and they feel ready to respond generously to the Lord in the words of the prophet: "Here I am, send me forth." They put their hope in the Lord, trusting that they may answer his call faithfully.

This call from the Lord should be recognized and understood from the daily signs which reveal God's will to men of discernment. When God chooses men to share in the ordained priesthood of Christ, he moves and helps them by his grace. At the same time, he entrusts us with the task of calling suitable and approved candidates and of consecrating them by a special seal of the Holy Spirit to the ministry of God and of the Church. By the sacrament of holy orders they will be appointed to share in the ministry of salvation that Christ accomplished in the world. When the time comes, they will be given a part in our ministry of service to the Church, and build up by word and sacrament the Christian communities to which they will be sent.

Our brothers here have already begun their preparation so that later they may be called to ordination by the bishop. Day by day they will learn to live the life of the Gospel and deepen their faith, hope, and love. In the practice of these virtues they will gain the spirit of prayer and grow in zeal to win the world to Christ.

Urged on by his love and strengthened by the Holy Spirit, they have come here to declare in public their desire to bind themselves to the service of God and of mankind.

When each one is called by name, he should come forward and declare his intention before the Church assembled here.

CALLING OF THE CANDIDATES

6. The appointed deacon or priest calls the candidates by name. Each one answers: **Present,** and goes to the bishop, before whom he makes a sign of reverence.

EXAMINATION

7. Then the bishop speaks to the candidates in these words or in others which the conference of bishops may determine:

My sons, the pastors and teachers in charge of your formation, and others who know you, have given a favorable account of you, and we have full confidence in their testimony.

In response to the Lord's call are you resolved to complete your preparation so that in due time you will be ready to be ordained for the ministry of the Church?
Together the candidates answer: **I am.**

The bishop:
Are you resolved to prepare yourselves in mind and spirit to give faithful service to Christ the Lord and his body, the Church?
The candidates: **I am.**

ACCEPTANCE OF THE CANDIDATES

If it wishes, the conference of bishops may determine the manner in which the bishop is to accept the candidates.

The bishop adds:
The Church receives your declaration with joy. May God who has begun the good work in you bring it to fulfillment.
All: **Amen.**

INVITATION TO PRAYER

8. Then all stand, and the bishop, without his miter, invites the people to pray:

Brothers and sisters, let us ask our God and Lord to pour out his grace and blessing on these servants of his

who desire to give their lives to the ministry of the Church.

INTERCESSIONS

9. The deacon or another qualified minister proposes the following intentions or others adapted to the circumstances. All respond with an appropriate acclamation.

Deacon or minister:
That our brothers may draw closer to Christ and be his witnesses in the world, let us pray to the Lord:
℟. **Lord, hear our prayer.**

Deacon or minister:
That they may share the burdens of others and always listen to the voice of the Holy Spirit, let us pray to the Lord:
℟. **Lord, hear our prayer.**

Deacon or minister:
That they may become ministers of the Church who will strengthen the faith of their brothers and sisters by word and example, and gather them together to share in the eucharist, let us pray to the Lord:
℟. **Lord, hear our prayer.**

CONCLUDING PRAYER

10. The bishop continues:

Lord,
hear our prayers for your sons
who wish to dedicate themselves
to your service and the service of your people
in the sacred ministry.
Bless them ✠ in your fatherly love,
that they may persevere in their vocation,
and through their loving fidelity to Christ the Priest
be worthy to carry out
the Church's apostolic mission.

We ask this through Christ our Lord.
℟. **Amen.**

Or:
**Lord,
help your servants
to understand and live the mystery of your love
more completely every day.
Deepen their sense of purpose
as they prepare for the sacred ministry of the Church
and fill them with the spirit of your love
so that they may be wholehearted
in bringing salvation to mankind
for the glory of your name.**

**We ask this through Christ our Lord.
℟. Amen.**

LITURGY OF THE EUCHARIST

11. If the rite of admission takes place during Mass, the celebration continues as usual. If it takes place during a celebration of the word, the bishop blesses the assembly and dismisses it in the usual way.

APOSTOLIC CONSTITUTION

APPROVAL OF NEW RITES FOR THE ORDINATION OF DEACONS, PRESBYTERS, AND BISHOPS

PAUL, BISHOP

Servant of the Servants of God for an Everlasting Memorial

The revision of the Roman Pontifical is prescribed in a general way by the Second Vatican Ecumenical Council[1] and is also governed by the specific conciliar directive ordering the revision of "both the ceremonies and texts" of the ordination rites.[2]

Among the rites of ordination the first to be considered are those that constitute the hierarchy through the sacrament of orders, conferred in its several degrees. "The divinely established ecclesiastical ministry is exercised at different levels by those who from antiquity have been called bishops, presbyters, and deacons."[3]

The revision of the rites for ordinations is to follow the general principles that must direct the entire reform of the liturgy according to the decrees of Vatican Council II. But in addition a supreme criterion for that revision must be the clear teaching of the Dogmatic Constitution on the Church concerning the nature and effects of the sacrament of orders. This teaching must of course receive expression through the liturgy itself in its own way, because "the texts and rites should be so drawn up that they express more clearly the holy things they signify and that the Christian people, as far as possible, are able to understand them with ease and to take part in the rites fully, actively, and as befits a community."[4]

The Council teaches that episcopal consecration bestows the fullness of the sacrament of orders, that fullness of power, namely, which in both the Church's liturgical practice and the language of the Fathers is called the high priesthood, the summit of the sacred ministry. But episcopal consecration,

[1] See SC art. 25 [DOL 1 no. 25].
[2] SC art. 76 [DOL 1 no. 76].
[3] LG no. 28 [DOL 4 no. 148].
[4] SC art. 21 [DOL 1 no. 21].

together with the office of sanctifying, also confers the offices of teaching and governing, offices that of their very nature can be exercised only in hierarchic communion with the head of the college and its members. For from tradition, expressed especially in liturgical rites and in the usage of the Church of both East and West, it is clear that the laying on of hands and the words of consecration bestow the grace of the Holy Spirit and impress a sacred character in such a way that bishops in an eminent and visible way carry on the role of Christ himself as teacher, shepherd, and high priest and act in his person.[5]

To these words must be added a number of important doctrinal points concerning the apostolic succession of bishops and their functions and duties. Even if these themes are already present in the rite of episcopal consecration, it still seems that they must be better and more precisely expressed. To ensure this, it was judged appropriate to take from ancient sources the consecratory prayer that is found in the document called the *Apostolic Tradition of Hippolytus of Rome*, written at the beginning of the third century. This consecratory prayer is still used, in large part, in the ordination rites of the Coptic and West Syrian liturgies. Thus in the very act of ordination there is a witness to the harmony of tradition in East and West concerning the apostolic office of bishops.

With regard to presbyters, the following should be especially recalled from the acts of the Council: "Even though they do not possess the fullness of the priesthood and in the exercise of their power are subordinate to the bishops, priests are nevertheless linked to the bishops in priestly dignity. By virtue of the sacrament of orders, in the image of Christ the eternal High Priest (see Heb 5:1–10 and 7–24, 9:11–28), they are consecrated to preach the Gospel, to shepherd the faithful, and to celebrate divine worship as true priests of the New Testament."[6] Elsewhere the Council says: "By ordination and the mission they receive from the bishops, presbyters are promoted to the service of Christ the Teacher, Priest, and King. They share in his ministry of unceasingly building up the Church on earth into the people of God, the Body of Christ, and the temple of the Holy Spirit."[7] In the ordination

[5]See LG no. 21 [DOL 4 no. 145].
[6]LG no. 28 [DOL 4 no. 148].

of presbyters, as formerly given in the Roman Pontifical, the mission and grace of the presbyter as a helper of the episcopal order were very clearly described. Yet it seemed necessary to reduce the entire rite, which had been divided into several parts, to a greater unity and to express more strikingly the central part of the ordination, that is, the laying on of hands and the consecratory prayer.

Finally, with regard to deacons, in addition to the content of our Motu Proprio *Sacrum Diaconatus Ordinem*, issued 18 June 1967, the following should be especially recalled: "At a lower level of the hierarchy are deacons, who receive the laying on of hands 'not unto priesthood, but only for a ministry service' (*Constitutions of the Church of Egypt* 3, 2). Strengthened by sacramental grace, they have as their service for the people of God, in communion with the bishop and his college of presbyters, the *diakonia* of liturgy, word, and charity."[8] In the ordination of deacons a few changes had to be made to satisfy the recent prescriptions about the diaconate as a distinct and permanent grade of the hierarchy in the Latin Church or to achieve a greater simplicity and clarity in the rites.

Among the other documents of the magisterium pertaining to sacred orders, we consider one worthy of particular mention, namely, the Apostolic Constitution *Sacramentum Ordinis* published by our predecessor, Pius XII, 30 November 1947. In this Constitution he declared that "the sole matter of the sacred orders of diaconate and presbyterate is the laying on of hands; likewise the sole form is the words determining the application of this matter, which unequivocally signify the sacramental effects—namely, the power of orders and the grace of the Holy Spirit—and are accepted and used as such by the Church."[9] After this, the document determines which laying on of hands and which words constitute the matter and form in the conferring of each order.

It was necessary in the revision of the rite to add, delete, or change certain things, in order to restore the texts of the rite to the form they had in antiquity, to clarify expressions, or to bring out more clearly the effects of the sacraments. We therefore think it necessary, so as to remove all controversy

[7]PO no. 1: AAS 58 (1966) 991; ConstDecrDecl 619–620.
[8]LG no. 29 [DOL 4 no. 149].
[9]AAS 40 (1948) 6.

and avoid perplexity of conscience, to declare what are to be
held as the essentials in each revised rite. By our supreme
apostolic authority we decree and establish the following
with regard to the matter and form in the conferring of each
order.

In the ordination of deacons, the matter is the laying of the
bishop's hands on the individual candidates that is done in
silence before the consecratory prayer; the form consists in
the words of the consecratory prayer, of which the following
belong to the essence and are consequently required for
validity:

Lord,
send forth upon them the Holy Spirit,
that they may be strengthened
by the gift of your sevenfold grace
to carry out faithfully the work of the ministry.

In the ordination of presbyters, the matter is likewise the laying of the bishop's hands on the individual candidates that is
done in silence before the consecratory prayer; the form consists in the words of the consecratory prayer, of which the
following belongs to the essence and are consequently required for validity:

Almighty Father,
grant to these servants of yours
the dignity of the priesthood.
Renew within them the Spirit of holiness.
As co-workers with the order of bishops
may they be faithful to the ministry
that they receive from you, Lord God,
and be to others a model of right conduct.

Finally, in the ordination of a bishop, the matter is the laying
of hands on the head of the bishop-elect by the consecrating
bishops, or at least by the principal consecrator, that is done
in silence before the consecratory prayer; the form consists in
the words of the consecratory prayer, of which the following
belong to the essence and are consequently required for
validity:

So now pour out upon this chosen one
that power which is from you,
the governing Spirit
whom you gave to your beloved Son, Jesus Christ,
the Spirit given by him to the holy apostles,
who founded the Church in every place to be your
    temple
for the unceasing glory and praise of your name.

This rite for the conferring of the orders of diaconate, presbyterate, and episcopate has been revised by the Consilium for the Implementation of the Constitution on the Sacred Liturgy "with the employment of experts and with the consultation of bishops, from various parts of the world."[10] By our apostolic authority we approve this rite so that it may be used in the future for the conferral of these orders in place of the rite now found in the Roman Pontifical.

It is our will that these our decrees and prescriptions be firm and effective now and in the future, notwithstanding, to the extent necessary, the apostolic constitutions and ordinances issued by our predecessors and other prescriptions, even those deserving particular mention and amendment.

Given at Rome, at Saint Peter's, 18 June 1968, the fifth year of our pontificate.

Paul VI

[10] SC art. 25 [DOL 1 no. 25].

CHAPTER II

ORDINATION OF A DEACON

INTRODUCTION

1. The ordination of a deacon should take place on a Sunday or holyday, when a large number of the faithful can attend, unless pastoral reasons suggest another day.

The public commitment to celibacy by the candidate for ordination as a priest and by an unmarried candidate for the diaconate, including a religious, must be made before the rite of ordination of a deacon (see no. 14 below).

2. The ordination should take place ordinarily at the *cathedra* or bishop's chair; or, to enable the faithful to participate more fully, a chair for the bishop may be placed before the altar or elsewhere. A seat for the one to be ordained should be placed so that the faithful may have a complete view of the liturgical rites.

3. The one to be ordained wears an alb (with amice and cincture unless other provisions are made).

4. In addition to what is needed for the celebration of Mass, there should be ready: (a) the Roman Pontifical; (b) stole and dalmatic for the candidate.

5. When everything is ready, the procession moves through the church to the altar in the usual way. A deacon carries the Book of the Gospels; he is followed by the candidate and finally by the bishop between two deacons.

LITURGY OF THE WORD

6. The liturgy of the word takes place according to the rubrics.

7. The readings may be taken in whole or in part from the Mass of the day or from the texts listed in Chapter VI.

8. The profession of faith is not said, nor are the general intercessions.

ORDINATION OF A DEACON

9. The ordination of a deacon begins after the gospel. The bishop, wearing his miter, sits at his chair.

CALLING OF THE CANDIDATE

10. The candidate is called by the deacon:
Let N. who is to be ordained deacon please come forward.

11. The candidate answers: **Present**, and goes to the bishop, before whom he makes a sign of reverence.

PRESENTATION OF THE CANDIDATE

12. When the candidate is in his place before the bishop, the priest designated by the bishop says:

Most Reverend Father, holy mother Church asks you to ordain this man, our brother, for service as deacon.

The bishop asks:
Do you judge him to be worthy?

He answers:
After inquiry among the people of Christ and upon recommendation of those concerned with his training, I testify that he has been found worthy.

ELECTION BY THE BISHOP
AND CONSENT OF THE PEOPLE

13. Bishop:
We rely on the help of the Lord God and our Savior Jesus Christ, and we choose this man, our brother, for the order of deacons.

All present say: **Thanks be to God**, or give their assent to the choice in some other way, according to local custom.

HOMILY

14. Then all sit, and the bishop gives the homily. He begins with the text of the readings from Scripture and then speaks to the people and the candidate about the office of deacon and the meaning and importance of celibacy in the Church. He may use these words:

This man, your relative and friend, is now to be raised to the order of deacons. Consider carefully the ministry to which he is to be promoted.

He will draw new strength from the gift of the Holy Spirit. He will help the bishop and his body of priests as a minister of the word, of the altar, and of charity. He will make himself a servant to all. As a minister of the altar he will proclaim the Gospel, prepare the sacrifice, and give the Lord's body and blood to the community of believers.

It will also be his duty, at the bishop's discretion, to bring God's word to believer and unbeliever alike, to preside over public prayer, to baptize, to assist at marriages and bless them, to give viaticum to the dying, and to lead the rites of burial. Once he is consecrated by the laying on of hands that comes to us from the apostles and is bound more closely to the altar, he will perform works of charity in the name of the bishop or the pastor. From the way he goes about these duties, may you recognize him as a disciple of Jesus, who came to serve, not to be served.

He then addresses the candidate:

My son, you are being raised to the order of deacons. The Lord has set an example for you to follow.

As a deacon you will serve Jesus Christ, who was known among his disciples as the one who served others. Do the will of God generously. Serve God and mankind in love and joy. Look upon all unchastity and avarice as worship of false gods; for no man can serve two masters.

Like the men the apostles chose for works of charity, you should be a man of good reputation, filled with wisdom and the Holy Spirit. Show before God and mankind that you are above every suspicion of blame, a true minister of Christ and of God's mysteries, a man firmly rooted in faith. Never turn away from the hope which the Gospel offers; now you must not only listen to God's word but also preach it. Hold the mystery of faith with a clear conscience. Express in action what you proclaim by word of mouth. Then the people of Christ, brought to life by the Spirit, will be an offering God accepts. Finally, on the last day, when you go to meet the Lord, you will hear him say: "Well done, good and faithful servant, enter into the joy of your Lord."

COMMITMENT TO CELIBACY

After the homily the candidate, if he is to manifest his intention of a commitment to celibacy, stands before the bishop. The bishop speaks to him in these or similar words:

By your own free choice you seek to enter the order of deacons. You shall exercise this ministry in the celibate state for celibacy is both a sign and a motive of pastoral charity, and a special source of spiritual fruitfulness in the world. By living in this state with total dedication, moved by a sincere love for Christ the Lord, you are consecrated to him in a new and special way. By this consecration you will adhere more easily to Christ with an undivided heart; you will be more freely at the service of God and mankind, and you will be more untrammeled in the ministry of Christian conversion and rebirth. By your life and character you will give witness to your brothers and sisters in faith that God must be loved above all else, and that it is he whom you serve in others.

Therefore, I ask you:
In the presence of God and the Church, are you resolved, as a sign of your interior dedication to Christ,

to remain celibate for the sake of the kingdom and in lifelong service to God and mankind?

The candidate answers: **I am.**

If it wishes, the conference of bishops may determine some external sign to express the intention of the candidate.

The bishop adds:
May the Lord help you to persevere in this commitment.

The candidate answers: **Amen.**

EXAMINATION OF THE CANDIDATE

15. The candidate then stands before the bishop who questions him:

My son, before you are ordained a deacon, you must declare before the people your intention to undertake this office.

Are you willing to be ordained for the Church's ministry by the laying on of hands and the gift of the Holy Spirit?
The candidate answers: **I am.**

Bishop:
Are you resolved to discharge the office of deacon with humility and love in order to assist the bishop and the priests and to serve the people of Christ?
Candidate: **I am.**

Bishop:
Are you resolved to hold the mystery of the faith with a clear conscience as the Apostle urges, and to proclaim this faith in word and action as it is taught by the Gospel and the Church's tradition?
Candidate: **I am.**

Bishop:
Are you resolved to maintain and deepen a spirit of prayer appropriate to your way of life and, in keeping with what is required of you, to celebrate faithfully the

liturgy of the hours for the Church and for the whole world?
Candidate: **I am.**

Bishop:
Are you resolved to shape your way of life always according to the example of Christ, whose body and blood you will give to the people?
Candidate: **I am, with the help of God.**

PROMISE OF OBEDIENCE

16. Then the candidate goes to the bishop and, kneeling before him, places his joined hands between those of the bishop. If this gesture seems less suitable in some places, the conference of bishops may choose another gesture or sign.

If the bishop is the candidate's own Ordinary, he asks:
Do you promise respect and obedience to me and my successors?
Candidate: **I do.**

If the bishop is not the candidate's own Ordinary, he asks:
Do you promise respect and obedience to your Ordinary?
Candidate: **I do.**

Bishop:
May God who has begun the good work in you bring it to fulfillment.

INVITATION TO PRAYER

17. Then all stand, and the bishop, without his miter, invites the people to pray:

My dear people, let us pray that the all-powerful Father will pour out his blessing on this servant of his, whom he receives into the holy order of deacons.

Deacon (except during the Easter season):
Let us kneel.

LITANY OF THE SAINTS

18. The candidate prostrates himself and, except during the Easter season, the rest kneel at their places.

The cantors begin the litany (see Chapter VI); they may add, at the proper place, names of other saints (for example, the patron saint, the titular of the church, the founder of the church, the patron saint of the one to be ordained) or petitions suitable to the occasion.

19. The bishop alone stands and, with his hands joined, sings or says:

**Lord God,
hear our petitions
and give your help to this act of our ministry.
We judge this man worthy to serve as deacon
and we ask you to bless him
and make him holy.**

**Grant this through Christ our Lord.
℟. Amen.**

Deacon: **Let us stand.**

LAYING ON OF HANDS

20. Then all stand. The candidate goes to the bishop and kneels before him. The bishop lays his hands on the candidate's head, in silence.

PRAYER OF CONSECRATION

21. The candidate kneels before the bishop. With his hands extended over the candidate, he sings the prayer of consecration or says it aloud:

**Almighty God,
be present with us by your power.
You are the source of all honor,
you assign to each his rank,
you give to each his ministry.**

You remain unchanged,
but you watch over all creation and make it new
through your Son, Jesus Christ, our Lord:
he is your Word, your power, and your wisdom.
You foresee all things in your eternal providence
and make due provision for every age.
You make the Church, Christ's body,
grow to its full stature as a new and greater temple.
You enrich it with every kind of grace
and perfect it with a diversity of members
to serve the whole body in a wonderful pattern of
    unity.

You established a threefold ministry of worship and
    service
for the glory of your name.
As ministers of your tabernacle you chose the sons
    of Levi
and gave them your blessing as their everlasting
    inheritance.
In the first days of your Church
under the inspiration of the Holy Spirit
the apostles of your Son appointed seven men of
    good repute
to assist them in the daily ministry,
so that they themselves might be more free for
    prayer and preaching.
By prayer and the laying on of the hands
the apostles entrusted to those chosen men the
    ministry of serving at tables.

Lord
look with favor on this servant of yours,
whom we now dedicate to the office of deacon,
to minister at your holy altar.

Lord,
send forth upon him the Holy Spirit,
that he may be strengthened
by the gift of your sevenfold grace
to carry out faithfully the work of the ministry.

May he excel in every virtue:
in love that is sincere,
in concern for the sick and the poor,
in unassuming authority,
in self-discipline,
and in holiness of life.
May his conduct exemplify your commandments
and lead your people to imitate his purity of life.
May he remain strong and steadfast in Christ,
giving to the world the witness of a pure conscience.
May he in this life imitate your Son,
who came, not to be served but to serve,
and one day reign with him in heaven.

We ask this through our Lord Jesus Christ, your Son,
who lives and reigns with you and the Holy Spirit,
one God, for ever and ever.
℟. Amen.

INVESTITURE WITH STOLE AND DALMATIC

22. After the prayer of consecration, the bishop, wearing his
miter, sits, and the newly ordained stands. An assisting
deacon or priest puts a deacon's stole and then a dalmatic
on him.

23. Meanwhile, the following antiphon may be sung with
Psalm 84.

Blessed are they who dwell in your house, O Lord.

The antiphon is repeated after every two verses. **Glory to the
Father** is not said. The psalm is interrupted and the antiphon
repeated when the dalmatic has been put on the deacon.

Any other appropriate song may be sung.

PRESENTATION OF THE BOOK OF THE GOSPELS

24. Vested as a deacon, the newly ordained goes to the
bishop and kneels before him. The bishop places the Book of
the Gospels in the hands of the newly ordained and says:

**Receive the Gospel of Christ,
whose herald you now are.**

**Believe what you read,
teach what you believe,
and practice what you teach.**

KISS OF PEACE

25. Lastly, the bishop stands and gives the kiss of peace to the new deacon, saying:

Peace be with you.

The deacon responds: **And also with you.**

If circumstances permit, the deacons present also give the kiss of peace to the newly ordained.

26. Meanwhile, the following antiphon may be sung with Psalm 146.

**If anyone serves me, says the Lord,
my Father in heaven will honor him.**

The antiphon is repeated after every two verses. **Glory to the Father** is not said. The psalm is interrupted and the antiphon repeated when all have received the kiss of peace.

Any other appropriate song may be sung.

LITURGY OF THE EUCHARIST

27. The Order of Mass is followed with these changes:
a) The new deacon brings the offerings for the celebration to the bishop and assists him at the altar.
b) In Eucharistic Prayer I, the special form of **Father, accept this offering** is said:

**Father, accept this offering
from your whole family
and from the one you have chosen for the order
   of deacons.**

Protect the gifts you have given him,
and let him yield a harvest worthy of you.

[Through Christ our Lord. Amen.]

28. The new deacon receives communion under both kinds and if necessary assists the bishop by ministering the cup. In any event he assists the bishop in giving communion to the people.

CHAPTER III

ORDINATION OF A PRIEST

INTRODUCTION

1. The ordination of a priest should take place on a Sunday or holyday, when a large number of the faithful can attend, unless pastoral reasons suggest another day.

2. The ordination should take place ordinarily at the *cathedra* or bishop's chair; or, to enable the faithful to participate more fully, a chair for the bishop may be placed before the altar or elsewhere. A seat for the one to be ordained should be placed so that the faithful may have a complete view of the liturgical rites.

3. The priest concelebrates with the bishop in his ordination Mass. It is most appropriate for the bishop to admit other priests to the concelebration; in this case and on this day the newly ordained priest takes the first place ahead of the others who concelebrate.

4. The one to be ordained wears an alb (with an amice and cincture unless other provisions are made) and a deacon's stole. In addition to what is needed for the concelebration of Mass, there should be ready: (a) the Roman Pontifical; (b) stoles for the priests who lay hands upon the candidate; (c) a chasuble for the candidate; (d) a linen gremial; (e) holy chrism; (f) whatever is needed for the washing of hands.

5. When everything is ready, the procession moves through the church to the altar in the usual way. A deacon carries the Book of the Gospels; he is followed by the candidate then the concelebrating priests, and finally the bishop between two deacons.

LITURGY OF THE WORD

6. The liturgy of the word takes place according to the rubrics.

7. The readings may be taken in whole or in part from the Mass of the day or from the texts listed in Chapter VI.

8. The profession of faith is not said, nor are the general intercesssions.

ORDINATION OF A PRIEST

9. The ordination of a priest begins after the gospel. The bishop, wearing his miter, sits at his chair.

CALLING OF THE CANDIDATE

10. The candidate is called by the deacon:
Let N. who is to be ordained priest please come forward.

11. The candidate answers: **Present**, and goes to the bishop, before whom he makes a sign of reverence.

PRESENTATION OF THE CANDIDATE

12. When the candidate is in his place before the bishop, the priest designated by the bishop says:

Most Reverend Father, holy mother Church asks you to ordain this man, our brother, for service as priest.

The bishop asks:
Do you judge him to be worthy?

He answers:
After inquiry among the people of Christ and upon recommendation of those concerned with his training, I testify that he has been found worthy.

ELECTION BY THE BISHOP
AND CONSENT OF THE PEOPLE

13. Bishop:
We rely on the help of the Lord God and our Savior Jesus Christ, and we choose this man, our brother, for priesthood in the presbyteral order.

All present say: **Thanks be to God**, or give their assent to the choice in some other way, according to local custom.

HOMILY

14. Then all sit, and the bishop addresses the people and the candidate on the duties of a priest. He may use these words:

This man, your relative and friend, is now to be raised to the order of priests. Consider carefully the position to which he is to be promoted in the Church.

It is true that God has made his entire people a royal priesthood in Christ. But our High Priest, Jesus Christ, also chose some of his followers to carry out publicly in the Church a priestly ministry in his name on behalf of mankind. He was sent by the Father, and he in turn sent the apostles into the world; through them and their successors, the bishops, he continues his work as Teacher, Priest, and Shepherd. Priests are co-workers of the order of bishops. They are joined to the bishops in the priestly office and are called to serve God's people.

Our brother has seriously considered this step and is now to be ordained to priesthood in the presbyteral order. He is to serve Christ the Teacher, Priest, and Shepherd in his ministry which is to make his own body, the Church, grow into the people of God, a holy temple.

He is called to share in the priesthood of the bishops and to be molded into the likeness of Christ, the supreme and eternal Priest. By consecration he will be made a true priest of the New Testament, to preach the Gospel, sustain God's people, and celebrate the liturgy, above all, the Lord's sacrifice.

He then addresses the candidate:

My son, you are now to be advanced to the order of the presbyterate. You must apply your energies to the duty of teaching in the name of Christ, the chief Teacher. Share with all mankind the word of God you have received with joy. Meditate on the law of God, believe what you read, teach what you believe, and put into practice what you teach.

Let the doctrine you teach be true nourishment for the people of God. Let the example of your life attract the followers of Christ, so that by word and action you may build up the house which is God's Church.

In the same way you must carry out your mission of sanctifying in the power of Christ. Your ministry will perfect the spiritual sacrifice of the faithful by uniting it to Christ's sacrifice, the sacrifice which is offered sacramentally through your hands. Know what you are doing and imitate the mystery you celebrate. In the memorial of the Lord's death and resurrection, make every effort to die to sin and to walk in the new life of Christ.

When you baptize, you will bring men and women into the people of God. In the sacrament of penance, you will forgive sins in the name of Christ and the Church. With holy oil you will relieve and console the sick. You will celebrate the liturgy and offer thanks and praise to God throughout the day, praying not only for the people of God but for the whole world. Remember that you are chosen from among God's people and appointed to act for them in relation to God. Do your part in the work of Christ the Priest with genuine joy and love, and attend to the concerns of Christ before your own.

Finally, conscious of sharing in the work of Christ, the Head and Shepherd of the Church, and united with the bishop and subject to him, seek to bring the faithful together into a unified family and to lead them effectively, through Christ and in the Holy Spirit, to God the Father. Always remember the example of the Good Shepherd who came not to be served but to serve, and to seek out and rescue those who were lost.

EXAMINATION OF THE CANDIDATE

15. The candidate then stands before the bishop, who questions him:

My son, before you proceed to the order of the presbyterate, declare before the people your intention to undertake this priestly office.

Are you resolved, with the help of the Holy Spirit, to discharge without fail the office of priesthood in the presbyteral order as a conscientious fellow worker with the bishops in caring for the Lord's flock?
The candidate answers: **I am.**

Bishop:
Are you resolved to celebrate the mysteries of Christ faithfully and religiously as the Church has handed them down to us for the glory of God and the sanctification of Christ's people?
Candidate: **I am.**

Bishop:
Are you resolved to exercise the ministry of the word worthily and wisely, preaching the Gospel and explaining the Catholic faith?
Candidate: **I am.**

Bishop:
Are you resolved to consecrate your life to God for the salvation of his people, and to unite yourself more closely every day to Christ the High Priest, who offered himself for us to the Father as a perfect sacrifice?
Candidate: **I am, with the help of God.**

PROMISE OF OBEDIENCE

16. Then the candidate goes to the bishop and, kneeling before him, places his joined hands between those of the bishop. If this gesture seems less suitable in some places, the conference of bishops may choose another gesture or sign.

If the bishop is the candidate's own Ordinary, he asks:
Do you promise respect and obedience to me and my successors?
Candidate: **I do.**

If the bishop is not the candidate's own Ordinary, he asks:
Do you promise respect and obedience to your Ordinary?
Candidate: **I do.**

Bishop:
May God who has begun the good work in you bring it to fulfillment.

INVITATION TO PRAYER

17. Then all stand, and the bishop, without his miter, invites the people to pray:

My dear people, let us pray, that the all-powerful Father may pour out the gifts of heaven on this servant of his, whom he has chosen to be a priest.

Deacon (except during the Easter season):
Let us kneel.

LITANY OF THE SAINTS

18. The candidate prostrates himself and, except during the Easter season, the rest kneel at their places.

The cantors begin the litany (see Chapter VI); they may add, at the proper place, names of other saints (for example, the patron saint, the titular of the church, the founder of the church, the patron saint of the one to be ordained) or petitions suitable to the occasion.

19. The bishop alone stands and, with his hands joined, sings or says:

**Hear us, Lord our God,
and pour out upon this servant of yours
the blessing of the Holy Spirit
and the grace and power of the priesthood.
In your sight we offer this man for ordination:
support him with your unfailing love.**

**We ask this through Christ our Lord.
℟. Amen.**

Deacon: **Let us stand.**

LAYING ON OF HANDS

20. Then all stand. The candidate goes to the bishop and kneels before him. The bishop lays his hands on the candidate's head, in silence.

21. Next all the priests present, wearing stoles, lay their hands upon the candidate in silence. After the laying on of hands, the priests remain on either side of the bishop until the prayer of consecration is completed.

PRAYER OF CONSECRATION

22. The candidate kneels before the bishop. With his hands extended over the candidate, the bishop sings the prayer of consecration or says it aloud:

**Come to our help,
Lord, holy Father, almighty and eternal God;
you are the source of every honor and dignity,
of all progress and stability.
You watch over the growing family of man
by your gift of wisdom and your pattern of order.
When you had appointed high priests to rule
    your people,
you chose other men next to them in rank and dignity
to be with them and to help them in their task;
and so there grew up
the ranks of priests and the offices of levites,
established by sacred rites.**

**In the desert
you extended the spirit of Moses to seventy wise men
who helped him to rule the great company of his
    people.
You shared among the sons of Aaron
the fullness of their father's power,
to provide worthy priests in sufficient number
for the increasing rites of sacrifice and worship.
With the same loving care
you gave companions to your Son's apostles
to help in teaching the faith:
they preached the Gospel to the whole world.**

**Lord,
grant also to us such fellow workers,
for we are weak and our need is greater.**

**Almighty Father,
grant to this servant of yours**

the dignity of the priesthood.
Renew within him the Spirit of holiness.
As a co-worker with the order of bishops
may he be faithful to the ministry
that he receives from you, Lord God,
and be to others a model of right conduct.

May he be faithful in working with the order of
     bishops,
so that the words of the Gospel may reach the ends of
     the earth,
and the family of nations,
made one in Christ,
may become God's one, holy people.

We ask this through our Lord Jesus Christ, your Son,
who lives and reigns with you and the Holy Spirit,
one God, for ever and ever.
℞. Amen.

INVESTITURE WITH STOLE AND CHASUBLE

23. After the prayer of consecration, the bishop, wearing his miter, sits, and the newly ordained stands. The assisting priests return to their places, but one of them arranges the stole of the newly ordained as it is worn by priests and vests him in a chasuble.

ANOINTING OF HANDS

24. Next the bishop receives a linen gremial and anoints with chrism the palms of the new priest as he kneels before him. The bishop says:

The Father anointed our Lord Jesus Christ
through the power of the Holy Spirit.
May Jesus preserve you to sanctify the Christian
     people
and to offer sacrifice to God.

25. While the new priest is being vested in stole and chasuble and the bishop is anointing his hands, the hymn **Veni, Creator Spiritus** or the following antiphon may be sung with Psalm 110.

**Christ the Lord,
a priest for ever in the line of Melchizedek,
offered bread and wine.**

The antiphon is repeated after every two verses. **Glory to the Father** is not said. The psalm is interrupted and the antiphon repeated when the hands of the priest have been anointed.

Any other appropriate song may be sung.

Then the bishop and the new priest wash their hands.

PRESENTATION OF THE GIFTS

26. The deacon assists the bishop in receiving the gifts of the people and he prepares the bread on the paten and the wine and water in the chalice for the celebration of Mass. He brings the paten and chalice to the bishop, who hands them to the new priest as he kneels before him. The bishop says:

Accept from the holy people of God the gifts to be offered to him.
Know what you are doing, and imitate the mystery you celebrate:
model your life on the mystery of the Lord's cross.

KISS OF PEACE

27. Lastly, the bishop stands and gives the kiss of peace to the new priest, saying:

Peace be with you.

The priest responds: **And also with you.**

If circumstances permit, the priests present also give the kiss of peace to the newly ordained.

28. Meanwhile, the following antiphon may be sung with Psalm 100.

You are my friends, says the Lord, if you do what I command you.

The antiphon is repeated after every two verses. **Glory to the Father** is not said. The psalm is interrupted and the antiphon repeated when all have received the kiss of peace.

Any other appropriate song may be sung, or:

No longer do I call you servants, but my friends, because you know all that I have done among you (alleluia).
—Receive the Holy Spirit as an Advocate among you: it is he whom the Father will send you (alleluia).
You are my friends if you do the things I command you.
—Receive the Holy Spirit as an Advocate among you. Glory to the Father...
—It is he whom the Father will send you (alleluia).

LITURGY OF THE EUCHARIST

29. The rite for the concelebration of Mass is followed with these changes:
a) The preparation of the chalice is omitted.
b) In Eucharistic Prayer I, the special form of **Father, accept this offering** is said:

Father, accept this offering
from your whole family
and from the one you have chosen for the order of
   priests.
Protect the gifts you have given him,
and let him yield a harvest worthy of you.

[Through Christ our Lord. Amen.]

CHAPTER IV

ORDINATION OF DEACONS AND PRIESTS IN THE SAME CELEBRATION

1. The preparations and the order of the liturgy of the word should follow what has been previously indicated for the individual ordinations.

2. After the gospel is read, the bishop, wearing his miter, sits at his chair.

ORDINATION OF DEACONS AND PRIESTS

FOR DEACONS

CALLING OF THE CANDIDATES

3. First the candidates for the order of deacons are called by the deacon:

Those to be ordained deacons please come forward.

Then their names are called by the deacon. Each one answers: **Present,** and goes to the bishop, before whom he makes a sign of reverence.

PRESENTATION OF THE CANDIDATES

4. When all the candidates are in their place before the bishop, the priest designated by the bishop says:

Most Reverend Father, holy mother Church asks you to ordain these men, our brothers, for service as deacons.

The bishop asks:
Do you judge them to be worthy?

He answers:
After inquiry among the people of Christ and upon recommendation of those concerned with their training, I testify that they have been found worthy.

ELECTION BY THE BISHOP
AND CONSENT OF THE PEOPLE

5. Bishop:

We rely on the help of the Lord God and our Savior Jesus Christ, and we choose these men, our brothers, for the order of deacons.

All present say: **Thanks be to God**, or give their assent to the choice in some other way, according to local custom.

FOR PRIESTS

CALLING OF THE CANDIDATES

6. Then the candidates for priesthood in the presbyteral order are called by the deacon:

Those to be ordained priests please come forward.

7. Then their names are called by the deacon. Each one answers: **Present**, and goes to the bishop, before whom he makes a sign of reverence.

PRESENTATION OF THE CANDIDATES

8. When the candidates are in their places before the bishop, the priest designated by the bishop says:

Most Reverend Father, holy mother Church asks you to ordain these men, our brothers for service as priests.

The bishop asks:
Do you judge them to be worthy?

He answers:
After inquiry among the people of Christ and upon recommendation of those concerned with their training, I testify that they have been found worthy.

ELECTION BY THE BISHOP
AND CONSENT OF THE PEOPLE

9. Bishop:

We rely on the help of the Lord God our Savior Jesus Christ, and we choose these men, our brothers, for priesthood in the presbyteral order.

All present say: **Thanks be to God**, or give their assent to the choice in some other way, according to local custom.

FOR DEACONS AND PRIESTS

HOMILY

10. Then all sit, and the bishop addresses the people and the candidates. He may use these words:

These men, our brothers, are now to be raised to the order of deacons and to the order of priests. Consider carefully the ministry to which they are to be promoted in the Church. They are to serve Christ the Teacher, Priest, and Pastor in his ministry which is to make his own body, the Church, grow incessantly into the people of God and the temple of the Holy Spirit. They are called to share in the priesthood of bishops. By consecration priests and deacons will preach the Gospel, sustain God's people, and celebrate the liturgy, above all, the Lord's sacrifice. From the way they go about these duties, may you recognize them as disciples of Jesus, who came to serve, not to be served.

FOR DEACONS

He then addresses the candidates:

My sons, you are being raised to the order of deacons. The Lord has set an example for you to follow.

As deacons you will serve Jesus Christ, who was known among his disciples as the one who served others. Do the will of God generously. Serve God and mankind in love and joy. Look upon all unchastity and avarice as worship of false gods; for no man can serve two masters.

Like the men the apostles chose for works of charity, you should be men of good reputation, filled with wisdom and the Holy Spirit. Show before God and mankind that you are above every suspicion of blame, true ministers of Christ and of God's mysteries, men

firmly rooted in faith. Never turn away from the hope which the Gospel offers; now you must not only listen to God's word but also preach it. Hold the mystery of faith with a clear conscience. Express in action what you proclaim by word of mouth. Then the people of Christ, brought to life by the Spirit, will be an offering God accepts. Finally, on the last day, when you go to meet the Lord, you will hear him say: "Well done, good and faithful servant, enter into the joy of your Lord."

COMMITMENT TO CELIBACY

Now the candidates who are to manifest their intention of a commitment to celibacy stand before the bishop. He speaks to them in these or similar words:

By your own free choice you seek to enter the order of deacons. You shall exercise this ministry in the celibate state: for celibacy is both a sign and a motive of pastoral charity, and a special source of spiritual fruitfulness in the world. By living in this state with total dedication, moved by a sincere love for Christ the Lord, you are consecrated to him in a new and special way. By this consecration you will adhere more easily to Christ with an undivided heart; you will be more freely at the service of God and mankind, and you will be more untrammeled in the ministry of Christian conversion and rebirth. By your life and character you will give witness to your brothers and sisters in faith that God must be loved above all else, and that it is he whom you serve in others.

Therefore, I ask you:
In the presence of God and the Church, are you resolved, as a sign of your interior dedication to Christ, to remain celibate for the sake of the kingdom and in lifelong service to God and mankind?

The candidates answer: I am.

If it wishes, the conference of bishops may determine some external sign to express the intention of the candidates.

The bishop adds:
May the Lord help you to persevere in this commitment.

The candidates answer: **Amen.**

FOR PRIESTS

The bishop now addresses the candidates for priesthood in the presbyteral order:

My sons, you are now to be advanced to the order of the presbyterate. You must apply your energies to the duty of teaching in the name of Christ, the chief Teacher. Share with all mankind the word of God you have received with joy. Meditate on the law of God, believe what you read, teach what you believe, and put into practice what you teach.

Let the doctrine you teach be true nourishment for the people of God. Let the example of your lives attract the followers of Christ, so that by word and action you may build up the house which is God's Church.

In the same way you must carry out your mission of sanctifying in the power of Christ. Your ministry will perfect the spiritual sacrifice of the faithful by uniting it to Christ's sacrifice, the sacrifice which is offered sacramentally through your hands. Know what you are doing and imitate the mystery you celebrate. In the memorial of the Lord's death and resurrection, make every effort to die to sin and to walk in the new life of Christ.

When you baptize, you will bring men and women into the people of God. In the sacrament of penance, you will forgive sins in the name of Christ and the Church. With holy oil you will relieve and console the sick. You will celebrate the liturgy and offer thanks and praise to God throughout the day, praying not only for the people of God but for the whole world. Remember that you are chosen from among God's people and appointed to act for them in relation to God. Do

your part in the work of Christ the Priest with genuine joy and love, and attend to the concerns of Christ before your own.

Finally, conscious of sharing in the work of Christ, the Head and Shepherd of the Church, and united with the bishop and subject to him, seek to bring the faithful together into a unified family and to lead them effectively, through Christ and in the Holy Spirit, to God the Father. Always remember the example of the Good Shepherd who came not to be served but to serve, and to seek out and rescue those who were lost.

FOR DEACONS

EXAMINATION OF THE CANDIDATES

11. The candidates for the order of deacons then stand before the bishop who questions all of them together:

My sons, before you are ordained deacons, you must declare before the people your intention to undertake the office.

Are you willing to be ordained for the Church's ministry by the laying on of hands and the gift of the Holy Spirit?
Together, all the candidates answer: I am.

Bishop:
Are you resolved to discharge the office of deacon with humility and love in order to assist the bishop and the priests and to serve the people of Christ?
Candidates: I am.

Bishop:
Are you resolved to hold the mystery of the faith with a clear conscience, as the Apostle urges, and to proclaim this faith in word and action as it is taught by the Gospel and the Church's tradition?
Candidates: I am.

Bishop:
Are you resolved to maintain and deepen a spirit of prayer appropriate to your way of life and, in keeping

with what is required of you, to celebrate faithfully the liturgy of the hours for the Church and for the whole world?
Candidates: **I am.**

Bishop:
Are you resolved to shape your way of life always according to the example of Christ, whose body and blood you will give to the people?
Candidates: **I am, with the help of God.**

PROMISE OF OBEDIENCE

12. Then each one of the candidates goes to the bishop and, kneeling before him, places his joined hands between those of the bishop. If this gesture seems less suitable in some places, the conference of bishops may choose another gesture or sign.

If the bishop is the candidate's own Ordinary, he asks:
Do you promise respect and obedience to me and my successors?
Candidate: **I do.**

If the bishop is not the candidate's own Ordinary, he asks:
Do you promise respect and obedience to your Ordinary?
Candidate: **I do.**

Bishop:
May God who has begun the good work in you bring it to fulfillment.

FOR PRIESTS

EXAMINATION

Then the candidates for priesthood in the presbyteral order stand before the bishop who questions all of them together:

My sons, before you proceed to the order of the presbyterate, declare before the people your intention to undertake this priestly office.

Are you resolved, with the help of the Holy Spirit, to discharge without fail the office of priesthood in the

presbyteral order as conscientious fellow workers with the bishops in caring for the Lord's flock?
Together, all the candidates answer: **I am.**

Bishop:
Are you resolved to celebrate the mysteries of Christ faithfully and religiously as the Church has handed them down to us, for the glory of God and the sanctification of Christ's people?
Candidates: **I am.**

Bishop:
Are you resolved to exercise the ministry of the word worthily and wisely, preaching the Gospel and explaining the Catholic faith?
Candidates: **I am.**

Bishop:
Are you resolved to consecrate your life to God for the salvation of his people, and to unite yourself more closely every day to Christ the High Priest, who offered himself for us to the Father as a perfect sacrifice?
Candidates: **I am, with the help of God.**

PROMISE OF OBEDIENCE
13. Then each of the candidates goes to the bishop and, kneeling before him, places his joined hands between those of the bishop. If this gesture seems less suitable in some places, the conference of bishops may choose another gesture or sign.

If the bishop is the candidate's own Ordinary, he asks:
Do you promise respect and obedience to me and my successors?
Candidate: **I do.**

If the bishop is not the candidate's own Ordinary, he asks:
Do you promise respect and obedience to your Ordinary?
Candidate: **I do.**

Bishop:
May God who has begun the good work in you bring it to fulfillment.

FOR DEACONS AND PRIESTS

INVITATION TO PRAYER

14. Then all stand, and the bishop, without his miter, invites the people to pray:

My dear people, let us pray that the all-powerful Father may pour out the gifts of heaven on these servants of his, whom he has chosen to be deacons and priests.

Deacon (except during the Easter season):
Let us kneel.

LITANY OF THE SAINTS

15. The candidates prostrate themselves and, except during the Easter season, the rest kneel at their places.

The cantors begin the litany (see Chapter VI); they may add, at the proper place, names of other saints (for example, the patron saint, the titular of the church, the founder of the church, the patron saints of those to be ordained) or petitions suitable to the occasions.

16. The bishop alone stands and, with his hands joined, sings or says:

**Lord God,
hear our petitions
and give your help to this act of our ministry.
We judge these men worthy to serve as deacons and
     priests
and we ask you to bless them
and make them holy.**

**Grant this through Christ our Lord.
℟. Amen.**

Deacon: **Let us stand.**

All stand. The candidates for priesthood in the presbyteral order return to their places, and the ordination of the deacons begins.

FOR DEACONS

LAYING ON OF HANDS

17. Then all stand. One by one the candidates go to the bishop and kneel before him. The bishop lays his hands on the head of each, in silence.

PRAYER OF CONSECRATION

18. The candidates kneel before the bishop. With his hands extended over them, he sings the prayer of consecration or says it aloud:

**Almighty God,
be present with us by your power.
You are the source of all honor,
you assign to each his rank,
you give to each his ministry.**

**You remain unchanged,
but you watch over all creation and make it new
through your Son, Jesus Christ, our Lord:
he is your Word, your power, and your wisdom.
You foresee all things in your eternal providence
and make due provision for every age.
You make the Church, Christ's body,
grow to its full stature as a new and greater temple.
You enrich it with every kind of grace
and perfect it with a diversity of members
to serve the whole body in a wonderful pattern of
   unity.
You established a threefold ministry of worship and
   service
for the glory of your name.
As ministers of your tabernacle you chose the sons of
   Levi
and gave them your blessing as their everlasting inheritance.
In the first days of your Church
under the inspiration of the Holy Spirit
the apostles of your Son appointed seven men of good
   repute**

to assist them in the daily ministry,
so that they themselves might be more free for prayer
  and preaching.
By prayer and the laying on of hands
the apostles entrusted to those chosen men the ministry
  of serving at tables.

Lord,
look with favor on these servants of yours,
whom we now dedicate to the office of deacon,
to minister at your holy altar.

Lord,
send forth upon them the Holy Spirit,
that they may be strengthened
by the gift of your sevenfold grace
to carry out faithfully the work of the ministry.

May they excel in every virtue:
in love that is sincere,
in concern for the sick and the poor,
in unassuming authority,
in self-discipline,
and in holiness of life.
May their conduct exemplify your commandments
and lead your people to imitate their purity of life.
May they remain strong and steadfast in Christ,
giving to the world the witness of a pure conscience.
May they in this life imitate your Son,
who came, not to be served but to serve,
and one day reign with him in heaven.

We ask this through our Lord Jesus Christ, your Son,
who lives and reigns with you and the Holy Spirit,
one God, for ever and ever.
℟. Amen.

INVESTITURE WITH STOLE AND DALMATIC

19. After the prayer of consecration, the bishop, wearing his miter, sits, and the newly ordained stand. Some of the assisting deacons or priests put a deacon's stole and then a dalmatic on each of them.

20. Meanwhile, the following antiphon may be sung with Psalm 84.

Blessed are they who dwell in your house, O Lord.

The antiphon is repeated after every two verses. **Glory to the Father** is not said. The psalm is interrupted and the antiphon repeated when dalmatics have been put on all of the deacons.

Any other appropriate song may be sung.

PRESENTATION OF THE BOOK OF THE GOSPELS

21. Vested as deacons, the newly ordained go to the bishop and kneel before him. He places the Book of the Gospels in the hands of each one and says:

Receive the Gospel of Christ,
whose herald you now are.
Believe what you read,
teach what you believe,
and practice what you teach.

22. The newly ordained deacons return to their places, and the candidates for priesthood in the presbyteral order come forward.

FOR PRIESTS

INVITATION TO PRAYER

23. Then all stand, and the bishop, without his miter, invites the people to pray:

My dear people, let us pray that the all-powerful Father may pour out the gifts of heaven on these servants of his, whom he has chosen to be priests.

Deacon: **Let us kneel.**

All kneel and in silence pray for the candidates.

PRAYER

The bishop alone stands and sings or says:

Hear us, Lord our God,
and pour out upon these servants of yours

the blessing of the Holy Spirit
and the grace and power of the priesthood.
In your sight we offer these men for ordination:
support them with your unfailing love.

We ask this through Christ our Lord.
℟. Amen.

Deacon: **Let us stand.**

LAYING ON OF HANDS

24. Then all stand. One by one the candidates go to the
bishop and kneel before him. The bishop lays his hands on
the head of each, in silence.

25. Next all the priests present, wearing stoles, lay their
hands upon each of the candidates, in silence. After laying on
of hands, the priests remain on either side of the bishop until
the prayer of consecration is completed.

PRAYER OF CONSECRATION

26. The candidates kneel before the bishop. With his hands
extended over them, he sings the prayer of consecration or
says it aloud:

Come to our help,
Lord, holy Father, almighty and eternal God;
you are the source of every honor and dignity,
of all progress and stability.
You watch over the growing family of man
by your gift of wisdom and your pattern of order.
When you had appointed high priests to rule your
    people,
you chose other men next to them in rank and dignity
to be with them and help them in their task;
and so there grew up
the ranks of priests and the offices of levites,
established by sacred rites.

In the desert
you extended the spirit of Moses to seventy wise men
who helped him to rule the great company of his
    people.

You shared among the sons of Aaron
the fullness of their father's power,
to provide worthy priests in sufficient number
for the increasing rites of sacrifice and worship.
With the same loving care
you gave companions to your Son's apostles
to help in teaching the faith:
they preached the Gospel to the whole world.

Lord,
grant also to us such fellow workers,
for we are weak and our need is greater.

Almighty Father,
grant to these servants of yours
the dignity of the priesthood.
Renew within them the Spirit of holiness.
As co-workers with the order of bishops
may they be faithful to the ministry
that they receive from you, Lord God,
and be to others a model of right conduct.

May they be faithful in working with the order of
   bishops,
so that the words of the Gospel may reach the ends of
   the earth,
and the family of nations,
made one in Christ,
may become God's one, holy people.

We ask this through our Lord Jesus Christ, your Son,
who lives and reigns with you and the Holy Spirit,
one God, for ever and ever.
℞. Amen.

INVESTITURE WITH STOLE AND CHASUBLE

27. After the prayer of consecration, the bishop, wearing his
miter, sits, and the newly ordained stand. The assisting
priests return to their places, but some of them arrange the
stoles of the newly ordained as they are worn by priests and
vest them in chasubles.

ANOINTING OF HANDS

28. Next the bishop receives a linen gremial and anoints with chrism the palms of each new priest as he kneels before him. The bishop says:

**The Father anointed our Lord Jesus Christ
through the power of the Holy Spirit.
May Jesus preserve you to sanctify the Christian
  people
and to offer sacrifice to God.**

29. While the new priests are being vested in stoles and chasubles and the bishop is anointing their hands, the hymn **Veni, Creator Spiritus** or the following antiphon may be sung with Psalm 110.

**Christ the Lord,
a priest for ever in the line of Melchizedek,
offered bread and wine.**

The antiphon is repeated after every two verses. **Glory to the Father** is not said. The psalm is interrupted and the antiphon repeated when the hands of all the priests have been anointed.

Any other appropriate song may be sung.

Then the bishop and the new priests wash their hands.

PRESENTATION OF THE GIFTS

30. The deacon assists the bishop in receiving the gifts of the people and then he prepares the bread on the paten and the wine and water in the chalice for the celebration of Mass. He brings the paten and chalice to the bishop, who hands them to each of the new priests as he kneels before him. The bishop says:

Accept from the holy people of God the gifts to be offered to him. Know what you are doing, and imitate the mystery you celebrate: model your life on the mystery of the Lord's cross.

FOR DEACONS AND PRIESTS

KISS OF PEACE

31. Lastly, the bishop stands and gives the kiss of peace to each of the newly ordained, first the priests, then the deacons, saying:

Peace be with you.

The priest/deacon responds: **And also with you.**

If circumstances permit, the priests and deacons present also give the kiss of peace to the newly ordained.

32. Meanwhile, the following antiphon may be sung with Psalm 100.

You are my friends, says the Lord, if you do what I command you.

The antiphon is repeated after every two verses. **Glory to the Father** is not said. The psalm is interrupted and the antiphon repeated when all have received the kiss of peace.

Any other appropriate song may be sung, or:

No longer do I call you servants, but my friends, because you know all that I have done among you (alleluia).
—Receive the Holy Spirit as an Advocate among you: it is he whom the Father will send you (alleluia).

You are my friends if you do the things I command you.
—Receive the Holy Spirit as an Advocate among you. Glory to the Father...
—It is he whom the Father will send you (alleluia).

LITURGY OF THE EUCHARIST

33. The rite for the concelebration of Mass is followed with these changes:
a) The preparation of the chalice is omitted.

b) In Eucharistic Prayer I, the special form of **Father, accept this offering** is said:

**Father, accept this offering
from your whole family
and from those you have chosen for the order of priests
   and deacons.
Protect the gifts you have given them,
and let them yield a harvest worthy of you.**

[Through Christ our Lord. Amen.]

34. The new deacons receive communion under both kinds. The deacon who assists the bishop ministers the cup.

35. Some of the new deacons assist the bishop in giving communion to the people.

CHAPTER V

ORDINATION OF A BISHOP

INTRODUCTION

1. The ordination of a bishop should take place on a Sunday or holyday when a large number of the faithful can attend, unless pastoral reasons suggest another day, such as the feast of an apostle.

2. The principal consecrator must be assisted by at least two other consecrating bishops, but it is fitting for all the bishops present together with the principal consecrator to ordain the bishop-elect.

3. Two priests assist the bishop-elect.

4. It is most appropriate for all the consecrating bishops and the priests assisting the bishop-elect to concelebrate the Mass with the principal consecrator and with the bishop-elect. If the ordination takes place in the bishop-elect's own church, some priests of his diocese should also concelebrate.

5. If the ordination takes place in the bishop-elect's own church, the principal consecrator may ask the newly ordained bishop to preside over the concelebration of the eucharistic liturgy. If the ordination does not take place in the bishop-elect's own church, the principal consecrator presides at the concelebration; in this case the new bishop takes the first place among the other celebrants.

6. The principal consecrator and the concelebrating bishops and priests wear the vestments required for Mass. The bishop-elect wears all the priestly vestments, the pectoral cross, and the dalmatic. If the consecrating bishops do not celebrate, they wear the rochet or alb, pectoral cross, stole, cope, and miter. If the priests assisting the bishop-elect do not concelebrate, they wear the cope over an alb or surplice.

7. The blessing of the ring, pastoral staff, and miter ordinarily takes place at a convenient time prior to the ordination service (see Appendix II).

8. In addition to what is needed for the concelebration of a pontifical Mass, there should be ready: a) the Roman Pontifical; b) copies of the consecratory prayer for the consecrating bishops; c) a linen gremial; d) holy chrism; e) a ring, staff, and miter for the bishop-elect.

9. Seats for the principal consecrator, consecrating bishops, the bishop-elect, and concelebrating priests are arranged as follows:

a) For the liturgy of the word, the principal consecrator should sit at the *cathedra* or bishop's chair, with the consecrating bishops near the chair. The bishop-elect sits between the assisting priests in an appropriate place within the sanctuary.

b) The ordination should usually take place at the bishop's chair; or, to enable the faithful to participate more fully, seats for the principal consecrator and consecrating bishops may be placed before the altar or elsewhere. Seats for the bishop-elect and his assisting priests should be placed so that the faithful may have a complete view of the liturgical rites.

10. When everything is ready, the procession moves through the church to the altar in the usual way. A deacon carries the Book of the Gospels; he is followed by the priests who will concelebrate, the bishop-elect between the priests assisting him, the consecrating bishops, and, finally, the principal consecrator between two deacons.

LITURGY OF THE WORD

11. The liturgy of the word takes place according to the rubrics.

12. The readings may be taken in whole or in part from the Mass of the day or from the texts listed in Chapter VI.

The profession of faith is not said, nor are the general intercessions.

ORDINATION OF A BISHOP

HYMN

13. The ordination of a bishop begins after the gospel. While all stand, the hymn **Veni, Creator Spiritus** is sung, or another hymn similar to it, depending on local custom.

14. The principal consecrator and the consecrating bishops, wearing their miters, go to the seats prepared for the ordination and sit.

15. The bishop-elect is led by his assisting priests to the chair of the principal consecrator, before whom he makes a sign of reverence.

PRESENTATION OF THE BISHOP-ELECT

16. One of the priests addresses the principal consecrator:
Most Reverend Father, the church of N. asks you to ordain this priest, N., for service as bishop.

If the bishop-elect is not to be ordained as a residential bishop:
Most Reverend Father, our holy mother the Catholic Church asks you to ordain this priest, N., for service as a bishop.

APOSTOLIC LETTER

The principal consecrator asks him:
Have you a mandate from the Holy See?

He replies: **We have.**

Principal consecrator: **Let it be read.**

Everyone sits while the document is read.

CONSENT OF THE PEOPLE

17. After the reading, all present say: **Thanks be to God**, or give their assent to the choice in some other way, according to local custom.

HOMILY

18. Then the principal consecrator, while all are sitting, briefly addresses the clergy, people, and the bishop-elect on the duties of a bishop. He may use these words:

Consider carefully the position in the Church to which our brother is about to be raised. Our Lord Jesus Christ, who was sent by the Father to redeem the human race, in turn sent twelve apostles into the world. These men were filled with the power of the Holy Spirit to preach the Gospel and gather every race and people into a single flock to be guided and governed in the way of holiness. Because this service was to continue to the end of time, the apostles selected others to help them. By the laying on of hands which confers the sacrament of orders in its fullness, the apostles passed on the gift of the Holy Spirit which they themselves had received from Christ. In that way, by a succession of bishops unbroken from one generation to the next, the powers conferred in the beginning were handed down, and the work of the Savior lives and grows in our time.

In the person of the bishop, with his priests around him, Jesus Christ, the Lord, who became High Priest for ever, is present among you. Through the ministry of the bishop, Christ himself continues to proclaim the Gospel and to confer the mysteries of faith on those who believe. Through the fatherly action of the bishop, Christ adds new members to his body. Through the bishop's wisdom and prudence, Christ guides you in your earthly pilgrimage toward eternal happiness.

Gladly and gratefully, therefore, receive our brother whom we are about to accept into the college of bishops by the laying on of hands. Respect him as a minister of Christ and a steward of the mysteries of God. He has been entrusted with the task of witnessing to the truth of the Gospel and fostering a spirit of justice and holiness. Remember the words of Christ spoken to the apostles: "Whoever listens to you listens

to me; whoever rejects you rejects me, and those who reject me reject the one who sent me."

He then addresses the bishop-elect:

You, dear brother, have been chosen by the Lord. Remember that you are chosen from among men and appointed to act for men and women in relation to God. The title of bishop is one not of honor but of function, and therefore a bishop should strive to serve rather than to rule. Such is the counsel of the Master: the greater should behave as is he were the least, and the leader as if he were the one who serves. Proclaim the message whether it is welcome or unwelcome; correct error with unfailing patience and teaching. Pray and offer sacrifice for the people committed to your care and so draw every kind of grace for them from the overflowing holiness of Christ.

As a steward of the mysteries of Christ in the church entrusted to you, be a faithful overseer and guardian. Since you are chosen by the Father to rule over his family, always be mindful of the Good Shepherd, who knows his sheep and is known by them and who did not hesitate to lay down his life for them.

As a father and a brother, love all those whom God places in your care. Love the priests and deacons who share with you the ministry of Christ. Love the poor and infirm, strangers and the homeless. Encourage the faithful to work with you in your apostolic task; listen willingly to what they have to say. Never relax your concern for those who do not yet belong to the one fold of Christ; they too are commended to you in the Lord. Never forget that in the Catholic Church, made one by the bond of Christian love, you are incorporated into the college of bishops. You should therefore have a constant concern for all the churches and gladly come to the aid and support of churches in need. Attend to the whole flock in which the Holy Spirit appoints you an overseer of the Church of God—in the name of the Father, whose image you personify in the Church—and in the name of his Son, Jesus Christ, whose role of

Teacher, Priest, and Shepherd you undertake—and in the name of the Holy Spirit, who gives life to the Church of Christ and supports our weakness with his strength.

EXAMINATION OF THE CANDIDATE

19. The bishop-elect then rises and stands in front of the principal consecrator, who questions him:

An age-old custom of the Fathers decrees that a bishop-elect is to be questioned before the people on his resolve to uphold the faith and to discharge his duties faithfully.

My brother, are you resolved by the grace of the Holy Spirit to discharge to the end of your life the office the apostles entrusted to us, which we now pass on to you by the laying on of hands?
The bishop-elect replies: I am.

Principal consecrator:
Are you resolved to be faithful and constant in proclaiming the Gospel of Christ?
Bishop-elect: I am.

Principal consecrator:
Are you resolved to maintain the deposit of faith, entire and incorrupt, as handed down by the apostles and professed by the Church everywhere and at all times?
Bishop-elect: I am.

Principal consecrator:
Are you resolved to build up the Church as the body of Christ and to remain united to it within the order of bishops under the authority of the successor of the apostle Peter?
Bishop-elect: I am.

Principal consecrator:
Are you resolved to be faithful in your obedience to the successor of the apostle Peter?
Bishop-elect: I am.

Principal consecrator:
Are you resolved as a devoted father to sustain the people of God and to guide them in the way of salvation in cooperation with the priests and deacons who share your ministry?
Bishop-elect: **I am.**

Principal consecrator:
Are you resolved to show kindness and compassion in the name of the Lord to the poor and to strangers and to all who are in need?
Bishop-elect: **I am.**

Principal consecrator:
Are you resolved as a good shepherd to seek out the sheep who stray and to gather them into the fold of the Lord?
Bishop-elect: **I am.**

Principal consecrator:
Are you resolved to pray for the people of God without ceasing, and to carry out the duties of one who has the fullness of the priesthood so as to afford no grounds for reproach?
Bishop-elect: **I am, with the help of God.**

Principal consecrator:
May God who has begun the good work in you bring it to fulfillment.

INVITATION TO PRAYER
20. Then all stand, and the bishop, without his miter, invites the people to pray:

My dear people, let us pray that almighty God in his goodness will pour out his grace upon this man whom he has chosen to provide for the needs of the Church.

Deacon (except during the Easter season):
Let us kneel.

LITANY OF THE SAINTS

21. The bishop-elect prostrates himself and, except during the Easter season, the rest kneel at their places.

The cantors begin the litany (see Chapter VI); they may add, at the proper place, names of other saints (for example, the patron saint, the titular of the church, the founder of the church, the patron saint of the one to be ordained) or petitions suitable to the occasion.

22. After the litany, the principal consecrator alone stands and, with hands joined sings or says:

Lord,
be moved by our prayers.
Anoint your servant with the fullness of priestly grace,
and bless him with spiritual power in all its richness.

We ask this through Christ our Lord.
℟. Amen.

Deacon: **Let us stand.**

LAYING ON OF HANDS

23. All rise. The principal consecrator and the consecrating bishops stand at their places, facing the people. The bishop-elect rises, goes to the principal consecrator, and kneels before him.

24. The principal consecrator lays his hands upon the head of the bishop-elect, in silence. After him, all the other bishops present do the same.

BOOK OF THE GOSPELS

25. Then the principal consecrator places the open Book of the Gospels upon the head of the bishop-elect; two deacons, standing at either side of the bishop-elect, hold the Book of the Gospels above his head until the prayer of consecration is completed.

PRAYER OF CONSECRATION

26. Next the principal consecrator, with his hands extended over the bishop-elect, sings the prayer of consecration or says it aloud:

God the Father of our Lord Jesus Christ,
Father of mercies and God of all consolation,
you dwell in heaven,
yet look with compassion on all that is humble.
You know all things before they come to be;
by your gracious word
you have established the plan of your Church.

From the beginning
you chose the descendants of Abraham to be your holy
    nation.
You established rulers and priests,
and did not leave your sanctuary without ministers to
    serve you.
From the creation of the world
you have been pleased to be glorified
by those whom you have chosen.

The following part of the prayer is recited by all the consecrating bishops, with hands joined:

So now pour out upon this chosen one
that power which is from you,
the governing Spirit
whom you gave to your beloved Son, Jesus Christ,
the Spirit given by him to the holy apostles,
who founded the Church in every place to be your
    temple
for the unceasing glory and praise of your name.

Then the principal consecrator continues alone:

Father, you know all hearts.
You have chosen your servant for the office of bishop.
May he be a shepherd to your holy flock,
and a high priest blameless in your sight,
ministering to you night and day;
may he always gain the blessing of your favor
and offer the gifts of your holy Church.
Through the Spirit who gives the grace of high priest-
    hood
grant him the power

to forgive sins as you have commanded,
to assign ministries as you have decreed,
and to loose every bond by the authority which you
    gave to your apostles.
May he be pleasing to you by his gentleness and purity
    of heart,
presenting a fragrant offering to you,
through Jesus Christ, your Son,
through whom glory and power and honor are yours
with the Holy Spirit
in your holy Church,
now and for ever.
℟. Amen.

27. After the prayer of consecration, the deacons remove the Book of the Gospels which they have been holding above the head of the new bishop. One of them holds the book until it is given to the bishop. The principal consecrator and the consecrating bishops, wearing their miters, sit.

ANOINTING OF THE BISHOP'S HEAD
28. The principal consecrator puts on a linen gremial, takes the chrism, and anoints the head of the bishop, who kneels before him. He says:

God has brought you to share the high priesthood
    of Christ,
May he pour out on you the oil of mystical anointing
and enrich you with spiritual blessings.

The principal consecrator washes his hands.

PRESENTATION OF THE BOOK OF THE GOSPELS
29. He then hands the Book of the Gospels to the newly ordained bishop, saying:

Receive the Gospel and preach the word of God with
unfailing patience and sound teaching.

Afterward the deacon takes the Book of the Gospels and returns it to its place.

INVESTITURE WITH RING, MITER, AND PASTORAL STAFF

30. The principal consecrator places the ring on the ring finger of the new bishop's right hand, saying:

**Take this ring, the seal of your fidelity.
With faith and love protect the bride of God, his holy Church.**

31. Then the principal consecrator places the miter on the head of the new bishop, in silence.

32. Lastly, he gives the pastoral staff to the bishop, and says:

**Take this staff as a sign of your pastoral office:
keep watch over the whole flock
in which the Holy Spirit has appointed you
to shepherd the Church of God.**

SEATING OF THE BISHOP

33. All stand. If the ordination takes place at the bishop's chair and if the new bishop is in his own church, the principal consecrator invites him to occupy the chair; in that case the principal consecrator sits at the right of the newly ordained bishop. If the new bishop is not in his own church, he is invited by the principal consecrator to take the first place among the concelebrating bishops.

If the ordination does not take place at the bishop's chair, the principal consecrator leads the newly ordained bishop to the chair or to a place prepared for him, and the consecrating bishops follow them.

KISS OF PEACE

34. The newly ordained then sets aside his staff and receives the kiss of peace from the principal consecrator and all the other bishops.

35. After the presentation of the staff, and until the end of the ordination rite, the following antiphon may be sung with Psalm 96.

Alleluia, go and teach all people my Gospel, alleluia.

The antiphon is repeated after every two verses. **Glory to the Father** is not said. The psalm is interrupted and the antiphon repeated when all have given the kiss of peace to the new bishop.

Any other appropriate song may be sung.

LITURGY OF THE EUCHARIST

36. The rite for the concelebration of Mass is followed with this change:

37. In Eucharistic Prayer I, the special form of **Father, accept this offering** is said:

Father, accept this offering
from your whole family
and from the one you have chosen for the order of
   bishops.
Protect the gifts you have given him,
and let him yield a harvest worthy of you.

[Through Christ our Lord. Amen.]

CONCLUDING RITE

HYMN OF THANKSGIVING AND BLESSING

38. At the conclusion of the prayer after communion, the hymn **Te Deum** is sung, or another hymn similar to it, depending on local custom. Meanwhile, the newly ordained bishop is led by the consecrating bishops through the church, and he blesses the congregation.

After the hymn, the new bishop may stand at the altar or at the chair with staff and miter and address the people briefly.

SOLEMN BLESSING

39. The following blessing may be used in place of the usual blessing. If the newly ordained bishop is the celebrant, he says:

Lord God,
you care for your people with kindness,
you rule them with love.
Give your Spirit of wisdom
to the bishops you have made teachers and pastors.
By advancing in holiness
may the flock become the eternal joy of the
    shepherds.
℞. Amen.

Lord God,
by your power you allot us
the number of our days and the measure of our
    years.
Look favorably upon the service we perform for you,
and give true, lasting peace in our time.
℞. Amen.

Lord God,
now that you have raised me to the order of bishops,
may I please you in the performance of my office.
Unite the hearts of people and bishop,
so that the shepherd may not be without the support of
    his flock,
or the flock without the loving concern of its shepherd.
℞. Amen.

May almighty God bless you,
the Father, and the Son, ✠ and the Holy Spirit.
℞. Amen.

If the principal consecrator presides over the eucharistic
liturgy, he says:

May the Lord bless and keep you.
He chose to make you a bishop for his people:
may you know happiness in this present life
and share unending joy.
℞. Amen.

The Lord has gathered his people and clergy in unity.
By his care and your stewardship

may they be governed happily for many years.
℟. Amen.

May they be obedient to God's law,
free from hardships,
rich in every blessing,
and loyally assist you in your ministry.
May they be blessed with peace and calm in this life
and come to share with you
the fellowship of the citizens of heaven.
℟. Amen.

May almighty God bless you,
the Father, and the Son, ✠ and the Holy Spirit.
℟. Amen.

CHAPTER VI

TEXTS FOR USE IN ORDINATIONS

BIBLICAL READINGS

ADMISSION TO CANDIDACY FOR ORDINATION AS DEACONS AND PRIESTS

The readings are taken in whole or in part from the Mass of the day or from the texts listed below.

READING FROM THE OLD TESTAMENT (L 775)

1. Deuteronomy 1:9-14
Choose wise, intelligent, and experienced men from each of your tribes, that I may appoint them as your leaders.

2. Sirach 39:1b, 5-8
He will give his heart early to the LORD, his maker.

3. Isaiah 6:1-2a, 3-8
Whom shall I send? Who will go for us?

4. Jeremiah 1:4-9
To whomever I send you, you shall go.

READING FROM THE NEW TESTAMENT (L 776)

1. Acts 14:21-23
They appointed presbyters for them in each Church.

2. 1 Corinthians 9:16-19, 22-23
Woe to me if I do not preach the Gospel!

3. 1 Corinthians 12:4-11
To each individual the manifestation of the Spirit is given for some benefit.

4. 2 Timothy 3:10-12, 14-15
Remain faithful to what you have learned.

RESPONSORIAL PSALM (L 777)

1. Psalm 16:1-2a and 5, 7-8, 11
℞. (see 5a) You are my inheritance, O Lord.

2. Psalm 24:1-2, 3-4ab, 5-6
℟. (see 6) **Lord, this is the people that longs to see your face.**

3. Psalm 98:1, 2-3ab, 3c-4, 5-6
℟. (2b) **The Lord has revealed to the nations his saving power.**

ALLELUIA VERSE AND VERSE BEFORE THE GOSPEL (L 778)

1. Mark 1:17
Come after me, says the Lord,
and I will make you fishers of men.

2. Luke 4:18
The Lord sent me to bring glad tidings to the poor,
and to proclaim liberty to captives.

3. John 12:26
Whoever serves me must follow me, says the Lord;
and where I am, there also will my servant be.

GOSPEL (L 779)

1. Matthew 9:35-38
Ask the master of the harvest to send out laborers for his harvest.

2. Mark 1:14-20
I will make you fishers of men.

3. Luke 5:1-11
At your command I will lower the nets.

4. John 1:35-42
Behold the Lamb of God. We have found the Messiah.

5. John 1:45-51
Here is a true child of Israel. There is no duplicity in him.

ORDINATION OF DEACONS, PRIESTS, AND BISHOPS

The readings may be taken in whole or in part from the Mass of the day or from the texts listed below.

Some of the readings are intended for a particular use. The others may be used at any ordination.

According to liturgical tradition, the Old Testament is not read during the Easter season; a preference is given, in the gospel, to the readings from John.

READING FROM THE OLD TESTAMENT (L 770)

1. Numbers 3:5-9
Summon the tribe of Levi and present them to Aaron the priest, as his assistants. [For deacons]

2. Numbers 11:11b-12, 14-17, 24-25
I will take some of the Spirit that is on you and I will bestow it on them. [For priests]

3. Isaiah 61:1-3abcd
The LORD has anointed me; he has sent me to bring glad tidings to the lowly and to give them the oil of gladness. [For bishops and priests]

4. Jeremiah 1:4-9
To whomever I send you, you shall go.

READING FROM THE OLD TESTAMENT (L 771)

1. Acts 6:1-7b
Select from among you seven reputable men. [For deacons]

2. Acts 8:26-40
Beginning with this Scripture passage, Philip proclaimed Jesus to him. [For deacons]

3. Acts 10:37-43
We are witnesses of all that he did both in the country of the Jews and in Jerusalem.

4. Acts 20:17-18a, 28-32, 36
Keep watch over yourselves and over the whole flock of which the Holy Spirit has apointed you overseers, in which you tend the Church of God. [For bishops and priests]

5. Romans 12:4-8
We have gifts that differ according to the grace given to us.

6. 2 Corinthians 4:1-2, 5-7
For we do not preach ourselves but Jesus Christ as Lord, and ourselves as your slaves for the sake of Jesus.

7. 2 Corinthians 5:14-20
He has given us the ministry of reconciliation.

8. Ephesians 4:1-7, 11-13
In the work of ministry, in building up the Body of Christ.

9. 1 Timothy 3:8-10, 12-13
Holding fast to the mystery of the faith with a clear conscience. [For deacons]

10. 1 Timothy 4:12-16
Do not neglect the gift you have, which was conferred on you with the imposition of hands by the presbyterate. [For priests] or: 1 Timothy 4:12b-16 [For bishops]

11. 2 Timothy 1:6-14
To stir into flame the gift of God that you have through the laying on of hands. [For bishops]

12. Hebrews 5:1-10
Christ was acclaimed by God as high priest, in the line of Melchizedek.

13. 1 Peter 4:7b-11
As good stewards of God's varied grace.

14. 1 Peter 5:1-4
Tend the flock of God in your midst.

RESPONSORIAL PSALM (L 772)

1. Psalm 23:1-3a, 3b-4, 5, 6
℟. (1) **The Lord is my shepherd; there is nothing I shall want.**

2. Psalm 84:3-4, 5, 11
℟. (5a) **Blessed are they who dwell in your house, O Lord.**

3. Psalm 89:21-22, 25 and 27
℟. (2a) **For ever I will sing the goodness of the Lord.**

4. Psalm 96:1-2a, 2b-3, 10
℟. **Go out to the world and teach all nations, alleluia.**

5. Psalm 100:1b-2, 3, 4, 5
℟. (John 15:14) **You are my friends, says the Lord, if you do not I command you.**

6. Psalm 110:1, 2, 3, 4
℟. **Christ the Lord, a priest for ever in the line of Melchizedek, offered bread and wine.**
or: ℟. (4b) **You are a priest for ever, in the line of Melchizedek.**

7. Psalm 116:12-13, 17-18
℟. (1 Corinthians 10:16) **Our blessing-cup is a communion with the blood of Christ.**
or: ℟. **Alleluia.**

8. Psalm 117:1, 2
℟. (Mark 16:15) **Go out to all the world, and tell the Good News.**
or: ℟. **Alleluia.**

ALLELUIA VERSE AND VERSE BEFORE THE GOSPEL
(L 773)

1. Matthew 28:19a, 20b
**Go and teach all nations, says the Lord;
I am with you always, until the end of the world.**

2. Luke 4:18
**The Lord sent me to bring glad tidings to the poor
and to proclaim liberty to captives.**

3. John 10:14
**I am the good shepherd, says the Lord;
I know my sheep, and mine know me.**

4. John 15:15b
**I call you my friends, says the Lord,
for I have made known to you all that the Father has told me.**

GOSPEL (L 774)

1. Matthew 5:13-16
You are the light of the world.

2. Matthew 9:35-38
Ask the master of the harvest to send out laborers for his harvest.

3. Matthew 10:1-5a
Jesus chose twelve Apostles and sent them out.

4. Matthew 20:25b-28
Whoever wishes to be first among you shall be your slave.

5. Luke 10:1-9
The harvest is abundant but the laborers are few.

6. Luke 12:35-44
Blessed are those servants whom the master finds awake on his arrival.

7. Luke 22:14-20, 24-30
Do this in memory of me. I am among you as the one who serves.

8. John 10:11-16
A good shepherd lays down his life for the sheep.

9. John 12:24-26
Whoever serves me must follow me.

10. John 15:9-17
It was not you who chose me, but I who chose you.

11. John 17:6, 14-19
I consecrate myself for them, so that they also may be consecrated in truth.

12. John 20:19-23
As the Father has sent me, so I send you. Receive the Holy Spirit.

13. John 21:15-17
Feed my lambs, feed my sheep.

LITANY OF THE SAINTS

The cantors begin the litany; they may add, at the proper place, names of other saints (for example, the patron saint, the titular of the church, the founder of the church, the patron saints of those to be ordained) or petitions suitable to the occasion.

Lord, have mercy   Lord, have mercy
Christ, have mercy   Christ, have mercy
Lord, have mercy   Lord, have mercy

Holy Mary, Mother of God   pray for us
Saint Michael   pray for us
Holy angels of God   pray for us
Saint John the Baptist   pray for us
Saint Joseph   pray for us
Saint Peter and Saint Paul   pray for us
Saint Andrew   pray for us
Saint John   pray for us
Saint Mary Magdalene   pray for us
Saint Stephen   pray for us
Saint Ignatius   pray for us

Saint Lawrence   pray for us
Saint Perpetua and Saint Felicity   pray for us
Saint Agnes   pray for us
Saint Gregory   pray for us
Saint Augustine   pray for us
Saint Athanasius   pray for us
Saint Basil   pray for us
Saint Martin   pray for us
Saint Benedict   pray for us
Saint Francis and Saint Dominic   pray for us
Saint Francis Xavier   pray for us
Saint John Vianney   pray for us
Saint Catherine   pray for us
Saint Teresa   pray for us
All holy men and women   pray for us

Lord, be merciful   Lord, save your people
From all evil   Lord, save your people
From every sin   Lord, save your people
From everlasting death   Lord, save your people
By your coming as man   Lord, save your people
By your death and rising to new life   Lord, save your
   people
By your gift of the Holy Spirit   Lord, save your people
Be merciful to us sinners   Lord, hear our prayer
Guide and protect your holy Church   Lord, hear our
   prayer
Keep the pope and all the clergy in faithful service
   to your Church   Lord, hear our prayer
Bring all peoples together in trust and peace
   Lord, hear our prayer
Strengthen us in your service
   Lord, hear our prayer

Bless these chosen men   Lord, hear our prayer
Bless these chosen men and make them holy   Lord,
   hear our prayer
Bless these chosen men, make them holy,
   and consecrate them for their sacred duties   Lord,
   hear our prayer

Bless this chosen man   Lord, hear our prayer
Bless this chosen man and make him holy   Lord, hear
our prayer
Bless this chosen man, make him holy,
and consecrate him for his sacred duties   Lord, hear
our prayer

Jesus, Son of the living God   Lord, hear our prayer
Christ, hear us   Christ, hear us
Lord Jesus, hear our prayer   Lord Jesus, hear our
prayer

CHAPTER VII

APPENDIX

BLESSING OF PONTIFICAL INSIGNIA

RECEPTION OF THE BISHOP IN THE CATHEDRAL CHURCH

Canonical Possession

Introductory Rites

Imposition of the Pallium

Greeting of the Bishop

Celebration of Mass

Participation of the Metropolitan

Reception of Coadjuter or Auxiliary Bishops

CHAPTER VII

BLESSING OF THE PONTIFICAL INSIGNIA

The pastoral ring, staff, and miter may be blessed at a convenient time prior to the ordination of the bishop or the blessing of the abbot.

℣. **Our help is in the name of the Lord.**
℟. **The Lord who made heaven and earth.**

℣. **The Lord be with you.**
℟. **And also with you.**

Let us pray.

Almighty, eternal God,
bless these symbols (this symbol)
of the pastoral office and the pontifical dignity.
May the one who uses them (it)
receive the reward of his faithfulness
and enter into eternal life
with Christ, the High Priest and Good Shepherd
who lives and reigns with you for ever and ever.
℟. **Amen.**

The pontifical insignia are then sprinkled with holy water.

RECEPTION OF THE BISHOP IN THE CATHEDRAL CHURCH

The ordination of a new bishop properly takes place in his cathedral church, in accord with the Roman Pontifical, and there is then no distinct rite for the reception or installation of the bishop. In some cases, however, the new bishop may have been ordained already as bishop of another church, or it may have been impossible for him to be ordained in his cathedral church. In these circumstances, the new bishop should be solemnly received in the cathedral church by the clergy and people of the local church when he first comes to the diocese.

This liturgical reception of the new bishop is sometimes called installation; its principal element is the eucharistic celebration at which the bishop presides for the first time with the college of priests and the deacons, and with people of the diocese taking full and active part.

CANONICAL POSSESSION

The new bishop may take canonical possession of the diocese before the liturgical reception. It is preferable, however, that this be done in the presence of the clergy and people, that is, by the presentation and reading of the apostolic letter at the beginning of Mass (below). The showing of the letter to the chapter of the cathedral church or to the board of consultors should be recorded by the chancellor.

INTRODUCTORY RITES

The bishop, vested for Mass, is received at the door of the cathedral church by the senior member of the presbyterium. This may be, for example, the senior member of the presbyteral council, the ranking dignitary of the chapter or board of consultors, the senior auxiliary bishop, or the rector of the church, according to local custom or circumstances.

The one who receives the bishop may offer him a crucifix to kiss and then give him the sprinkler with holy water. The bishop sprinkles himself and all who are present The entrance procession through the church takes place as usual, while the entrance song is sung. (If the bishop has not vested for Mass, he may visit the chapel of the Blessed Sacrament with the priests, deacons, and other ministers and then go to the vesting chapel, sacristy, or other convenient place.)

When he has arrived at his chair or *cathedra*, the bishop greets the people and, wearing the miter, sits. One of the deacons reads the apostolic letter at the lectern. All sit and listen; at the end they say **Thanks be to God** or make some other appropriate acclamation or response.

IMPOSITION OF THE PALLIUM

In the case of the reception of the metropolitan (or other bishop who is to receive the pallium), it is appropriate that the imposition of the pallium take place on the occasion of the liturgical reception in the cathedral church. In this case the pallium is carried in the entrance procession by one of the deacons and placed upon the altar. The senior suffragan bishop or other bishop who is to impose the pallium takes a position in a suitable place in the sanctuary. After the reading of the apostolic letter the metropolitan goes to him, kneels, and makes the prescribed profession of faith and oath.

The bishop who is to impose the pallium then rises without the miter, takes the pallium from the deacon, and places it on the shoulders of the bishop. He says:

**To the glory of almighty God
and the praise of the Blessed Virgin Mary
and of the apostles Peter and Paul,
in the name of Pope N., Bishop of Rome,
and of the holy Roman Church,
for the honor of the Church of N.,
which has been placed in your care,
and as a symbol of your authority as metropolitan
archbishop:
we confer on you the pallium taken from the tomb of
Peter
to wear within the limits of your ecclesiastical province.**

May this pallium be a symbol of unity
and a sign of your communion with the Apostolic See,
a bond of love, and an incentive to courage.
On the day of the coming and manifestation of our
    great God and chief shepherd, Jesus Christ,
may you and the flock entrusted to you
be clothed with immortality and glory.
In the name of the Father, and of the Son, and of the
    Holy Spirit.
℟. Amen.

GREETING OF THE BISHOP

The penitential rite and **Kyrie** are omitted.

After the apostolic letter has been read (or after the imposition of the pallium), the bishop is greeted, according to local custom, by the one who received him at the door of the church and then by the chapter or board of consultors, representatives of the presbyteral and pastoral councils, and at least some of the priests, deacons, and lay people of the local church, and, depending on circumstances, by members of other churches and ecclesial communities, religious bodies, civil authorities, and others.

Then the **Gloria** is sung, or another appropriate song if the **Gloria** is not permitted.

CELEBRATION OF MASS

The bishop then invites the people to pray, and, after a period of silent prayer, sings or says the opening prayer of Mass.

The liturgy of the word and the liturgy of the eucharist are celebrated in the usual way. After the gospel, the bishop addresses the people of the local church for the first time.

PARTICIPATION OF THE METROPOLITAN

If the metropolitan brings the new bishop to the cathedral church, he presents the bishop to the one who is to receive him at the door of the church. The metropolitan presides over the introductory liturgical rite. After the entrance procession he goes to the bishop's chair, greets the people, and asks that the apostolic letter be read.

After the reading and the acclamation, the metropolitan invites the bishop to take his place at the chair, and the **Gloria** is sung, as described above.

The metropolitan goes to his own place within the sanctuary and joins the new bishop in the eucharistic celebration.

RECEPTION OF COADJUTOR OR AUXILIARY BISHOPS

The ordination of a coadjutor or auxiliary bishop properly takes place in the cathedral church of the bishop whom he will assist in the pastoral ministry. If, however, the coadjutor or auxiliary bishop has been ordained already, it is appropriate that he be introduced to the people of the local church by the bishop of the diocese, during the celebration of the eucharist, after the greeting of the people. The coadjutor or auxiliary bishop then joins the bishop of the diocese in the eucharistic celebration.

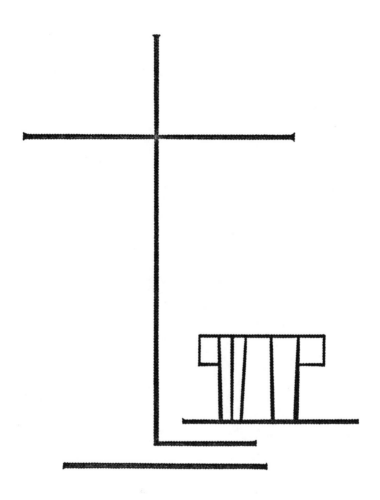

INSTITUTION OF MINISTERS
AND THE BLESSING OF PERSONS

INSTITUTION OF READERS AND ACOLYTES

Decree
Apostolic Letter

CHAPTER I
INSTITUTION OF READERS

Introduction (1)

Liturgy of the Word (2)

Institution of Readers (3-7)
    Calling of the Candidates (3)
    Homily (4)
    Invitation to Prayer (5)
    Prayer (6)
    Institution (7)

Liturgy of the Eucharist (8)

CHAPTER II
INSTITUTION OF ACOLYTES

Introduction (1)

Liturgy of the Word (2)

Institution of Acolytes (3-7)
    Calling of the Candidates (3)
    Homily (4)
    Invitation to Prayer (5)
    Prayer (6)
    Institution (7)

Liturgy of the Eucharist (8-10)

CHAPTER III
BIBLICAL READINGS

SACRED CONGREGATION FOR DIVINE WORSHIP

Prot. n. 1500/72

DECREE

The discipline for ministries was established by Pope Paul VI on 15 August 1972 through the Motu Proprio *Ministeria quaedam;* on the same day the norms were laid down for the diaconate, whether transitional or permanent, through the Motu Proprio *Ad pascendum.* The Congregation for Divine Worship has therefore duly prepared the rite of institution of readers and acolytes, the rite of admission to candidacy for ordination as deacons and priests, and the rite of commitment to celibacy.

Pope Paul VI by his authority has approved these rites and ordered their publication for use in Latin beginning on 1 January 1973. They are to be used in the vernacular beginning on a date to be established by the conferences of bishops for their own regions, after they have approved the translations and have obtained the Apostolic See's confirmation.

Anything to the contrary notwithstanding.

From the office of the Congregation for Divine Worship, 3 December 1972, the memorial of Saint Francis Xavier.

Arthuro Cardinal Tabera
Prefect

✠ Annibale Bugnini
Titular Archbishop of Diocletiana
Secretary

APOSTOLIC LETTER

ISSUED *MOTU PROPRIO* BY WHICH THE DISCIPLINE OF FIRST TONSURE, MINOR ORDERS, AND SUBDIACONATE IN THE LATIN CHURCH IS REFORMED

POPE PAUL VI

Certain ministries were established by the Church even in the most ancient times for the purpose of suitably giving worship to God and for offering service to the people of God according to their needs. By these ministries, the offices to be carried out in the liturgy and the practice of charity, deemed suitable to varying circumstances, were entrusted to the faithful. The conferring of these functions often took place by a special rite, in which, after God's blessing had been implored, a Christian was established in a special class or rank for the fulfillment of some ecclesiastical function.

Some of these functions, which were more closely connected with the liturgical celebration, slowly came to be considered as a training in preparation for the reception of sacred orders. As a result, the offices of porter, reader, exorcist, and acolyte were called minor orders in the Latin Church in relation to the subdiaconate, diaconate, and priesthood, which were called major orders. Generally, though not everywhere, these minor orders were reserved to those who received them as steps toward the priesthood.

Nevertheless, since the minor orders have not always been the same and many functions connected with them, as at present, have also been exercised by the laity, it seems fitting to reexamine this practice and to adapt it to contemporary needs. What is obsolete in these offices will thus be removed and what is useful retained; also anything new that is needed will be introduced and at the same time the requirements for candidates for holy orders will be established.

While Vatican Council II was in preparation, many bishops of the Church requested that the minor orders and subdiaconate be revised. Although the Council did not decree anything concerning this for the Latin Church, it stated certain principles for resolving the issue. There is no doubt that the norms laid down by the Council regarding the general and orderly reform of the liturgy[1] also include those areas that concern ministries in the liturgical assembly, so that the very arrangement of the celebration itself makes the Church stand out as being formed in a structure of different orders and ministries.[2] Thus Vatican Council II decreed that "in liturgical celebrations each one, minister or layperson, who has an office to perform, should do all of, but only, those parts which pertain to that office by the nature of the rite and the principles of liturgy."[3]

With this assertion is closely connected what was written a little earlier in the same Constitution: "The Church earnestly desires that all the faithful be led to that full, conscious, and active participation in liturgical celebrations called for by the very nature of the liturgy. Such participation by the Christian people as 'a chosen race, a royal priesthood, a holy nation, a purchased people' (1 Pt 2:9; see 2:4–5) is their right and duty by reason of their baptism. In the reform and promotion of the liturgy, this full and active participation by all the people is the aim to be considered before all else. For it is the primary and indispensable source from which the faithful are to derive the true Christian spirit and therefore pastors must zealously strive in all their pastoral work to achieve such participation by means of the necessary instruction."[4]

Among the particular offices to be preserved and adapted to contemporary needs are those that are in a special way more closely connected with the ministries of the word and of the altar and that in the Latin Church are called the offices of *reader* and *acolyte* and the subdiaconate. It is fitting to preserve and adapt these in such a way, that from this time on there will be two offices: that of reader and that of acolyte, which will include the functions of the subdiaconate.

In addition to the offices universal in the Latin Church, the conferences of bishops may request others of the Apostolic

---

[1]See SC art. 62 [DOL 1 no. 62]; see also art. 21 [DOL 1 no. 21].
[2]See GIRM no. 58 [DOL 208 no. 1448].
[3]SC art. 28 [DOL 1 no. 28].
[4]SC art. 14 [DOL 1 no. 14].

See, if they judge the establishment of such offices in their region to be necessary or very useful because of special reasons. To these belong, for example, the ministries of *porter, exorcist, catechist,*[5] as well as others to be conferred on those who are dedicated to works of charity, where this ministry had not been assigned to deacons.

It is in accordance with the reality itself and with the contemporary outlook that the above-mentioned ministries should no longer be called minor orders; their conferral will not be called *ordination,* but *institution.* Only those who have received the diaconate, however, will be clerics in the true sense and will be so regarded. This arrangement will bring out more clearly the distinction between clergy and laity, between what is proper and reserved to the clergy and what can be entrusted to the laity. This will also bring out more clearly that mutuality by which "the universal priesthood of believers and the ministerial or hierarchic priesthood, though they differ from one another in essence and not only in degree, are nonetheless interrelated: each of them in its own special way is a sharing in the one priesthood of Christ."[6]

After weighing every aspect of the question, seeking the opinion of experts, consulting with the conferences of bishops and taking their views into account, and after taking counsel with our esteemed brothers who are members of the congregations competent in this matter, by our apostolic authority we enact the following norms, amending—if and insofar as is necessary—provisions of the *Codex Iuris Canonici* now in force, and we promulgate them through this Motu Proprio.

1. First tonsure is no longer conferred; entrance into the clerical state is joined to the diaconate.

2. What up to now were called minor orders are henceforth to be called *ministries.*

[5] See AG no. 15: AAS 58 (1966) 965; ConstDecrDecl 574; see also AG no. 17 [DOL 17 no. 249].
[6] LG no. 10 [DOL 4 no. 140].

3. Ministries may be assigned to lay Christians; hence they are no longer to be considered as reserved to candidates for the sacrament of orders.

4. Two ministries, adapted to present-day needs, are to be preserved in the whole Latin Church, namely, those of reader and acolyte. The functions heretofore assigned to the subdeacon are entrusted to the reader and the acolyte; consequently, the major order of subdiaconate no longer exists in the Latin Church. There is, however, no reason why the acolyte cannot be called a subdeacon in some places, at the discretion of the conference of bishops.

5. The reader is appointed for a function proper to him, that of reading the word of God in the liturgical assembly. Accordingly, he is to proclaim the readings from sacred Scripture, except for the gospel in the Mass and other sacred celebrations; he is to recite the psalm between the readings when there is no psalmist; he is to present the intentions for the general intercessions in the absence of a deacon or cantor; he is to direct the singing and the participation by the faithful; he is to instruct the faithful for the worthy reception of the sacraments. He may also, insofar as may be necessary, take care of preparing other faithful who are appointed on a temporary basis to read the Scriptures in liturgical celebrations. That he may more fittingly and perfectly fulfill these functions, he is to meditate assiduously on sacred Scripture.

Aware of the office he has undertaken, the reader is to make every effort and employ suitable means to acquire that increasingly warm and living love[7] and knowledge of Scripture that will make him a more perfect disciple of the Lord.

6. The acolyte is appointed in order to aid the deacon and to minister to the priest. It is his duty therefore to attend to the service of the altar and to assist the deacon and the priest in liturgical celebrations, especially in the celebration of Mass; he is also to distribute communion as a special minister when the ministers spoken of in the *Codex Iuris Canonici* can.

[7]See SC art. 24 [DOL 1 no. 24]; DV no. 25 [DOL 14 no. 227].

845 are not available or are prevented by ill health, age, or another pastoral ministry from performing this function, or when the number of communicants is so great that the celebration of Mass would be unduly prolonged. In the same extraordinary circumstances an acolyte may be entrusted with publicly exposing the blessed sacrament for adoration by the faithful and afterward replacing it, but not with blessing the people. He may also, to the extent needed, take care of instructing other faithful who on a temporary basis are appointed to assist the priest or deacon in liturgical celebrations by carrying the missal, cross, candles, etc., or by performing other such duties. He will perform these functions more worthily if he participates in the holy eucharist with increasingly fervent devotion, receives nourishment from it, and deepens his knowledge about it.

As one set aside in a special way for the service of the altar, the acolyte should learn all matters concerning public divine worship and strive to grasp their inner spiritual meaning: in that way he will be able each day to offer himself entirely to God, be an example to all by his gravity and reverence in church, and have a sincere love for the Mystical Body of Christ, the people of God, especially for the weak and the sick.

7. In accordance with the ancient tradition of the Church, institution to the ministries of reader and acolyte is reserved to men.

8. The following are requirements for admission to the ministries:
a) the presentation of a petition that has been freely made out and signed by the aspirant to the Ordinary (the bishop and, in clerical institutes, the major superior) who has the right to accept the petition;
b) a suitable age and special qualities to be determined by the conference of bishops;
c) a firm will to give faithful service to God and the Christian people.

9. The ministries are conferred by the Ordinary (the bishop and, in clerical institutes, the major superior) through the li-

turgical rite *De institutione lectoris* and *De institutione acolythi* as revised by the Apostolic See.

10. An interval, determined by the Holy See or the conferences of bishops, shall be observed between the conferring of the ministries of reader and acolyte whenever more than one ministry is conferred on the same person.

11. Unless they have already done so, candidates for ordination as deacons and priests are to receive the ministries of reader and acolyte and are to exercise them for a suitable time, in order to be better disposed for the future service of the word and of the altar. Dispensation from receiving these ministries on the part of such candidates is reserved to the Holy See.

12. The conferring of ministries does not bring with it the right to support or remuneration from the Church.

13. The rite of institution of readers and acolytes will soon be published by the competent department of the Roman Curia.

The effective date of these norms is 1 January 1973.

We command as established and confirmed whatever this Motu Proprio has decreed, all things to the contrary notwithstanding.

Given in Rome, at Saint Peter's, on 15 August 1972, the Solemnity of the Assumption, the tenth year of our pontification.

Paul VI

CHAPTER I

INSTITUTION OF READERS

INTRODUCTION

1. The bishop or the major superior of a clerical religious institute carries out the institution of readers, either within Mass or at a celebration of the word of God.

LITURGY OF THE WORD

2. The readings are taken in whole or in part from the liturgy of the day or, alternatively, from the texts listed in Chapter III.

INSTITUTION OF READERS

CALLING OF THE CANDIDATES

3. After the gospel, the bishop, wearing his miter, sits, and the appointed deacon or priest calls the candidates:

Those to be instituted in the ministry of reader please come forward.

The candidates are called by name, and each one answers: **Present,** and goes to the bishop, before whom he makes a sign of reverence.

HOMILY

4. Then all sit, and the bishop gives the homily, which he concludes by speaking to the candidates in these or similar words:

Dear sons in Christ, through his Son, who became man for us, God the Father has revealed the mystery of salvation and brought it to fulfillment. Jesus Christ made all things known to us and then entrusted his Church with the mission of preaching the Gospel to the whole world.

As readers and bearers of God's word, you will assist in this mission, and so take on a special office within the Christian community; you will be given a respon-

sibility in the service of the faith, which is rooted in the word of God. You will proclaim that word in the liturgical assembly, instruct children and adults in the faith, and prepare them to receive the sacraments worthily. You will bring the message of salvation to those who have not yet received it. Thus with your help men and women will come to know God our Father and his Son Jesus Christ, whom he sent, and so be able to reach eternal life.

In proclaiming God's word to others, accept it yourselves in obedience to the Holy Spirit. Meditate on it constantly, so that each day you will have a deeper love of the Scriptures, and in all you say and do show forth to the world our Savior, Jesus Christ.

INVITATION TO PRAYER

5. Then all stand, and the bishop, without his miter, invites the people to pray:

Brothers and sisters, let us ask God our Father to bless these servants who have been chosen for the ministry of reader. Let us pray that they may be faithful to the work entrusted to them, proclaim Christ to the world, and so give glory to our Father in heaven.

All pray in silence for a brief period.

PRAYER

6. Then the bishop, with hands joined, continues:

Lord God,
source of all goodness and light,
you sent your only Son, the Word of life,
to reveal to mankind the mystery of your love.

Bless ✠ our brothers
who have been chosen for the ministry of reader.
Grant that as they meditate constantly on your word
they may grow in its wisdom
and faithfully proclaim it to your people.

We ask this through Christ our Lord.
℟. Amen.

INSTITUTION

7. Each candidate goes to the bishop, who gives him the Bible, saying:

**Take this book of holy Scripture
and be faithful in handing on the word of God,
so that it may grow strong in the hearts of his people.**
The reader answers: **Amen.**

Meanwhile, Psalm 19 or another appropriate song may be sung, especially if there are many candidates.

LITURGY OF THE EUCHARIST

8. If the institution of readers takes place during Mass, the Mass continues as usual. If the institution takes place during a celebration of the word, the bishop blesses the assembly and dismisses it in the usual manner.

CHAPTER II

INSTITUTION OF ACOLYTES

INTRODUCTION

1. The bishop or the major superior of a clerical religious institute carries out the institution of acolytes, within Mass.

LITURGY OF THE WORD

2. The readings are taken in whole or in part from the liturgy of the day or, alternatively, from the texts listed in Chapter III.

INSTITUTION OF ACOLYTES

CALLING OF THE CANDIDATES

3. After the gospel, the bishop, wearing his miter, sits, and the appointed deacon or priest calls the candidates:

Those to be instituted in the ministry of acolyte please come forward.

The candidates are called by name, and each one answers: **Present**, and goes to the bishop, before whom he makes a sign of reverence.

HOMILY

4. Then all sit, and the bishop gives the homily, which he concludes by speaking to the candidates in these or similar words:

Dear sons in Christ, as people chosen for the ministry of acolyte, you will have a special role in the Church's ministry. The summit and source of the Church's life is the eucharist, which builds up the Christian community and makes it grow. It is your responsibility to assist priests and deacons in carrying out their ministry, and as special ministers to give holy communion to the faithful at the liturgy and to the sick. Because you are specially called to this ministry, you should strive

to live more fully by the Lord's sacrifice and to be molded more perfectly in its likeness. You should seek to understand the deep spiritual meaning of what you do, so that you may offer yourselves daily to God as spiritual sacrifices acceptable to him through Jesus Christ.

In performing your ministry bear in mind that, as you share the one bread with your brothers and sisters, so you form one body with them. Show a sincere love for Christ's Mystical Body, God's holy people, and especially for the weak and the sick. Be obedient to the commandment which the Lord gave to his apostles at the Last Supper: "Love one another as I also have loved you."

INVITATION TO PRAYER

5. Then all stand, and the bishop, without his miter, invites the people to pray:

Brothers and sisters, let us pray to the Lord for those chosen by him to serve in the ministry of acolyte. Let us ask him to fill them with his blessing and strengthen them for faithful service in his Church.

All pray in silence for a brief period.

PRAYER

6. Then the bishop, with hands joined, continues:

God of mercy
through your only Son
you entrusted the bread of life to your Church.
Bless ✠ our brothers
who have been chosen for the ministry of acolyte.
Grant that they may be faithful
in the service of your altar
and in giving to others the bread of life;
may they grow always in faith and love,
and so build up your Church.

We ask this through Christ our Lord.
℟. Amen.

INSTITUTION

7. Each candidate goes to the bishop, who gives him a vessel with the bread or wine to be consecrated, saying:

**Take this vessel with bread (wine)
for the celebration of the eucharist.
Make your life worthy of your service
at the table of the Lord and of his Church.**
The acolyte answers: **Amen.**

LITURGY OF THE EUCHARIST

8. At the preparation of the gifts, the acolytes (or some of them, if the number is large) present the patens with the bread and the chalice with the wine.

9. The acolytes receive communion immediately after the deacons.

10. In the Mass of institution the bishop may direct the acolyte as a special minister to help in giving communion to the faithful.

CHAPTER III

BIBLICAL READINGS

FOR THE INSTITUTION OF READERS

READING FROM THE OLD TESTAMENT (L 780)

1. Deuteronomy 6:3-9
Take to heart these words.

2. Deuteronomy 30:10-14
It is something very near to you. You have only to carry it out.

3. Nehemiah 8:2-4a, 5-6, 8-10
Ezra read plainly from the book of the law, interpreting it.

4. Isaiah 55:10-11
The rain watered the earth, making it fertile.

READING FROM THE NEW TESTAMENT (L 781)

1. 1 Corinthians 2:1-5
Proclaiming the mystery of God.

2. 2 Timothy 3:14-17
All Scripture is inspired by God and is useful for teaching.

3. 2 Timothy 4:1-5
Perform the work of an evangelist; fulfill your ministry.

4. Hebrews 4:12-13
The word of God is able to discern reflections and thoughts of the heart.

5. 1 John 1:1-4
What we have seen and heard we now proclaim to you.

RESPONSORIAL PSALM (L 782)

1. Psalm 19:8, 9, 10, 11
℞. (see John 6:64b) **Your words, Lord, are spirit and life.**

2. Psalm 119:9, 10, 11, 12
℞. (12b) **Lord, teach me your statutes.**

3. Psalm 147:15-16, 17-18, 19-20
℞. (12) **Praise the Lord, Jerusalem.**

ALLELUIA VERSE AND VERSE BEFORE THE GOSPEL (L 783)

1. Luke 4:18
The Spirit of the Lord is upon me
he has sent me to bring glad tidings to the poor.

2. See John 6:63c, 68c
Your words, Lord, are Spirit and life;
you have the words of everlasting life.

3. See Acts 16:14b
Open our hearts, O Lord,
to listen to the words of your Son.

4.
The seed is the word of God, Christ is the sower;
all who come to him will live for ever.

GOSPEL (L 784)

1. Matthew 5:14-19
You are the light of the world

2. Mark 1:35-39
He went into their synagogues, preaching.

3. Luke 4:16-21
The Spirit of the Lord is upon me.

4. Luke 24:44-48
Jesus sent the Apostles to preach repentance, for the forgive-
ness of sins.

5. John 7:14-18
My teaching is not my own, but is from the One who sent me.

FOR THE INSTITUTION OF ACOLYTES

READING FROM THE OLD TESTAMENT (L 785)

1. Genesis 14:18-20
Melchizedek brought out bread and wine.

2. Exodus 16:2-4, 12-15
I will rain down bread from heaven for you.

3. Exodus 24:3-8
This is the blood of the covenant that the Lord has made
with you.

4. Deuteronomy 8:2-3, 14b-16a
He fed you with manna, a food unknown to you and your fathers.

5. 1 Kings 19:4-8
He walked forty days and forty nights to the mountain of God.

6. Proverbs 9:1-6
Come, eat my food, and drink the wine I have mixed.

READING FROM THE NEW TESTAMENT (L 786)

1. Acts 2:42-47
They devoted themselves to meeting together and breaking bread.

2. Acts 10:34a, 37-43
To us, who ate and drank with him after he rose from the dead.

3. 1 Corinthians 10:16-17
Because the loaf of bread is one, we, though many, are one Body.

4. 1 Corinthians 11:23-26
As often as you eat this bread and drink the cup, you proclaim the death of the Lord.

5. Hebrews 9:11-15
The Blood of Christ will cleanse our conscience.

RESPONSORIAL PSALM (L 787)

1. Psalm 23:1-3a, 3b-4, 5, 6
℟. **(1) The Lord is my shepherd; there is nothing I shall want.**

2. Psalm 34:2-3, 4-5, 6-7, 8-9, 10-11
℟. **(9a) Taste and see the goodness of the Lord.**

3. Psalm 78:3 and 4bc, 23-24, 25, 54
℟. **(24b) The Lord gave them bread from heaven.**

4. Psalm 110:1, 2, 3, 4
℟. **(4bc) You are a priest for ever, in the line of Melchizedek.**

5. Psalm 116:12-13, 15 and 16bc, 17-18
℟. (13) **I will take the cup of salvation, and call on the name of the Lord.**

6. Psalm 145:10-11, 15-16, 17-18
℟. (see 16) **You open your hand to feed us, Lord; you answer all our needs.**

7. Psalm 147:12-13, 14-15, 19-20
℟. (John 6:58c) **Whoever eats this bread will live forever.**

ALLELUIA VERSE AND VERSE BEFORE THE GOSPEL (L 788)

1. John 6:35
I am the bread of life, says the Lord;
whoever comes to me will never hunger,
and whoever believes in me will never thirst.

2. John 6:51
I am the living bread that came down from heaven,
says the Lord; whoever eats this bread will live forever.

3. John 6:56
Whoever eats my Flesh and drinks my Blood
remains in me and I in him, says the Lord.

4. John 6:57
Just as the living Father sent me and I have life because
    of the Father,
so also the one who feeds on me will have life because of
    me.

GOSPEL

1. Mark 14:12-16, 22-26
This is my Body. This is my Blood.

2. Luke 9:11b-17
They all ate and were satisfied.

3. Luke 24:13-35
He was made known to them in the breaking of the
bread.

4. John 6:1-15
Jesus distributed to those who were reclining, as much as
they wanted.

5. John 6:24-35
Whoever comes to me will never hunger, and whoever believes in me will never thirst.

6. John 6:41-51
I am the living bread that came down from heaven.

7. John 6:51-59
My Flesh is true food and my Blood true drink.

8. John 21:1-14
Jesus took the bread and gave it to them.

BLESSING OF PERSONS

BLESSING OF PERSONS

ORDER FOR THE BLESSING OF THOSE WHO EXERCISE
PASTORAL SERVICE
Introduction (1808-1810)

I. Order of Blessing within Mass (1811)
General Intercessions (1812)
Prayer of Blessing (1813)

II. Order of Blessing within a Celebration of the Word of God
(1814)
Introductory Rites (1815-1817)
Reading of the Word of God (1818-1821)
Intercessions (1822-1823)
Prayer of Blessing (1824)
Concluding Rites (1825-1826)

ORDER FOR THE BLESSING OF READERS
Introduction (1827-1830)

I. Order of Blessing within Mass (1831)
General Intercessions (1832)
Prayer of Blessing (1833)

II. Order of Blessing within a Celebration of the Word of God
(1834)
Introductory Rites (1835-1837)
Reading of the Word of God (1838-1841)
Intercessions (1842-1843)
Prayer of Blessing (1844)
Concluding Rites (1845-1846)

ORDER FOR THE BLESSING OF ALTAR SERVERS, SAC-
RISTANS, MUSICIANS, AND USHERS
Introduction (1847-1851)

I. Order of Blessing within Mass (1852)
General Intercesssions (1853)
Prayer of Blessing (1854)

II. Order of Blessing within Celebration of the Word (1855)
Introductory Rites (1856-1857)

Introduction (1858)
Reading of the Word of God (1859-1866)
Intercessions (1866-1867)
Prayer of Blessing (1868)
Concluding Rite (1869-1870)

ORDER FOR THE COMMISSIONING OF EXTRAORDINARY MINISTERS OF HOLY COMMUNION
Introduction (1871-1873)

I. Order of Commissioning within Mass (1874)
Presentation of the Candidates (1875)
Examination (1876)
Prayer of Blessing (1877-1878)
General Intercessions (1879-1880)
Liturgy of the Eucharist (1881)

II. Order of Commissioning within a Celebration of the Word of God
Introductory Rites (1882-1884)
Reading of the Word of God (1885-1888)
Presentation of the Candidates (1889)
Examination (1890)
Prayer of Blessing (1891-1892)
Intercessions (1893-1894)
Concluding Rites (1895-1896)

ORDER FOR THE BLESSING OF THOSE WHO EXERCISE PASTORAL SERVICE

INTRODUCTION

1808. In the life of a parish there is a diversity of services that are exercised by lay persons. It is fitting that as people publicly begin their service they receive the blessing of God who gives the gifts needed to carry out this work.

1809. This order may be celebrated during Mass or during a celebration of the word of God.

1810. This blessing may be given by a priest or a deacon.

I. ORDER OF BLESSING WITHIN MASS

1811. After the gospel reading, the celebrant in the homily, based on the sacred text and pertinent to the particular place and the people involved, explains the meaning of the celebration.

GENERAL INTERCESSIONS

1812. The general intercessions follow, either in the form usual at Mass or in the form provided here. The celebrant concludes the intercessions with the prayer of blessing. From the following intentions those best for the occasion may be used or adapted, or other intentions that apply to the particular circumstances may be composed.

The celebrant says:

Let us now ask God to strengthen and bless our brothers and sisters as they begin their new pastoral service in this parish.

℟. Lord, hear our prayer.

Or:

℟. We beseech you, hear us.

Assisting minister:

That those who exercise a pastoral service may grow to a greater love of Christ, let us pray to the Lord. ℟.

Assisting minister:

That they may lighten the burdens of the others and assist them in their struggles, let us pray to the Lord. ℟.

Assisting minister:

That the Holy Spirit may strengthen their hearts and enlighten their minds, let us pray to the Lord. ℟.

Assisting minister:

That through their endeavors this parish may grow in faith, hope, and love, let us pray to the Lord. ℟.

PRAYER OF BLESSING

1813. With hands extended over the new ministers, the celebrant says immediately:

Lord God,
in your loving kindness
you sent your Son to be our shepherd and guide.
Continue to send workers into your vineyard
to sustain and direct your people.

Bless N.N. and N.N.
Let your Spirit uphold them always
as they take up their new responsibility
among the people of this parish.

We ask this through Christ our Lord.
℟. Amen.

II. ORDER OF BLESSING WITHIN A CELEBRATION OF THE WORD OF GOD

1814. The present order may be used by a priest or a deacon.

INTRODUCTORY RITES

1815. When the community has gathered, a suitable song may be sung. After the singing, the minister says:

In the name of the Father, and of the Son, and of the Holy Spirit.

All make the sign of the cross and reply:

Amen.

1816. The minister greets those present in the following or other suitable words, taken mainly from sacred Scripture.

May the God of love and peace be with you all.

And all reply:

And also with you.

1817. In the following or similar words, the minister prepares those present for the blessing.

The needs of the Church are many and varied but God shows his goodness by sending pastoral workers to care for the Church. Today we ask God to bless our brothers and sisters who have declared their willingness to serve the Church.

READING OF THE WORD OF GOD

1818. A reader, another person present, or the minister reads a text of sacred Scripture.

Brothers and sisters, listen to the words of the holy gospel according to Matthew: 5:1-12

Rejoice, for your reward in heaven is great.

When Jesus saw the crowds, he went up the mountain, and after he had sat down, his disciples came to him. He began to teach them, saying:

**"Blessed are the poor in the spirit,
for theirs is the kingdom of heaven.
Blessed are they who mourn,
for they will be comforted.
Blessed are the meek,
for they will inherit the land.
Blessed are they who hunger and thirst for righteousness,
for they will be satisfied.
Blessed are the merciful,
for they will be shown mercy.
Blessed are the clean of heart,
for they will see God.
Blessed are the peacemakers,
for they will be called children of God.**

Blessed are they who are persecuted for the sake of
   righteousness,
for theirs is the kingdom of heaven.

Blessed are you when they insult you and persecute you
and utter every kind of evil against you falsely because
of me. Rejoice and be glad, for your reward will be great
in heaven. Thus they persecuted the prophets who were
before you."

1819. Or:

Jeremiah 1:4-9
To whomever I send you, you shall go.

Romans 10:9-18
How will they hear without someone preaching?

Mark 16:15-20
Go into the whole world and preach the gospel.

1820. As circumstances suggest, one of the following responsorial psalms may be sung, or some other suitable song.
℟. Happy are those who trust in the Lord.

Psalm 96
Sing to the LORD a new song;
sing to the LORD, all you lands.
Sing to the LORD, bless his name. ℟.

Announce his salvation, day after day.
Tell his glory among the nations;
among all peoples, his wondrous deeds. ℟.

Give to the LORD, you families of nations,
give to the LORD glory and praise;
give to the LORD the glory due his name! ℟.

Psalm 121:1-2, 3-4, 5-6, 7-8
℟. (v. 2) Our help is from the Lord, who made heaven and
earth.

1821. As circumstances suggest, the minister may give those present a brief explanation of the biblical text, so that they may understand through faith the meaning of the celebration.

INTERCESSIONS

1822. The intercessions are then said. The minister introduces them and an assisting minister or one of those present announces the intentions. From the following those best suited to the occasion may be used or adapted, or other intentions that apply to the particular circumstances may be composed.

The minister says:

Let us now ask God to strengthen and bless our brothers and sisters as they begin their new pastoral service in this parish.

℟. We beseech you, hear us.

Assisting minister:

That those who exercise a pastoral service may grow to a greater love of Christ, let us pray to the Lord. ℟.

Assisting minister:

That they may lighten the burdens of others and assist them in their struggles, let us pray to the Lord. ℟.

Assisting minister:

That the Holy Spirit may strengthen their hearts and enlighten their minds, let us pray to the Lord. ℟.

Assisting minister:

That through their endeavors this parish may grow in faith, hope, and love, let us pray to the Lord. ℟.

1823. After the intercessions the minister, in the following or similar words, invites all present to sing or say the Lord's Prayer.

Let us pray to the Father in the words Jesus gave us:

All:

Our Father . . .

PRAYER OF BLESSING

1824. The minister says the prayer of blessing with hands out-stretched over the new ministers.

Lord God,
in your loving kindness
you sent your Son to be our shepherd and guide.
Continue to send workers into your vineyard
to sustain and direct your people.

Bless N.N. and N.N.
Let your Spirit uphold them always
as they take up their new responsibility
among the people of this parish.

We ask this through Christ our Lord.
R̸. Amen.

CONCLUDING RITE

1825. The minister concludes the rite by saying:

May almighty God bless you in his mercy,
and make you aware of his saving wisdom.
R̸. Amen.

May he strengthen your faith with proofs of his love,
so that you may persevere in good works.
R̸. Amen.

May he direct your steps to himself
and show you how to walk in charity and peace.
R̸. Amen.

Then he blesses all present.

And may almighty God bless you all,
the Father, and Son, ✠ and the Holy Spirit.
R̸. Amen.

1826. It is preferable to end the celebration with a suitable song.

ORDER FOR THE BLESSING OF READERS

INTRODUCTION

1827. The word of God, as proclaimed in the sacred Scripture, lies at the heart of our Christian life and is integral to all our liturgical celebrations.

1828. This order is not intended for the institution of readers by the bishop, who uses the rite contained in the Roman Pontifical. Rather, this blessing is for parish readers who have the responsibility of proclaiming the Scriptures at Mass and other liturgical services. Care should be taken to see that readers are properly prepared for the exercise of their ministry before receiving this blessing. The functions of the reader are given in no. 66 of the General Instruction of the Roman Missal.

1829. If desired, each new reader may be presented with a lectionary or bible after the prayer of blessing.

1830. This blessing is given by the pastor, who may also delegate it to another priest or a deacon.

I. ORDER OF BLESSING WITHIN MASS

1831. After the gospel reading, the celebrant in the homily, based on the sacred text and pertinent to the particular place and the people involved, explains the meaning of the celebration.

GENERAL INTERCESSIONS

1832. The general intercessions follow, either in the form usual at Mass or in the form provided here. The celebrant concludes the intercessions with the prayer of blessing. From the following intentions those best for the occasion may be used or adapted, or other intentions that apply to the particular circumstances may be composed.

The celebrant says:

The word of God calls us out of darkness into the light of faith. With the confidence of God's children let us ask the Lord to hear our prayers and to bless these readers:

℟. **Lord, hear our prayer.**

Or:
℟. **Lord, graciously hear us.**

Assisting minister:
For the Church, that we may continue to respond to the word of God which is proclaimed in our midst, we pray to the Lord. ℟.

Assisting minister:
For all who listen as the Scriptures are proclaimed, that God's word may find in them a fruitful field, we pray to the Lord. ℟.

Assisting minister:
For those who have not heard the message of Christ, that we may be willing to bring them the good news of salvation, we pray to the Lord. ℟.

Assisting minister:
For our readers, that with deep faith and confident voice they may announce God's saving word, we pray to the Lord. ℟.

PRAYER OF BLESSING
1833. With hands extended over the new readers the celebrant says immediately:
Everlasting God,
when he read in the synagogue at Nazareth,
your Son proclaimed the good news of salvation
for which he would give up his life.

Bless these readers.
As they proclaim your words of life,
strengthen their faith
that they may read with conviction and boldness,
and put into practice what they read.

We ask this through Christ our Lord.
℟. **Amen.**

II. ORDER OF BLESSING WITHIN A CELEBRATION OF THE WORD OF GOD

1834. The present order may be used by a priest or a deacon.

INTRODUCTORY RITES

1835. When the community has gathered, a suitable song may be sung. After the singing, the minister says:

In the name of the Father, and of the Son, and of the Holy Spirit.

All make the sign of the cross and reply:

Amen.

1836. The minister greets those present in the following or other suitable words, taken mainly from sacred Scripture.

May the Lord, whose word dwells in your hearts, be with you.

And all reply:

And also with you.

1837. In the following or similar words, the minister prepares those present for the blessing.

The word of God, proclaimed in the sacred Scripture, enlightens our minds and hearts. When the Scriptures are read in the liturgical assembly, God speaks to us and calls us to respond in faith and love. The ministry of the reader, then, is important to the life of the Church, for the reader proclaims God's living word. We ask God to bless these readers and all of us who now listen to the word of the Lord.

READING OF THE WORD OF GOD

1838. A reader proclaims a text of sacred Scripture.

Brothers and sisters, listen to the words of the second letter of Paul to Timothy: 3:14-17

All Scripture is inspired by God and can be used for teaching.

But you, remain faithful to what you have learned and believed, because you know from whom you learned it, and that from infancy you have known the sacred scriptures, which are capable of giving you wisdom for salvation through faith in Christ Jesus. All scripture is inspired by God and is useful for teaching, for refutation, for correction, and for training in righteousness, so that one who belongs to God may be competent, equipped for every good work.

1839. Or:

Isaiah 55:10-11
The rain makes the earth fruitful.

Nehemiah 8:1-4a, 5-6, 8-10
They read from the book of the Law and understood what was read.

2 Timothy 4:1-5
Preach the Good News.

1 John 1:1-4
What we have seen and heard we are making known to you.

Matthew 5:14-19
You are the light of the world.

John 7:14-18
My teaching is not mine, but of him who sent me.

1840. As circumstances suggest, one of the following responsorial psalms may be sung, or some other suitable song.

℟. **Your words, Lord, are spirit and life.**

Psalm 19
**The law of the LORD is perfect,
refreshing the soul;
the decree of the LORD is trustworthy,
giving wisdom to the simple. ℟.**

**The precepts of the LORD are right,
rejoicing the heart;**

The command of the LORD is clear,
enlightening the eye. ℟.

The fear of the LORD is pure,
enduring forever;
The ordinances of the LORD are true,
all of them just. ℟.

They are more precious than gold,
than a heap of purest gold;
Sweeter also than syrup
or honey from the comb. ℟.

Psalm 119:9, 10, 11, 12
℟. (v. 12b) Lord, teach me your decrees.

1841. As circumstances suggest, the minister may give those present a brief explanation of the biblical text, so that they may understand through faith the meaning of the celebration.

INTERCESSIONS
1842. The intercessions are then said. The minister introduces them and an assisting minister or one of those present announces the intentions. From the following those best suited to the occasion may be used or adapted, or other intentions that apply to the particular circumstances may be composed.

The minister says:
The word of God calls us out of darkness into the light of faith. With the confidence of God's children let us ask the Lord to hear our prayers and to bless these readers:

℟. **Lord, graciously hear us.**

Assisting minister:
For the Church, that we may continue to respond to the word of God which is proclaimed in our midst, we pray to the Lord. ℟.

Assisting minister:

For all who listen as the Scriptures are proclaimed, that God's word may find in them a fruitful field, we pray to the Lord. ℟.

Assisting minister:

For those who have not heard the message of Christ, that we may be willing to bring them the good news of salvation, we pray to the Lord. ℟.

Assisting minister:

For our readers, that with deep faith and confident voice they may announce God's saving word, we pray to the Lord. ℟.

1843. After the intercessions the minister, in the following or similar words, invites all present to sing or say the Lord's Prayer.

With one voice we dare to say:

All:

Our Father . . .

PRAYER OF BLESSING

1844. The minister says the prayer of blessing with hands outstretched over the new readers:

**Everlasting God,
when he read in the synagogue at Nazareth,
your Son proclaimed the good news of salvation
for which he would give up his life.**

**Bless these readers.
As they proclaim your words of life,
strengthen their faith
that they may read with conviction and boldness
and put into practice what they read.**

**We ask this through Christ our Lord.
℟. Amen.**

CONCLUDING RITE

1845. The minister concludes the rite by saying:

May the word of God in all its richness
dwell in your hearts and minds,
now and for ever.
R̶. Amen.

Then he blesses all present.

And may almighty God bless you all,
the Father, and the Son, ✠ and the Holy Spirit.
R̶. Amen.

1846. It is preferable to end the celebration with a suitable song.

ORDER FOR THE BLESSING OF ALTAR SERVERS, SACRISTANS, MUSICIANS, AND USHERS

INTRODUCTION

1847. The Church earnestly desires that all the faithful be led to that full, conscious, and active participation in liturgical celebrations called for by the very nature of the liturgy (Constitution on the Liturgy, art. 14). Within the community of the baptized, individual members are called to participate in the liturgy by undertaking liturgical roles.

1848. Among the liturgical ministries exercised by lay persons are those of altar server (acolyte), sacristan, musician, and usher (or minister of hospitality).

1849. Those who are to receive this blessing should be properly prepared for the exercise of their new ministry. The various functions of these liturgical ministers are described in nos. 63-73 of the General Instruction of the Roman Missal.

1850. This order may be used during Mass or in a celebration of the word of God.

1851. This blessing is normally given by the pastor. If necessary, he may delegate another priest or deacon to give the blessing.

I. ORDER OF BLESSING WITHIN MASS

1852. After the gospel reading, the celebrant in the homily, based on the sacred text and pertinent to the particular place and the people involved, explains the meaning of the celebration.

GENERAL INTERCESSIONS

1853. The general intercessions follow, either in the form usual at Mass or in the form provided here. The celebrant concludes the intercessions with the prayer of blessing. From the following intentions those best for the occasion may be used or adapted, or other intentions that apply to the particular circumstances may be composed.

The celebrant says:

God provides the Church with suitable ministers to assist in divine worship. Let us pray for these new liturgical ministers, that God may bless them as they undertake their new roles of service to this parish.

℟. Lord, hear our prayer.

Or:

℟. Lord, graciously hear us.

Assisting minister:

For the Church of Christ and for this parish of N., that all Christians may offer themselves as living sacrifices, we pray to the Lord. ℟.

Assisting minister:

For all the liturgical ministers of our parish, that they may deepen their commitment to serve God and their neighbor, we pray to the Lord. ℟.

Assisting minister:

For altar servers

For these altar servers, that the light of Christ may shine in their hearts, we pray to the Lord. ℟.

Assisting minister:

For sacristans

For these sacristans, that the preparations they make for the celebration of the liturgy may remind us to prepare our hearts for worship, we pray to the Lord. ℟.

Assisting minister:

For musicians

For these parish musicians, that the beauty which they create in song and praise may echo always in our hearts, we pray to the Lord. ℟.

Assisting minister:

For ushers

For these ushers, that their presence may make all who
enter this church always feel welcome in God's house,
we pray to the Lord. ℟.

PRAYER OF BLESSING
1854. With hands extended over the new ministers the celebrant
says immediately:
**God of glory,
your beloved Son has shown us
that true worship comes from humble and contrite hearts.**

**Bless our brothers and sisters,
who have responded to the needs of our parish
and wish to commit themselves to your service as (altar
servers, sacristans, musicians, ushers).
Grant that their ministry may be fruitful
and our worship pleasing in your sight.**

**We ask this through Christ our Lord.
℟. Amen.**

II. ORDER OF BLESSING WITHIN A CELEBRA-
TION OF THE WORD OF GOD

1855. The present order may be used by a priest or a deacon.

INTRODUCTORY RITES
1856. When the community has gathered, a suitable song may be
sung. After the singing, the minister says:
**In the name of the Father, and of the Son, and of the
Holy Spirit.**

All make the sign of the cross and reply:
Amen.

1857. The minister greets those present in the following or other
suitable words, taken mainly from sacred Scripture.
**The grace and favor of our Lord Jesus Christ be with you
always.**

And all reply:
And also with you.

INTRODUCTION

1858. In the following or similar words, the minister prepares those present for the blessing.

In the body of Christ there exists a wonderful variety of ministries, which are especially evident when we gather around the altar to worship God. By virtue of our baptism in Christ some of us are called to serve as ministers of the liturgical assembly: altar servers assist the priest and deacon, sacristans prepare and maintain that which is necessary for divine worship, musicians help to raise our spirits in joyful praise, and ushers provide welcome and dignified order to the celebration. Today we ask God to bless abundantly these new (altar servers, sacristans, musicians, ushers) as they begin their liturgical ministry in our parish.

READING OF THE WORD OF GOD

1859. A reader, another person present, or the minister reads a text of sacred Scripture.

For altar servers

Brothers and sisters, listen to the words of the book of Numbers: 3:5-9

The Levites carried out their duties.

Now the LORD said to Moses: "Summon the tribe of Levi and present them to Aaron the priest, as his assistants. They shall discharge his obligations and those of the whole community before the meeting tent by serving at the Dwelling. They shall have custody of all the furnishings of the meeting tent and discharge the duties of the Israelites in the service of the Dwelling. You shall give the Levites to Aaron and his sons; they have been set aside from among the Israelites as dedicated to me."

1860. Or

Acts 4:32-35

The community of believers were of one heart and mind.

1 Corinthians 12:1-31

Set your hearts on the greater gifts.

1 John 3:14-18
Let us love in deed and in truth.

Matthew 5:1-12
The beatitudes.

John 15:12-16
The commandment of love

1861. For sacristans

Brothers and sisters, listen to the words of the book of Numbers: 4:4-14
Preparation of the meeting tent.

The LORD said to Moses and Aaron: "The service of the Kohathites in the meeting tent concerns the most sacred objects. In breaking camp, Aaron and his sons shall go in and take down the screening curtain and cover the ark of the commandments with it. Over these they shall put a cover of tahash skin, and on top of this spread an all-violet cloth. They shall then put the poles in place. On the table of the Presence they shall spread a violet cloth and put on it the plates and cups, as well as the bowls and pitchers for libations; the established bread offering shall remain on the table. Over these they shall spread a scarlet cloth and cover all this with tahash skin. They shall then put the poles in place. They shall use a violet cloth to cover the lampstand with its lamps, trimming shears, and trays, as well as the various containers of oil from which it is supplied. The lampstand with all its utensils they shall then enclose in a covering of tahash skin, and place on a litter. Over the golden altar they shall spread a violet cloth, and cover this also with a covering of tahash skin. They shall then put the poles in place. Taking the utensils of the sanctuary service, they shall wrap them all in violet cloth and cover them with tahash skin. They shall then place them on a litter. After cleansing the altar of its ashes, they shall spread a purple cloth over it. On this they shall put all the utensils with which it is served: the fire pans, forks, shovels, basins, and all the utensils of the altar. They shall then spread a

covering of tahash skin over this, and put the poles in place."

1862. For musicians

Brothers and sisters, listen to the words of the apostle Paul to the Colossians: 3:15-17

Sing to God from your hearts.

And let the peace of Christ control your hearts, the peace into which you were also called in one body. And be thankful. Let the word of Christ dwell in you richly, as in all wisdom you teach and admonish one another, singing psalms, hymns, and spiritual songs with gratitude in your hearts to God. And whatever you do, in word or in deed, do everything in the name of the Lord Jesus, giving thanks to God the Father through him.

1863. For ushers

Brothers and sisters, listen to the words of the first letter of Paul to the Corinthians: 13:1-13

Hymn to love.

If I speak in human and angelic tongues, but do not have love, I am a resounding gong or a clashing cymbal. And if I have the gift of prophecy, and comprehend all mysteries and all knowledge; if I have all faith so as to move mountains, but do not have love, I am nothing. If I give away everything I own, and if I hand my body over so that I may boast but do not have love, I gain nothing.

Love is patient, love is kind. It is not jealous, love is not pompous, it is not inflated, it is not rude, it does not seek its own interest, it is not quick-tempered, it does not brood over injury, it does not rejoice over wrongdoing but rejoices with the truth. It bears all things, believes all things, hopes all things, endures all things.

Love never fails. If there are prophecies, they will be brought to nothing; if tongues, they will cease; if knowledge, it will be brought to nothing. For we know partially and we prophesy partially, but when the perfect comes, the partial will pass away. When I was a child, I used to talk as a child, think as a child, reason as a child; when I became a man, I put aside childish things. At present we see indistinctly, as in a mirror, but then face to face. At present I know partially; then I shall know fully as I am fully known. So faith, hope, love remain, these three; but the greatest of these is love.

1864. As circumstances suggest, one of the following responsorial psalms may be sung, or some other suitable song.
℟. O Lord, my allotted portion and my cup,
    you it is who hold fast my lot.

Psalm 16
Keep me, O God, for in you I take refuge;
I say to the LORD, "My Lord are you.
Apart from you I have no good." ℟.

O LORD, my allotted portion and my cup,
you it is who hold fast my lot. ℟.

I bless the LORD who counsels me;
even in the night my heart exhorts me.
I set the LORD ever before me;
with him at my right hand I shall not be disturbed. ℟.

You will show me the path to life,
fullness of joys in your presence,
the delights at your right hand forever. ℟.

Psalm 19:8, 10, 12
℟. (see John 6:63b) Your words, O Lord, are spirit and life.

Psalm 34:2-3, 4-5, 6-7, 10-11, 12-13
℟. (v. 9) Taste and see the goodness of the Lord.

Psalm 112:1-2, 3-4, 5-7, 8-9
℟. (v. 1) Happy those who fear the Lord,
    who greatly delight in his commands.

Psalm 147: 1, 2, 3, 7, 12-13
℟. (v. 1) Praise the Lord, for he is good.

Psalm 149:1, 2, 3, 4, 5, 6
℟. (v. 1) **Sing to the Lord a new song.**

Psalm 150
℟. **(v. 6) Alleluia.**
Or:

℟. **Let everything that has breath praise the Lord.**

1865. As circumstances suggest, the minister may give those present a brief explanation of the biblical text, so that they may understand through faith the meaning of the celebration.

INTERCESSIONS
1866. The intercessions are then said. The minister introduces them and an assisting minister or one of those present announces the intentions. From the following those best suited to the occasion may be used or adapted, or other intentions that apply to the particular circumstances may be composed.

The minister says:

God provides the Church with suitable ministers to assist in divine worship. Let us pray for these new liturgical ministers, that God may bless them as they undertake their new roles of service to this parish.

℟. **Lord, graciously hear us.**

Assisting minister:

For the Church of Christ and for this parish of N., that all Christians may offer themselves as living sacrifices, we pray to the Lord. ℟.

Assisting minister:

For all the liturgical ministers of our parish, that they may deepen their commitment to serve God and their neighbor, we pray to the Lord. ℟.

Assisting minister:

For altar servers

For these altar servers, that the light of Christ may shine in their hearts, we pray to the Lord. ℟.

Assisting minister:

For sacristans

For these sacristans, that the preparations they make for the celebration of the liturgy may remind us to prepare our hearts for worship, we pray to the Lord. ℟.

Assisting minister:

For musicians

For these parish musicians, that the beauty which they create in song and praise may echo always in our hearts, we pray to the Lord. ℟.

Assisting minister:

For ushers

For these ushers, that their presence may make all who enter this church always feel welcome in God's house, we pray to the Lord. ℟.

1867. After the intercessions the minister, in the following or similar words, invites all present to sing or say the Lord's Prayer.

In the spirit of our common baptism, we cry out:

All:

Our Father . . .

PRAYER OF BLESSING

1868. The minister says the prayer of blessing with hands outstretched over the new ministers.

God of glory,
your beloved Son has shown us
that true worship comes from humble and contrite hearts.

Bless our brothers and sisters,
who have responded to the needs of our parish
and wish to commit themselves to your service as (altar servers, sacristans, musicians, ushers).

**Grant that their ministry may be fruitful
and our worship pleasing in your sight.**

We ask this through Christ our Lord.
℟. Amen.

CONCLUDING RITE

1869. The minister concludes the rite by saying:

**Lord God,
you give to each person
the gift of your Spirit for the building up of the Church.
Bless us and keep us all in your love.**

We ask this through Christ our Lord.
℟. Amen.

Then he blessses all present.

**And may almighty God bless you all,
the Father, and the Son, ✠ and the Holy Spirit.**
℟. Amen.

1870. It is preferable to end the celebration with a suitable song.

ORDER FOR THE COMMISSIONING OF EX-TRAORDINARY MINISTERS OF HOLY COMMUNION[2]

INTRODUCTION

1871. It is, first of all, the office of the priest and deacon to minister holy communion to the faithful who ask to receive it.[3] It is most fitting, therefore, that they give a suitable part of their time to this ministry of their order, depending on the needs of the faithful.[4]

It is the office of an acolyte who has been properly instituted to give communion as an extraordinary minister when the priest and deacon are absent or impeded by sickness, old age, or pastoral ministry or when the number of the faithful at the holy table is so great that the Mass or other service may be unreasonably protracted.[5]

The local Ordinary may give other extraordinary ministers the faculty to give communion whenever it seems necessary for the pastoral benefit of the faithful and a priest, deacon, or acolyte is not available.[6]

1872. Persons authorized to distribute holy communion in special circumstances should be commissioned by the local Ordinary or his delegate[7] according to the following rite. The rite should take place in the presence of the people during Mass or outside Mass.

1873. The pastor is the usual minister of this rite. However, he may delegate another priest to celebrate it, or a deacon when it is celebrated outside Mass.

NOTES

[2] This order is taken from the *Rite of Commissioning Special Ministers of Holy Communion.*

[3] See Congregation of Rites, instruction *Eucharisticum mysterium*, no. 31: AAS 64 (1967).

[4] Roman Ritual, *Holy Communion and Worship of the Eucharist outside Mass*, no. 17.

[5] Roman Ritual, *Holy Communion and Worship of the Eucharist outside Mass*, no. 17; see Paul VI, apostolic letter *Ministeria quaedam*, August 15, 1972, no. VI: AAS 64 (1972) 532.

[6] Roman Ritual, *Holy Communion and Worship of the Eucharist outside Mass*, no. 17; see Congregation for the Discipline of the Sacraments, instruction *Immensae caritatis*, January 29, 1973, 1, I and II.

[7] See instruction *Immensae caritatis* I, nos. 1, 6.

I. ORDER OF COMMISSIONING WITHIN MASS

1874. After the gospel reading, the celebrant in the homily, based on the sacred text and pertinent to the particular place and the people involved, explains the meaning of the celebration.

PRESENTATION OF THE CANDIDATES

1875. Then he presents to the people those chosen to serve as special ministers, using these or similar words:

Dear friends in Christ, our brothers and sisters N. and N. are to be entrusted with administering the eucharist, with taking communion to the sick and with giving it as viaticum to the dying.

The celebrant pauses, and then addresses the candidates:

**In this ministry, you must be examples of Christian living in faith and conduct; you must strive to grow in holiness through this sacrament of unity and love.
Remember that, though many, we are one body because we share the one bread and one cup.**

As ministers of holy communion be, therefore, especially observant of the Lord's command to love your neighbor. For when he gave his body as food to his disciples, he said to them: "This is my commandment, that you should love one another as I have loved you."

EXAMINATION

1876. After the address the candidates stand before the celebrant, who asks them these questions:

Are you resolved to undertake the office of giving the body and blood of the Lord to your brothers and sisters, and so serve to build up the Church?

℟. **I am.**

Are you resolved to administer the holy eucharist with
the utmost care and reverence?

℟. I am.

PRAYER OF BLESSING
1877. All stand. The candidates kneel and the celebrant invites
the faithful to pray:
Dear friends in Christ, let us pray with confidence to the
Father; let us ask him to bestow his blessings on our
brothers and sisters, chosen to be ministers of the eucharist.

Pause for silent prayer. The celebrant then continues:
Merciful Father,
creator and guide of your family,
bless ✠ our brother and sisters N. and N.

May they faithfully give the bread of life to your people.

Strengthened by this sacrament,
may they come at last to the banquet of heaven.

We ask this through Christ our Lord.
℟. Amen.

1878. Or:
Gracious Lord,
you nourish us with the body and blood of your Son,
that we might have eternal life.

Bless ✠ our brothers and sisters who have been chosen
to give the bread of heaven and the cup of salvation
to your faithful people.

May the saving mysteries they distribute
lead them to the joys of eternal life.

We ask this through Christ our Lord.
℟. Amen.

GENERAL INTERCESSIONS

1879. The general intercessions follow, either in the form usual at Mass or in the form provided here. The celebrant concludes the intercessions with the prayer of blessing. From the following intentions those best for the occasion may be used or adapted, or other intentions that apply to the particular circumstances may be composed.

The celebrant says:

The Lord feeds and nourishes us with his life-giving body and blood. Let us pray that these ministers of communion be ever faithful to their responsibility of distributing holy communion in our community.

℟. **Lord, hear our prayer.**

Or:

℟. **Hear us, O Lord.**

Assisting minister:

For our ministers of communion, that they witness by their deep faith in the eucharist to the saving mystery of Christ, let us pray to the Lord. ℟.

Assisting minister:

For the Church, that the eucharist we celebrate always be a bond of unity and a sacrament of love for all who partake, let us pray to the Lord. ℟.

Assisting minister:

For the sick who will receive holy communion from these ministers, that Christ heal and strengthen them, let us pray to the Lord. ℟.

Assisting minister:

For all who are present here, that the bread of life and cup of salvation we receive at the altar always be our nourishment, let us pray to the Lord. ℟.

1880. The celebrant then says:

**Lord our God,
teach us to cherish in our hearts**

the paschal mystery of your Son,
by which you redeemed the world.

Watch over the gifts of grace your love has given us
and bring them to fulfillment in the glory of heaven.

We ask this through Christ our Lord.
R̲. Amen.

LITURGY OF THE EUCHARIST

1881. In the procession at the presentation of gifts, the newly commissioned ministers carry the vessels with the bread and wine, and at communion may receive the eucharist under both kinds.

II. ORDER OF COMMISSIONING WITHIN A CELEBRATION OF THE WORD OF GOD

INTRODUCTORY RITES

1882. When the community has gathered a suitable song may be sung. After the singing, the minister says:

In the name of the Father, and of the Son, and of the Holy Spirit.

All make the sign of the cross and reply:

Amen.

1883. The minister greets those present in the following or other suitable words, taken mainly from sacred Scripture.

May the Lord, who nourishes us with the bread of life, be with you.

And all reply:

And also with you.

1884. In the following or similar words, the minister prepares those present for the blessing.

Our brothers and sisters who have been chosen as extraordinary ministers of holy communion will be commissioned through our prayer and God's blessing. We pray that they may exercise this ministry with faith, devotion, and love.

READING OF THE WORD OF GOD

1885. A reader, another person present, or the minister reads a text of sacred Scripture.

Brothers and sisters, listen to the words of the first letter of Paul to the Corinthians: 10:16-17
Though we are many, we form a single body because we share this one loaf.
The cup of blessing that we bless, is it not a participation in the blood of Christ? The bread that we break, is it not a participation in the body of Christ? Because the loaf of bread is one, we, though many, are one body, for we all partake of the one loaf.

1886. Or:

Genesis 14:18-20
Melchizedek brought bread and wine.

Exodus 16:2-4, 12-15
I will rain bread from heaven upon you.

Exodus 24:3-8
This is the blood of the covenant that the Lord has made with you.

Deuteronomy 8:2-3, 14b-16a
He gave you food which you and your fathers did not know.

1 Kings 19:4-8
Strengthened by the food, he walked to the mountain of the Lord.

Proverbs 9:1-6
Come and eat my bread, drink the wine I have prepared.

Acts 2:42-47
All who believed shared everything in common.

Acts 10:34a, 37-43
We have eaten and drunk with him after his resurrection from the dead.

1 Corinthians 11: 23-26
Until the Lord comes, every time you eat this bread and drink this cup, you proclaim his death.

Hebrews 9: 11-15
The blood of Christ will purify our inner selves.

Mark 14:12-16, 22-26
This is my body. This is my blood.

Luke 9:11b-17
They all ate and were filled.

Luke 24:13-35
They had recognized him in the breaking of the bread.

John 6: 1-15
He distributed to those who were seated as much as they wanted.

John 6:24-35
Anyone who comes to me will never be hungry; anyone who believes in me will never thirst.

John 6:41-52
I am the living bread that came down from heaven.

John 6:51-59
My flesh is real food and my blood is real drink.

John 21:1-14
Jesus came and took the bread and gave it to them.

1887. As circumstances suggest, one of the following responsorial psalms may be sung, or some other suitable song.
℟. **The Lord is my shepherd; there is nothing I shall want.**

Psalm 23
The LORD is my shepherd; I shall not want.
In verdant pastures he gives me repose;
Beside restful waters he leads me;
he refreshes my soul. ℟.

He guides me in right paths
for his name's sake.
Even though I walk in the dark valley
I fear no evil; for you are at my side
With your rod and your staff
that give me courage. ℟.

You spread the table before me
in the sight of my foes;
You anoint my head with oil;
my cup overflows.
Only goodness and kindness follow me
all the days of my life;
And I shall dwell in the house of the LORD
for years to come. ℟.

Psalm 34:2-3, 4-5, 6-7
℟. (v. 9a) Taste and see the goodness of the Lord.

Psalm 78:3, 4bc, 23-24, 25, 54
℟. (v. 24) The Lord gave them bread from heaven.

Psalm 145:10-11, 15-16, 17-18
℟. (v. 16) The hand of the Lord feeds us; he answers all
our needs.

Psalm 147:12-13, 14-15, 19-20
℟. (see John 6:58b) Whoever eats this bread will live for
ever.

1888. In the homily the minister first explains the reason for this
ministry.

PRESENTATION OF THE CANDIDATES

1889. Then he presents to the people those chosen to serve as extraordinary ministers, using these or similar words:

**Dear friends in Christ, our brothers and sisters N. and N.
are to be entrusted with administering the eucharist,
with taking communion to the sick, and with giving it as
viaticum to the dying.**

The minister pauses, and addresses the candidates:

**In this ministry, you must be examples of Christian liv-
ing in faith and conduct; you must strive to grow in holiness through this sacrament of unity and love.
Remember that, though many, we are one body because
we share the one bread and one cup.**

As ministers of holy communion be, therefore, especially observant of the Lord's command to love your neighbor. For when he gave his body as food to his disciples, he said to them: "This is my commandment, that you should love one another as I have loved you."

EXAMINATION
1890. After the address the candidates stand before the minister, who asks them these questions:
Are you resolved to undertake the office of giving the body and blood of the Lord to you brothers and sisters, and so serve to build up the Church?

℟. I am.

Are you resolved to administer the holy eucharist with the utmost care and reverence?

℟. I am.

PRAYER OF BLESSING
1891. All stand. The candidates kneel and the minister invites the faithful to pray:
Dear friends in Christ, let us pray with confidence to the Father; let us ask him to bestow his blessings on our brothers and sisters, chosen to be ministers of the eucharist.

Pause for silent prayer. The minister then continues:
Merciful Father,
creator and guide of your family,
bless ✠ our brothers and sisters N. and N.

May they faithfully give the bread of life to your people.

Strengthened by this sacrament,
may they come at last to the banquet of heaven.
We ask this through Christ our Lord.
℟. Amen.

1892. Or:

Gracious Lord,
you nourish us with the body and blood of your Son,
that we might have eternal life.

Bless ✛ our brothers and sisters who have been chosen
to give the bread of heaven and the cup of salvation
to your faithful people.

May the saving mysteries they distribute
lead them to the joys of eternal life.

We ask this through Christ our Lord.
℞. Amen.

INTERCESSIONS

1893. The intercessions are then said. The minister introduces
them and an assisting minister or one of those present announces the intentions. From the following those best suited to
the occasion may be used or adapted, or other intentions that
apply to the particular circumstances may be composed.

The minister says:

The Lord feeds and nourishes us with his life-giving
body and blood. Let us pray that these ministers of communion be ever faithful to their responsibility of distributing holy communion in our community.

℞. Hear us, O Lord.

Assisting minister:

For our ministers of communion, that they witness by
their deep faith in the eucharist to the saving mystery of
Christ, let us pray to the Lord. ℞.

For the Church, that the eucharist we celebrate always be
a bond of unity and a sacrament of love for all who partake, let us pray to the Lord. ℞.

Assisting minister:

For the sick who will receive holy communion from
these ministers, that Christ heal and strengthen them, let
us pray to the Lord. ℞.

For all who are present here, that the bread of life and cup of salvation we receive at the altar always be our nourishment, let us pray to the Lord. ℟.

1894. After the intercessions the minister, in the following or similar words, invites all present to sing or say the Lord's Prayer.
Let us pray to the Father in the words our Savior gave us.

All:
Our Father . . .

CONCLUDING RITE
1895. The minister concludes the rite by saying:
**Lord our God,
teach us to cherish in our hearts
the paschal mystery of your Son,
by which you redeemed the world.
Watch over the gifts of grace your love has given us
and bring them to fulfillment in the glory of heaven.**

**We ask this through Christ our Lord.
℟. Amen.**

Then he blesses all present.
**And may almighty God bless you all,
the Father, and the Son, ✠ and the Holy Spirit.
℟. Amen.**

1896. It is preferable to end the celebration with a suitable song.

CONSECRATION TO A LIFE
OF VIRGINITY

CONSECRATION TO A LIFE OF VIRGINITY

Introduction (1-10)

Nature and Value of Consecration to Virginity (1)

Principal Duties of Those Consecrated (2)

Those Who May Be Consecrated (3-5)

Minister of the Rule (6)

Form of the Rite (7)

Mass for the Consecration to a Life of Virginity (8-10)

A. CONSECRATION TO A LIFE OF VIRGINITY FOR WOMEN LIVING IN THE WORLD

Introduction (1-8)

Introductory Rites (9-11)

Liturgy of the Word (12)

Consecration (13-31)

Calling of the Candidates (13-15)

Homily (16)

Examination (17)

Invitation to Prayer (18-19)

Litany of the Saints (20-21)

Renewal of Intention (22-23)

Prayer of Consecration (24)

Presentation of the Insignia of Consecration (25-27)

Presentation of the Liturgy of the Hours (28-31)

Liturgy of the Eucharist (32-35)

Concluding Rite (36-38)

Solemn Blessing (36-38)

B. CONSECRATION TO A LIFE OF VIRGINITY TOGETHER WITH RELIGIOUS PROFESSION FOR NUNS

Introduction (39-47)

Introductory Rites (48-49)

Liturgy of the Word (50)

Consecration Together with Religious Profession (51-72)

Calling of the Candidates (51-53)

Homily (54)

Examination (55-56)

Invitation to Prayer (57-58)

Litany of the Saints (59-60)

Profession (61-63)

Prayer of Consecration (64)

Presentation of the Insignia of Consecration (65-67)

Presentation of the Liturgy of the Hours (68-69)

Sign of Acceptance (70-72)

Liturgy of the Eucharist (73-76)

Concluding Rite (77, 155, 156, 80)

Solemn Blessing (77, 155, 156, 80)

Appendix

CHAPTER I

CONSECRATION TO A LIFE OF VIRGINITY

INTRODUCTION

NATURE AND IMPORT OF CONSECRATION TO VIRGINITY

1. The custom of consecrating women to a life of virginity flourished even in the early Church. It led to the formation of a solemn rite constituting the candidate a sacred person, a surpassing sign of the Church's love for Christ, and an eschatological image of the world to come and the glory of the heavenly Bride of Christ. In the rite of consecration the Church reveals its love of virginity, begs God's grace on those who are consecrated, and prays with fervor for an outpouring of the Holy Spirit.

THE MAIN DUTIES OF THOSE CONSECRATED

2. Those who consecrate their chastity under the inspiration of the Holy Spirit do so for the sake of a more fervent love of Christ and of greater freedom in the service of their brothers and sisters.

They are to spend their time in works of penance and of mercy, in apostolic activity, and in prayer, according to their state of life and spiritual gifts.

To fulfill their duty of prayer they are strongly advised to recite the liturgy of the hours each day, especially morning prayer and evening prayer. In this way, by joining their voice to those of Christ the High Priest and of his Church, they will offer unending praise to their heavenly Father and pray for the salvation of the whole world.

THOSE WHO MAY BE CONSECRATED

3. This consecration may be received by nuns or by women living in the world.

4. In the case of nuns it is required:
a) that they have never married or lived in public or flagrant violation of chastity;

b) that they have made their final profession, either in the same rite or on an earlier occasion;

c) that their religious family uses this rite because of long-established custom or by new permission of the competent authority.

5. In the case of women living in the world it is required:

a) that they have never been married or lived in public or flagrant violation of chastity;

b) that by their age, prudence, and universally attested good character they give assurance of perseverance in a life of chastity dedicated to the service of the Church and of their neighbor;

c) that they be admitted to this consecration by the bishop who is the local Ordinary.

It is for the bishop to decide on the conditions under which women living in the world are to undertake a life of perpetual virginity.

THE MINISTER OF THE RITE

6. The minister of the rite of consecration is the bishop who is the local Ordinary.

THE FORM OF THE RITE

7. For the consecration of women living in the world the rite described in Chapter I of this ritual is to be used.

For the consecration of nuns the rite found in Chapter II of this ritual is to be followed. This integrates religious profession with the consecration. For a good reason, however, these two rites may be separated, for example, when this is in accordance with long-established custom. But care should be taken not to duplicate parts of the rite; the two liturgical services should be so arranged that the rite of religious profession omits any prayer of consecration, retaining only those elements that belong to the religious profession. But the prayer, *Loving Father, chaste bodies* and the ritual elements with a nuptial significance (for example, the presentation of the ring) are to be preserved for the rite of consecration.

The rite consists of these parts:

a) the calling of the candidates;

b) the homily or address, instructing the candidates and the people on the grace of virginity;

c) the examination by which the bishop asks the candidates about their readiness to persevere in their intention and to receive the consecration;

d) the litanies, in which prayer is offered to God the Father and the intercession of the Blessed Virgin Mary and all the saints is invoked;

e) the renewal of the intention of chastity (or the making of religious profession);

f) the solemn blessing or consecration by which the Church asks our heavenly Father to pour out the gifts of the Holy Spirit on the candidates;

g) the presentation of the insignia of consecration as outward signs of a spiritual dedication.

MASS FOR THE CONSECRATION TO A LIFE OF VIRGINITY

8. It is appropriate to use the ritual Mass for the day of consecration to a life of virginity. On a solemnity or a Sunday of Advent, Lent, or the Easter season the Mass of the day is used, but the special formularies for the eucharistic prayer and the final blessing may be used.

9. The liturgy of the word for the rite of consecration to a life of virginity can be a help in understanding the importance and place of virginity in the Church. Therefore it is lawful, when the Mass for the day of consecration to a life of virginity is not permitted, to take one reading from the special list of readings for this rite. But this may not be done during the Easter triduum, on the Solemnities of Christmas, Epiphany, Ascension, Pentecost, or Corpus Christi, or on other solemnities of obligation.

10. White vestments are worn for the ritual Mass for the day of consecration.

A. CONSECRATION TO A LIFE OF VIRGINITY FOR WOMEN LIVING IN THE WORLD

INTRODUCTION

1. It is appropriate for the rite of consecration to take place during the octave of Easter, on solemnities, especially those which celebrate the incarnation, on Sundays, or on feasts of the Blessed Virgin Mary or of holy virgins.

2. On a day scheduled close to the day of the rite of consecration, or at least on the day before the consecration, the candidates are presented to the bishop, so that the father of the diocese may begin a pastoral dialogue with his spiritual daughters.

3. It is at the discretion of the bishop and by his authority that women living in the world are admitted to this consecration, and often they take part in the good works of the diocese. It is therefore fitting that the rite of consecration should take place in the cathedral, unless local circumstances or custom suggest otherwise.

4. As occasion offers, and especially to promote an esteem for chastity, to deepen understanding of the Church, and to encourage a greater attendance of the people, the faithful should be notified of the celebration in good time.

5. The Mass of the day or the ritual Mass for the day of consecration is celebrated in accordance with the rubrics (see Introduction, nos. 8-10).

6. The consecration ordinarily takes place at the chair. To enable the faithful to take part more easily, the bishop's chair may be placed in front of the altar. Seats for the candidates should be so arranged in the sanctuary that the faithful may have a complete view of the liturgical rites.

7. For the eucharistic celebration enough bread and wine should be prepared for the ministers, the candidates, their parents, relatives, and friends. If only one chalice is used, it should be sufficiently large.

8. In addition to what is needed for the celebration of Mass, there should be ready: a) the Roman Pontifical; b) veils, rings, or other insignia of bridal consecration to be presented in accordance with local rules or approved customs.

INTRODUCTORY RITES

9. When the people are assembled and everything is ready, the procession moves through the church to the altar in the usual way, while the choir and people sing the entrance song of the Mass. The candidates may join in the procession.

10. It is appropriate for two women—either consecrated themselves or chosen from the laity—to accompany the candidates to the altar.

11. When they come to the sanctuary, all make the customary reverence to the altar. The candidates go to their places in the body of the church and Mass continues.

LITURGY OF THE WORD

12. The liturgy of the word takes place as usual, except for the following:
a) the readings may be taken from the Mass of the day or from the texts listed in Chapter V (see Introduction, nos. 8-9);
b) the profession of faith is not said, even if prescribed by the rubrics of the day;
c) the general intercessions are omitted, since they are included in the litany.

CONSECRATION

CALLING OF THE CANDIDATES

13. After the gospel, if the consecration takes place in front of the altar, the bishop goes to the chair prepared for him and sits.

When candles are not used see no. 15 below.

If candles are used, the choir sings the following antiphon:

Be wise: make ready your lamps.
Behold, the Bridegroom comes;
go out to meet him.

Any other appropriate song may be sung.

The candidates then light their lamps or candles and, accompanied by the two women mentioned above (see no. 10), approach the sanctuary and stand outside it.

14. Then the bishop calls the candidates; he sings or says aloud:

Come, listen to me, my children;
I will teach you reverence for the Lord.

The candidates reply by singing this antiphon or some other appropriate song:

Now with all our hearts we follow you,
we reverence you and seek your presence.
Lord, fulfill our hope:
show us your loving kindness,
the greatness of your mercy.

As they sing the antiphon, the candidates enter the sanctuary and take up their positions so that everyone may have a complete view of the liturgical rites. They place their candles in a candelabrum, or give them to the ministers until they are returned at the end of Mass. They then sit in the places prepared for them.

15. Or, when candles are not used:
[138] The deacon calls each of the candidates by name. Each candidate, on hearing her name, rises and replies: **Lord, you have called me.** The candidate may make some other suitable reply. Then she goes to the sanctuary and stands outside it.

[139] After the calling of the candidates, the bishop invites them in these or similar words:

Come, daughters,
that through me, his servant,
the Lord may consecrate
the resolution you have formed in your hearts.

The candidates reply by singing this antiphon or some other appropriate song:

**Now with all our hearts we follow you,
we reverence you and seek your presence.
Lord, fulfill our hope:
show us your loving kindness,
the greatness of your mercy.**

As they sing the antiphon, the candidates enter the sanctuary, accompanied by the two women mentioned above (see no. 10), and take up their positions so that everyone may have a complete view of the liturgical rites. They then sit in the places prepared for them.

HOMILY

16. The bishop then gives a short homily to the candidates and the people on the gift of virginity and its role in the sanctification of those called to virginity and the welfare of the whole Church. He does so in these or similar words:

Dear brothers and sisters, today the Church consecrates these candidates to a life of virginity. They come from God's holy people, from your own families. They are your daughters, your sisters, your relatives, joined by the ties of family or friendship.

God has called them to be more closely united to himself and to be dedicated to the service of the Church and of mankind. Their consecration is a call to greater fervor in spreading the kingdom of God and in giving to the world the spirit of Christ. Think of the good they will accomplish by their prayers and good works, and the abundant blessings they will obtain from God for holy Church, for human society, and for your families.

He then addresses the candidates:

And now we speak to you, dear daughters. Our words are not words of command but encouragement from the heart. The life you seek to follow has its home in heaven. God himself is its source. It is he, infinitely pure and holy, who gives the grace of virginity. Those to whom he gives it are seen by the Fathers of the Church as images of the eternal and all-holy God.

When the fullness of time had come, the almighty
Father showed, in the mystery of the incarnation, his
love for this great virtue. In the chaste womb of the
Blessed Virgin Mary, by the power of the Holy Spirit,
the Word was made flesh, in a marriage covenant uniting two natures, human and divine.

Our Lord himself taught us the high calling of such a
life, consecrated to God and chosen for the sake of the
kingdom of heaven. By his whole life, and especially
by his labors, his preaching, and, above all, by his
paschal mystery, he brought his Church into being. He
desired it to be a virgin, a bride, and a mother: a virgin,
to keep the faith whole and entire; a bride, to be one
with him for ever; and a mother, to raise up the family
of the Church.

The Holy Spirit, the Paraclete, through baptism has
already made you temples of God's glory and children
of the Father. Today through our ministry he anoints
you with a new grace and consecrates you to God by a
new title. He gives each one of you the dignity of being
a bride of Christ and binds you to the Son of God in a
covenant to last for ever.

The Church is the bride of Christ. This title of the
Church was given by the fathers and doctors of the
Church to those like you who speak to us of the world
to come, where there is not marrying or giving in marriage. You are a sign of the great mystery of salvation,
proclaimed at the beginning of human history and fulfilled in the marriage covenant between Christ and his
Church.

Make your whole life reflect your vocation and your
dignity. Our holy mother the Church sees in you a
chosen company within the flock of Christ. Through
you the Church's motherhood of grace bears its abundant fruit. Imitate the mother of God; desire to be
called and to be handmaids of the Lord. Preserve the
fullness of your faith, the steadfastness of your hope,
the single-heartedness of your love. Be prudent and
watch: keep the glory of your virginity uncorrupted by

pride. Nourish your love of God by feeding on the body of Christ; strengthen it by self-denial; build it up by study of the Scriptures, by untiring prayer, by works of mercy. Let your thoughts be on the things of God. Let your life be hidden with Christ in God. Make it your concern to pray fervently for the spread of the Christian faith and for the unity of all Christians. Pray earnestly to God for the welfare of the married. Remember also those who have forgotten their Father's goodness and have abandoned his love, so that God's mercy may forgive where his justice must condemn.

Never forget that you are given over entirely to the service of the Church and of all your brothers and sisters. You are apostles in the Church and in the world, in the things of the Spirit and in the things of the world. Let your light then shine before men and women, that your Father in heaven may be glorified, and his plan of making all things one in Christ come to perfection. Love everyone, especially those in need. Help the poor, care for the weak, teach the ignorant, protect the young, minister to the old, bring strength and comfort to widows and all in adversity.

You have renounced marriage for the sake of Christ. Your motherhood will be a motherhood of the spirit, as you do the will of your Father and work with others in a spirit of charity, so that a great family of children may be born, or reborn, to the life of grace.

Your joy and your crown, even here on earth, will be Christ, the Son of the Virgin and the Bridegroom of virgins. He will call you to his presence and into his kingdom, where you will sing a new song as you follow the Lamb of God wherever he leads you.

EXAMINATION

17. After the homily the candidates stand and the bishop questions them in these or similar words:

Are you resolved to persevere to the end of your days in the holy state of virginity and in the service of God and his Church?
Together, all the candidates answer: **I am.**

Bishop:
Are you so resolved to follow Christ in the spirit of the Gospel that your whole life may be a faithful witness to God's love and a convincing sign of the kingdom of heaven?
Candidates: **I am.**

Bishop:
Are you resolved to accept solemn consecration as a bride of our Lord Jesus Christ, the Son of God?
Candidates: **I am.**

Bishop and all present: **Thanks be to God.**

INVITATION TO PRAYER
18. Then all stand, and the bishop, without his miter, invites the people to pray:

Dearly beloved, let us pray to God the almighty Father through his Son, our Lord Jesus Christ, that, by the intercession of the Blessed Virgin Mary and all the saints, he will pour out the Holy Spirit of his love on these servants of his whom he has chosen to be consecrated to his service.

19. Deacon (except during the Easter season):
Let us kneel.

LITANY OF THE SAINTS
Then the bishop, the ministers, the candidates, and the people kneel (except during the Easter season, when all stand). Where it is customary for the candidates to prostrate themselves, this may be done.

20. The cantors then sing the litany (Chapter V). At the proper place they may add the names of other saints who are

specially venerated by the people, or petitions suitable to the occasion.

21. Then the bishop alone rises and, with hands joined, sings or says:

Lord,
hear the prayers of your Church.
Look with favor on your handmaids
whom you have called in your love.
Set them on the way of eternal salvation;
may they seek only what is pleasing to you,
and fulfill it with watchful care.

We ask this through Christ our Lord.
All: **Amen.**

Deacon: **Let us stand.**

All stand.

RENEWAL OF INTENTION

22. Then, if it seems suitable, the candidates offer themselves to God at the hands of the bishop. This may be done, for example, in the following way: the candidates come one by one before the bishop. Each one kneels, places her joined hands between his hands and says:

Father, receive my resolution to follow Christ in a life
of perfect chastity which, with God's help, I here pro-
fess before you and God's holy people.

If there are many candidates, the bishop may allow all to remain kneeling in their places and to say together:

Father, receive our resolution to follow Christ in a life
of perfect chastity which, with God's help, we here
profess before you and God's holy people.

23. Another suitable rite, in accordance with local custom, may be substituted.

PRAYER OF CONSECRATION

24. After the renewal of intention, the candidates return to their places in the sanctuary and kneel. The bishop extends

his hands over them, and sings or says the prayer of consecration. The words in brackets may be omitted.

Loving Father,
chaste bodies are your temple;
you delight in sinless hearts.
Our nature was corrupted
when the devil deceived our first parents,
but you have restored it in Christ.
He is your Word, through whom all things were made.
He has made our nature whole again,
and made it possible for mortal people to reflect the
    life of angels.

Lord,
look with favor on your handmaids.
They place in your hands their resolve to live in
    chastity.
You inspire them to take this vow;
now they give you their hearts.
[Only you can kindle this flame of love, and feed its
    brightness,
giving strength and perseverance to our will.
Without you our flesh is weak,
bound by the law of nature,
free with false freedom,
imprisoned by habit,
softened by the spirit of the age.]

You have poured out your grace upon all peoples.
You have adopted as heirs of the new covenant
sons and daughters from every nation under heaven,
countless as the stars.
Your children are born, not of human birth,
nor of man's desire,
but of your Spirit.
Among your many gifts
you give to some the grace of virginity.
Yet the honor of marriage is in no way lessened.
As it was in the beginning,
your first blessing still remains upon this holy union.
Yet your loving wisdom chooses those

who make sacrifice of marriage
for the sake of the love of which it is the sign.
They renounce the joys of human marriage,
but cherish all that it foreshadows.

[Those who choose chastity have looked upon the face
   of Christ,
its origin and inspiration.
They give themselves wholly to Christ,
the Son of the ever-virgin Mary,
and the heavenly Bridegroom of those
who in his honor dedicate themselves to lasting
   virginity.]

Lord,
protect those who seek your help.
They desire to be strengthened by your blessing and
   consecration.
Defend them from the cunning and deceit of the
   enemy.
Keep them vigilant and on their guard;
may nothing tarnish the glory of perfect virginity,
or the vocation of purity which is shared by those who
   are married.

Through the gift of your Spirit, Lord,
give them modesty with right judgment,
kindness with true wisdom,
gentleness with strength of character,
freedom with the grace of chastity.
Give them the warmth of love,
to love you above all others.
Make their lives deserve our praise,
without seeking to be praised.
May they give you glory
by holiness of action and purity of heart.
May they love you and fear you;
may they love you and serve you.

Be yourself their glory, their joy, their whole desire.
Be their comfort in sorrow,
their wisdom in perplexity,

their protection in the midst of injustice,
their patience in adversity,
their riches in poverty,
their food in fasting,
their remedy in time of sickness.

They have chosen you above all things;
may they find all things in possessing you.

We ask this through our Lord Jesus Christ, your Son,
who lives and reigns with you and the Holy Spirit,
one God, for ever and ever.
All: Amen.

PRESENTATION OF THE INSIGNIA OF CONSECRATION

One of the following forms, nos. 25 to 29 or nos. 151 to 154, is
used.

25. After the prayer of consecration, the bishop and the
people sit. The newly consecrated stand and, accompanied
by the two consecrated or lay women mentioned above, come
before the bishop. He says once for all of them:

If the veil is given:
Dearest daughters,
receive the veil and the ring
that are the insignia of your consecration.
Keep unstained your fidelity to your Bridegroom,
and never forget that you are bound
to the service of Christ and of his body, the Church.
They all reply together: Amen.

26. Or, if the veil is not given:
Receive the ring
that marks you as a bride of Christ.
Keep unstained your fidelity to your Bridegroom,
that you may one day be admitted to the wedding feast
    of everlasting joy.
They all reply together: Amen.

27. While the newly consecrated kneel, the bishop gives the
ring to each one and, if customary, the veil and other insignia
of consecration.

Meanwhile, the choir and the people may sing the following antiphon with Psalm 45.

To you, O Lord, I lift my soul;
come and rescue me, for you are my refuge and my
strength.

The antiphon is repeated after every two verses. **Glory to the Father** is not said. The psalm is interrupted and the antiphon repeated when the presentation of the insignia is completed.

Any other appropriate song may be sung.

PRESENTATION OF THE LITURGY OF THE HOURS

28. Then, if it seems appropriate, the bishop gives the newly consecrated the book containing the prayer of the Church, saying these or similar words:

Receive the book of the liturgy of the hours,
the prayer of the Church;
may the praise of our heavenly Father
be always on your lips;
pray without ceasing
for the salvation of the whole world.
All reply together: **Amen.**

The newly consecrated come before the bishop, who gives each a copy of the liturgy of the hours. After receiving it, they return to their places and remain standing.

---

29. Then, if appropriate, this or some suitable antiphon is sung.

I am espoused to him whom the angels serve;
sun and moon stand in wonder at his glory.

If possible, all those newly consecrated sing the antiphon together; otherwise the choir sings it.

Or:
[151] (For the giving of the veil. The rite is omitted if those consecrated have already received the veil canonically.) After the prayer of consecration the bishop and the people sit. The newly consecrated stand and, accompanied by the consecrated or lay women mentioned above, come before the bishop. He gives the veil to each one, saying:

Receive this veil,
by which you are to show
that you have been chosen from other women
to be dedicated to the service of Christ
and of his body, which is the Church.
Each one replies: **Amen.**

After receiving the veil each one returns to her place and remains standing. When all have received their veils, they sing the antiphon:

I will raise my mind and heart to you, O Lord,
that I may be holy in body and in spirit.

The choir may begin the antiphon after the veil has been given to the first or second one. It may be repeated after one or more verses of a suitable psalm or canticle.

[152] (For the giving of the ring.) When all have received the veil, the rings are given in the following way: those consecrated come before the bishop in the same order as before. Then he gives each one her ring, saying:

Receive the ring
that marks you as a bride of Christ.
Keep unstained your fidelity to your Bridegroom,
that you may one day be admitted to the wedding feast
**   of everlasting joy.**
Each one replies: **Amen.**

PRESENTATION OF THE LITURGY OF THE HOURS

[153] Then, if it seems appropriate, the bishop gives the newly consecrated the book containing the prayer of the Church, saying these or similar words:

Receive the book of the liturgy of the hours,
the prayer of the Church;
may the praise of our heavenly Father
be always on your lips;
pray without ceasing
for the salvation of the world.
Each replies: **Amen.**

Each returns to her place.

---

[154] After all have received the insignia of profession, those consecrated sing the antiphon:

I am espoused to him whom the angels serve;
sun and moon stand in wonder at his glory.

If appropriate the choir may sing the antiphon after the ring has been given to the first or second person. It may be repeated after one or more verses of a suitable psalm or canticle.

31. After this the newly consecrated return to their places in the sanctuary and the Mass continues.

LITURGY OF THE EUCHARIST

32. During the preparation of the gifts, some of the newly consecrated may bring to the altar the bread, wine, and water for the eucharistic sacrifice.

33. In the eucharistic prayer the offering of those newly consecrated may be mentioned (see Ritual Masses, Consecration to a Life of Virginity).

34. After **The peace of the Lord be always with you,** the bishop gives an appropriate sign of peace to those newly consecrated.

35. After the bishop has received the body and blood of Christ, the newly consecrated come to the altar to receive communion under both kinds.

Their parents, relatives, and friends may also receive communion under both kinds.

CONCLUDING RITE

SOLEMN BLESSING

36. When the prayer after communion has been said, those newly consecrated stand before the altar. The bishop faces them and sings or says one of the following:

The almighty Father
has poured into your hearts
the desire to live a life of holy virginity.

May he keep you safe under his protection.
℟. Amen.

May the Lord Jesus Christ,
with whose sacred heart
the hearts of virgins are united,
fill you with his divine love.
℟. Amen.

May the Holy Spirit,
by whom the Virgin Mary conceived her Son,
today consecrate your hearts
and fill you with a burning desire
to serve God and his Church.
℟. Amen.

Finally he blesses the whole congregation:
May almighty God,
the Father, and the Son, ✠ and the Holy Spirit,
bless all of you who have taken part in this celebration.
℟. Amen.

Or [155, 156]:
God inspires all holy desires and brings them
    to fulfillment.
May he protect you always by his grace
so that you may fulfill the duties of your vocation
with a faithful heart.
℟. Amen.

May he make each of you a witness
and sign of his love for all people.
℟. Amen.

May he make those bonds
with which he has bound you to Christ on earth
endure for ever in heavenly love.
℟. Amen.

Finally he blesses the whole congregation:
May almighty God,
the Father, and the Son, ✠ and the Holy Spirit,
bless all of you who have taken part in this celebration.
℟. Amen.

38. After the blessing by the bishop, the newly consecrated may take their candles. The choir and the people sing an appropriate song or a canticle of praise, and the procession is formed as at the beginning.

B. CONSECRATION TO A LIFE OF VIRGINITY TOGETHER WITH RELIGIOUS PROFESSION FOR NUNS

INTRODUCTION

39. It is appropriate for the rite of consecration combined with that of perpetual profession to take place during the octave of Easter, on solemnities, especially those which celebrate the incarnation, on Sundays, or on feasts of the Blessed Virgin Mary, holy virgins or saints distinguished in the living of the religious life.

40. On a day scheduled close to the day of the rite of consecration, or at least on the day before the consecration, the candidates are presented to the bishop, so that the father of the diocese may begin a pastoral dialogue with his spiritual daughters.

41. The consecration ordinarily takes place in the monastery church.

42. Sufficient announcement should be made to the faithful of the date and time so that they may attend in greater numbers.

43. The Mass of the day or the ritual Mass for the day of consecration is celebrated, in accordance with the rubrics (see Introduction, nos. 8-10).

44. The consecration ordinarily takes place at the chair. To enable the faithful to take part more easily, the bishop's chair may be placed in front of the altar. A chair for the superior who is to receive the profession is to be prepared in a suitable place in the sanctuary. Seats for the candidates should be so arranged in the sanctuary that the faithful may have a complete view of the liturgical rites.

45. As the nature of the rite demands, the whole liturgical service should be celebrated with fitting solemnity, but any appearance of lavishness unbecoming to religious poverty should be avoided.

46. For the eucharistic celebration enough bread and wine should be prepared for the ministers, the candidates, their parents, relatives, friends, and fellow religious. If only one chalice is used, it should be sufficiently large.

47. In addition to what is needed for the celebration of Mass, there should be ready: a) the Roman Pontifical; b) veils, rings, or other insignia of consecration or religious profession to be presented in accordance with local rules or customs of the religious family.

INTRODUCTORY RITES

48. When the people are assembled and everything is ready, the procession moves through the church to the altar in the usual way, while the choir and people sing the entrance song of the Mass. The candidates may fittingly join in the procession, accompanied by the superior and novice mistress.

49. When they come to the sanctuary, all make the customary reverence to the altar. The candidates go to their places in the body of the church and Mass continues.

LITURGY OF THE WORD

50. The liturgy of the word takes place as usual, except for the following:
a) the readings may be taken from the Mass of the day or from the texts listed in the Appendix (see Introduction, nos. 8-9);
b) the profession of faith is not said, even if prescribed by the rubrics of the day;
c) the general intercessions are omitted, since they are included in the litany.

CONSECRATION TOGETHER WITH RELIGIOUS PROFESSION

CALLING OF THE CANDIDATES

51. After the gospel, if the consecration takes place in front of the altar, the bishop goes to the chair prepared for him and sits.

When candles are not used see no. 53 below.

If candles are used, the choir sings the following antiphon:

Be wise: make ready your lamps.
Behold, the Bridegroom comes;
go out to meet him.

Any other appropriate song may be sung.

The candidates then light their lamps or candles and, accompanied by the novice mistress and another nun assigned to this task, approach the sanctuary and stand outside it.

52. Then the bishop calls the candidates; he sings or says aloud:

Come, listen to me, my children;
I will teach you reverence for the Lord.

The candidates reply by singing this antiphon or some other appropriate song:

Now with all our hearts we follow you,
we reverence you and seek your presence.
Lord, fulfill our hope:
show us your loving kindness,
the greatness of your mercy.

As they sing the antiphon, the candidates enter the sanctuary and take up their positions so that everyone may have a complete view of the liturgical rites. They place their candles in a candelabrum, or give them to the ministers until they are returned at the end of Mass. They then sit in the places prepared for them.

53. Or, when candles are not used:
[138] The deacon calls each of the candidates by name. Each candidate, on hearing her name, rises and replies: **Lord, you have called me.** The candidate may make some other suitable reply. Then she goes to the sanctuary and stands outside it.

[139] After the calling of the candidates, the bishop invites them in these or similar words:

Come, daughters,
that through me, his servant,

**the Lord may consecrate
the resolution you have formed in your hearts.**

The candidates reply by singing this antiphon or some other appropriate song:

**Now with all our hearts we follow you,
we reverence you and seek your presence.
Lord, fulfill our hope:
show us your loving kindness,
the greatness of your mercy.**

As they sing the antiphon, the candidates enter the sanctuary, accompanied by the two women, and take up their positions so that everyone may have a complete view of the liturgical rites. They then sit in the places prepared for them.

HOMILY

54. The bishop then gives a short homily to the candidates and the people, developing the Scripture readings and the theme of virginity as a gift and religious life as a responsibility, and how it sanctifies those called to it and promotes the good of the Church and the whole human family.

EXAMINATION

55. After the homily the candidates stand; the bishop then questions them on their readiness to dedicate themselves to God and to seek perfect charity, according to the rule or constitutions of the religious community. The questions may be changed or in part omitted, to suit the spirit and character of each religious institute. He uses these or similar words:

Dear sisters (daughters), in baptism you have already died to sin and have been set aside for God's service. Are you now resolved to unite yourself more closely to God by the bond of perpetual profession?
Together, all the candidates answer: **I am.**

Bishop:
Are you resolved to strive steadfastly for perfection in the love of God and of your neighbor by living the Gospel with all your heart and keeping the rule of this religious community?
Candidates: **I am.**

Bishop:

Are you resolved to give yourself to God alone, in solitude and silence, in persevering prayer and willing penance, in humble labor and good works?
Candidates: **I am.**

Are you resolved to accept solemn consecration as a bride of our Lord Jesus Christ, the Son of God?
Candidates: **I am.**

56. At the end of the questions, the bishop confirms the intention of those to be professed in these or similar words:

May God who has begun the good work in you bring it to fulfillment before the day of Christ Jesus.
All: **Amen.**

INVITATION TO PRAYER

57. Then all stand, and the bishop, without his miter, invites the people to pray:

Dearly beloved, let us pray to God the almighty Father through his Son, our Lord Jesus Christ, that, by the intercession of the Blessed Virgin Mary and all the saints, he will pour out the Holy Spirit of his love on these servants of his whom he has chosen to be consecrated to his service.

58. Deacon (except during the Easter season):
Let us kneel.

LITANY OF THE SAINTS

Then the bishop, the ministers, the candidates, and the people kneel (except during the Easter season, when all stand). Where it is customary for the candidates to prostrate themselves, this may be done.

59. The cantors then sing the litany (Chapter V). At the proper place they may add the names of other saints who are specially venerated by the people, or petitions suitable to the occasion.

60. Then the bishop alone rises and, with hands joined, sings or says:

Lord,
hear the prayers of your Church.
Look with favor on your handmaids
whom you have called in your love.
Set them on the way of eternal salvation;
may they seek only what is pleasing to you,
and fulfill it with watchful care.

We ask this through Christ our Lord.
All: **Amen.**

Deacon: **Let us stand.**

All stand.

PROFESSION

61. After the litany, if it is the custom of the religious community, two consecrated and professed members of the community come to the chair of the superior and, standing, act as witnesses. Those to be professed come, one by one, to the superior and read the formula of profession, which they themselves have written out beforehand.

62. Then the newly professed may fittingly go to the altar, one by one, to place on it the formula of profession; if it can be done conveniently, each of them should sign the document of profession upon the altar itself. After this, each goes back to her place.

63. Afterward, if it is the practice of the community, the newly professed may stand and sing the following antiphon or another song expressing the spirit of self-giving and joy:

Uphold me, Lord, according to your promise
and I shall live;
and do not bring to nothing all my hope.

PRAYER OF CONSECRATION

64. Then the candidates kneel, and the bishop extends his hands over them, and sings or says the prayer of consecration. The words in brackets may be omitted.

Loving Father,
chaste bodies are your temple;
you delight in sinless hearts.
Our nature was corrupted
when the devil deceived our first parents,
but you have restored it in Christ.
He is your Word, through whom all things were made.
He has made our nature whole again,
and made it possible for mortal people to reflect the
    life of angels.

Lord,
look with favor on your handmaids.
They place in your hands their resolve to live in
    chastity.
You inspire them to take this vow;
now they give you their hearts.

[Only you can kindle this flame of love, and feed its
    brightness,
giving strength and perseverance to our will.
Without you our flesh is weak,
bound by the law of nature,
free with false freedom,
imprisoned by habit,
softened by the spirit of the age.]

You have poured out your grace upon all peoples.
You have adopted as heirs of the new covenant
sons and daughters from every nation under heaven,
countless as the stars.
Your children are born, not of human birth,
nor of man's desire,
but of your Spirit.
Among your many gifts
you give to some the grace of virginity.
Yet the honor of marriage is in no way lessened.
As it was in the beginning,
your first blessing still remains upon this holy union.
Yet your loving wisdom chooses those
who make sacrifice of marriage
for the sake of the love of which it is the sign.

They renounce the joys of human marriage,
but cherish all that it foreshadows.

[Those who choose chastity have looked upon the face
    of Christ,
its origin and inspiration.
They give themselves wholly to Christ,
the Son of the ever-virgin Mary,
and the heavenly Bridegroom of those
who in his honor dedicate themselves to lasting
    virginity.]

Lord,
protect those who seek your help.
They desire to be strengthened by your blessing and
    consecration.
Defend them from the cunning and deceit of the
    enemy.
Keep them vigilant and on their guard;
may nothing tarnish the glory of perfect virginity,
or the vocation of purity which is shared by those who
    are married.

Through the gift of your Spirit, Lord,
give them modesty with right judgment,
kindness with true wisdom,
gentleness with strength of character,
freedom with the grace of chastity.
Give them the warmth of love,
to love you above all others.
Make their lives deserve our praise,
without seeking to be praised.
May they give you glory
by holiness of action and purity of heart.
May they love you and fear you;
may they love you and serve you.

Be yourself their glory, their joy, their whole desire.
Be their comfort in sorrow,
their wisdom in perplexity,
their protection in the midst of injustice,
their patience in adversity,

their riches in poverty,
their food in fasting,
their remedy in time of sickness.

They have chosen you above all things; may they find
all things in possessing you.

We ask this through our Lord Jesus Christ, your Son,
who lives and reigns with you and the Holy Spirit,
one God, for ever and ever.
All: Amen.

PRESENTATION OF THE INSIGNIA OF CONSECRATION

One of the following forms, nos. 65 to 69 or nos. 151 to 154, is
used.

65. After the prayer of consecration, the bishop and the
people sit. The newly consecrated stand and, accompanied
by the novice mistress and the other nun assigned to this
task, come before the bishop. He says, once for all of them:

If the veil is given:
Dearest daughters,
receive the veil and the ring
that are the insignia of your consecration.
Keep unstained your fidelity to your Bridegroom,
and never forget that you are bound
to the service of Christ and of his body, the Church.
They all reply together: Amen.

66. Or, if the veil is not given:
Receive the ring
that marks you as a bride of Christ.
Keep unstained your fidelity to your Bridegroom,
that you may one day be admitted to the wedding feast
    of everlasting joy.
They all reply together: Amen.

67. While the newly consecrated kneel, the bishop gives the
ring to each one and, if customary, the veil and other insignia
of consecration.

Meanwhile, the choir and the people may sing the following
antiphon with Psalm 45.

To you, O Lord, I lift my soul;
come and rescue me, for you are my refuge and my
strength.

The antiphon is repeated after every two verses. **Glory to the Father** is not said. The psalm is interrupted and the antiphon repeated when the presentation of the insignia is completed.

Any other appropriate song may be sung.

PRESENTATION OF THE LITURGY OF THE HOURS

68. Then, if it seems appropriate, the bishop gives the newly consecrated the book containing the prayer of the Church, saying these or similar words:

Receive the book of the liturgy of the hours,
the prayer of the Church;
may the praise of our heavenly Father
be always on your lips;
pray without ceasing
for the salvation of the whole world.
All reply together: **Amen.**

The newly consecrated come before the bishop, who gives each a copy of the liturgy of the hours. After receiving it, they return to their places and remain standing.

---

69. Then, if appropriate, this or some other suitable antiphon is sung.

I am espoused to him whom the angels serve;
sun and moon stand in wonder at his glory.

If possible, all those newly consecrated sing the antiphon together, otherwise the choir sings it.

Or:
[151] (For the giving of the veil. The rite is omitted if those consecrated have already received the veil canonically.) After the prayer of consecration the bishop and the people sit. The newly consecrated stand and, accompanied by the consecrated or lay women mentioned above, come before the bishop. He gives the veil to each one, saying:

Receive this veil,
by which you are to show
that you have been chosen from other women
to be dedicated to the service of Christ
and of his body, which is the Church.
Each one replies: **Amen.**

After receiving the veil each one returns to her place and remains standing. When all have received their veils, they sing the antiphon:

I will raise my mind and heart to you, O Lord,
that I may be holy in body and in spirit.

The choir may begin the antiphon after the veil has been given to the first or second one. It may be repeated after one or more verses of a suitable psalm or canticle.

[152] (For the giving of the ring.) When all have received the veil, the rings are given in the following way: those consecrated come before the bishop in the same order as before. Then he gives each one her ring, saying:

Receive the ring
that marks you as a bride of Christ.
Keep unstained your fidelity to your Bridegroom,
that you may one day be admitted to the wedding feast
of everlasting joy.
Each one replies: **Amen.**

PRESENTATION OF THE LITURGY OF THE HOURS

[153] Then, if it seems appropriate, the bishop gives the newly consecrated the book containing the prayer of the Church, saying these or similar words:

Receive the book of the liturgy of the hours,
the prayer of the Church;
may the praise of our heavenly Father
be always on your lips;
pray without ceasing
for the salvation of the whole world.
Each replies: **Amen.**

Each returns to her place.

[154] After all have received the insignia of profession, those consecrated sing the antiphon:

I am espoused to him whom the angels serve; sun and moon stand in wonder at his glory.

If appropriate the choir may sing the antiphon after the ring has been given to the first or second person. It may be repeated after one or more verses of a suitable psalm or canticle.

SIGN OF ACCEPTANCE

70. After this, if it is customary or seems opportune, there may be a ceremony to mark the fact that the newly professed religious have been admitted as lifelong members of the religious family. This can take the form of a suitable statement by the superior or of the sign of peace.

The superior says these or similar words:
We confirm that you are now one with us as members of this religious community of N., sharing all things common with us now and in the future.

The members of the community manifest their assent, saying:
Amen.

Or:
71. The above may be omitted, and the bishop may give the sign of peace. The superior expresses sisterly love for the newly professed by the sign of peace or in some other way, according to the custom of the religious community or monastery. Meanwhile the choir and the people may sing the following antiphon with Psalm 84.

**How lovely is your dwelling place, O Lord of power and might.
My soul is longing and fainting for the courts of the Lord.**

Any other appropriate song may be sung.

If the sign of peace is given here, it is omitted before communion.

72. After this the newly consecrated return to their places in the sanctuary and the Mass continues.

LITURGY OF THE EUCHARIST

73. During the preparation of the gifts, some of those newly consecrated may bring to the altar the bread, wine, and water for the eucharistic sacrifice.

74. In the eucharistic prayers the offering of those newly consecrated may be mentioned (see Ritual Masses, Consecration to a Life of Virginity).

75. If the sign of peace has not already been given, the bishop now gives it in some suitable form to those newly consecrated.

76. After the bishop has received the body and blood of Christ, the newly consecrated come to the altar to receive communion under both kinds.

Their parents, relatives, friends, and fellow religious may also receive communion under both kinds.

CONCLUDING RITE

SOLEMN BLESSING

77. When the prayer after communion has been said, the newly consecrated stand before the altar. The bishop faces them and sings or says one of the following:

**The almighty Father
has poured into your hearts
the desire to live a life of holy virginity.
May he keep you safe under his protection.
℟. Amen.**

**May the Lord Jesus Christ,
with whose sacred heart
the hearts of virgins are united,
fill you with his divine love.
℟. Amen.**

**May the Holy Spirit,
by whom the Virgin Mary conceived her Son,
today consecrated your hearts**

and fill you with a burning desire
to serve God and his Church.
℟. Amen.

Finally he blesses the whole congregation:
May almighty God,
the Father, and the Son, ✠ and the Holy Spirit,
bless all of you who have taken part in this celebration.
℟. Amen.

Or [155, 156]:
God inspires all holy desires and brings them to ful-
    fillment.
May he protect you always by his grace
so that you may fulfill the duties of your vocation
with a faithful heart.
℟. Amen.

May he make those bonds
with which he has bound you to Christ on earth
endure for ever in heavenly love.
℟. Amen.

Finally he blesses the whole congregation:
May almighty God,
the Father, and the Son, ✠ and the Holy Spirit,
bless all of you who have taken part in this celebration.
℟. Amen.

80. After the blessing by the bishop, those newly consecrated
may take their candles. The choir and the people sing an
appropriate song or a canticle of praise, and the procession is
formed as at the beginning.

APPENDIX

CONSECRATION TO A LIFE OF VIRGINITY

The readings are taken in whole or in part from the Mass of the day or from the texts listed below.

READING FROM THE OLD TESTAMENT (L 811)

1. Genesis 12:1-4a
Go forth from the land of your kinsfolk and from your father's home.

2. 1 Samuel 3:1-10
Speak, Lord, for your servant is listening.

3. 1 Kings 19:4-9a, 11-15a
Go out and stand on the mountain before the Lord.

4. 1 Kings 19:16b, 19-21
Then he left and followed Elijah as his attendant.

5. Song of Songs 2:8-14
Arise, my beloved, my beautiful one, and come!

6. Song of Songs 8:6-7
Stern as death is love.

7. Isaiah 44:1-5
One shall say, "I am the LORD's."

8. Isaiah 61:9-11
I rejoice heartily in the LORD.

9. Jeremiah 31:31-37
A new covenant

10. Hosea 2:16, 21-22
I will espouse you to me forever.

READING FROM THE NEW TESTAMENT (L 812)

1. Acts 2:42-47
All who believed were together and had all things in common.

2. Acts 4:32-35
The community of believers was of one heart and mind.

3. Romans 6:3-11
So that we too might live in newness of life.

4. Romans 12:1-13
Offer your bodies as a living sacrifice, holy and pleasing to God.

5. 1 Corinthians 1:22-31
We proclaim Christ crucified.

6. 1 Corinthians 7:25-35
A virgin is anxious about the things of the Lord.

7. Ephesians 1:3-14
God chose us in Christ to be holy and without blemish before him in love.

8. Philippians 2:1-4
Being of the same mind, with the same love.

9. Philippians 3:8-14
I consider them so much rubbish, that I may gain Christ.

10. Colossians 3:1-4
Think of what is above, not of what is on earth.

11. Colossians 3:12-17
Over all these put on love, that is, the bond of perfection.

12. 1 Thessalonians 4:1-3, 7-12
This is the will of God, your holiness.

13. 1 Peter 1:3-9
Although you have not seen him you love him.

14. 1 John 4:7-16
If we love one another, God remains in us.

15. Revelation 3:14b, 20-22
I will dine with him and he with me.

16. Revelation 22:12-14, 16-17, 20
Come, Lord Jesus!

RESPONSORIAL PSALM (L 813)

1. Psalm 24:1bc-2, 3-4ab, 5-6
℞. (see 6) **Lord, this is the people that longs to see your face.**

2. Psalm 27:1, 4, 5, 8-9abc, 11
℞. (8b) **I long to see your face, O Lord.**

3. Psalm 33:2-3, 4-5, 11-12, 13-14, 18-19, 20-21
℟. (12) Blessed the people the Lord has chosen to be his own.

4. Psalm 34:2-3, 4-5, 6-7, 8-9
or: Psalm 34:10-11, 12-13, 14-15, 17 and 19
℟. (2a) I will bless the Lord at all times.
or: ℟. (9a) Taste and see the goodness of the Lord.

5. Psalm 40:2 and 4ab, 7-8a, 8b-9, 10, 12
℟. (8a and 9a) Here I am, Lord: I come to do your will.

6. Psalm 45:11-12, 14-15, 16-17
℟. (Matthew 25:6) The bridegroom is here; let us go out to meet Christ the Lord.

7. Psalm 63:2, 3-4, 5-6, 8-9
℟. (2b) My soul is thirsting for you, O Lord my God.

8. Psalm 84:3, 4, 5-6a and 8a, 11, 12
℟. (2) How lovely is your dwelling place, Lord, mighty God!

9. Psalm 100:2, 3, 4, 5
℟. (2c) Come with joy into the presence of the Lord.

ALLELUIA VERSE AND VERSE BEFORE THE GOSPEL
(L 814)
1. Psalm 133:1
Behold, how good it is, and how pleasant,
when brothers and sisters dwell as one!

2. See Matthew 11:25
Blessed are you, Father, Lord of heaven and earth;
you have revealed to little ones the mysteries of the
    Kingdom.

3. John 13:34
I give you a new commandment:
love one another as I have loved you.

4. John 15:5
I am the vine, you are the branches, says the Lord:
whoever remains in me and I in him will bear much fruit.

5. 2 Corinthians 8:9
Jesus Christ became poor although he was rich,
so that by his poverty you might become rich.

6. Galatians 6:14
May I never boast except in the cross of our Lord Jesus
   Christ,
through which the world has been crucified to me and I
   to the world.

7. Philippians 3:8-9
I consider all things so much rubbish
that I may gain Christ and be found in him.

GOSPEL (L 815)

1. Matthew 5:1-12a
Blessed are you . . . rejoice and be glad.

2. Matthew 11:25-30
You have hidden these things from the wise and the
learned and you have revealed them to the childlike.

3. Matthew 16:24-27
Whoever loses his life for my sake will find it.

4. Matthew 19:3-12
For the sake of the Kingdom of heaven.

5. Matthew 19:16-26
If you wish to be perfect, go sell what you have and follow
me.

6. Matthew 25:1-13
Behold the bridegroom! Come out to meet him!

7. Mark 3:31-35
Whoever does the will of God is my brother and sister
and mother.

8. Mark 10:24b-30
We have given up everything and followed you.

9. Luke 1:26-38
"Behold, I am the handmaid of the Lord."

10. Luke 9:57-62
No one who sets a hand to the plow and looks to what
was left behind is fit for the Kingdom of God.

11. Luke 10:38-42
Martha welcomed him. Mary has chosen the better part.

12. Luke 11:27-28
Blessed are those who hear the word of God and observe it.

13. John 12:24-26
If a grain of wheat dies, it produces much fruit.

14. John 15:1-8
Remain in me, as I remain in you.

15. John 15:9-17
You are my friends if you do what I command you.

16. John 17:20-26
I wish that where I am, they also may be with me.

CONSECRATION TO A LIFE OF VIRGINITY

The cantors begin the litany. At the proper place they may add the names of other saints who are specially venerated by the people or petitions suitable to the occasion.

Lord, have mercy   Lord, have mercy
Christ, have mercy   Christ, have mercy
Lord, have mercy   Lord, have mercy

Holy Mary   pray for us
Mother of God   pray for us
Most honored of all virgins   pray for us
Saint Michael   pray for us
Holy angels of God   pray for us
Saint John the Baptist   pray for us
Saint Joseph   pray for us
Saint Peter and Saint Paul   pray for us
Saint John   pray for us
Saint Mary Magdalene   pray for us
Saint Stephen and Saint Lawrence   pray for us
Saint Perpetua and Saint Felicity   pray for us
Saint Agnes   pray for us
Saint Maria Goretti   pray for us
Saint Athanasius   pray for us
Saint Ambrose   pray for us
Saint Augustine   pray for us
Saint Jerome   pray for us
Saint Benedict   pray for us
Saint Dominic and Saint Francis   pray for us
Saint Macrina   pray for us
Saint Scholastica   pray for us
Saint Clare and Saint Catherine   pray for us
Saint Teresa of Avila   pray for us
Saint Rose of Lima   pray for us
Saint Louise Marillac   pray for us
Saint Margaret Mary Alacoque   pray for us
All holy men and women   pray for us

Lord, be merciful   Lord, save your people
From all evil   Lord, save your people
From every sin   Lord, save your people
From everlasting death   Lord, save your people
By your coming as man   Lord, save your people
By your death and rising to new life   Lord, save your
     people
By your gift of the Holy Spirit   Lord, save your people
Be merciful to us sinners   Lord, hear our prayer
Give to your servant Pope N., and to all other bishops,
     the grace of growing daily in the likeness of Christ,
     Bridegroom of the Church   Lord, hear our prayer
Maintain and foster in your Church love for holy vir-
     ginity   Lord, hear our prayer
Strengthen in Christ's faithful people hope of a glori-
     ous resurrection and of the life of the world to
     come   Lord, hear our prayer
Give to all nations true harmony and peace   Lord,
     hear our prayer
Increase in holiness and in number those who follow
     the counsels of the Gospel   Lord, hear our prayer
Reward a hundredfold the parents of your handmaids
     for the sacrifice they have made   Lord, hear our
     prayer
Bless these handmaids, make them holy, and conse-
     crate them to your service   Lord, hear our prayer
Jesus, Son of the living God   Lord, hear our prayer
Christ, hear us   Christ, hear us
Lord Jesus, hear our prayer   Lord Jesus, hear our
     prayer

RITE OF RELIGIOUS PROFESSION

RITE OF RELIGIOUS PROFESSION

PART I: RITE OF RELIGIOUS PROFESSION FOR MEN

CHAPTER I
NORMS FOR THE RITE OF INITIATION INTO THE RELIGIOUS LIFE
Introductory Rites
Greeting or Song (6)
Questioning of the Postulants or Request for Admission (7)
Opening Prayer (9)

Celebration of the Word of God (10)

Concluding Rites
General Intercessions (12)
Lord's Prayer (12)
Concluding Prayer (12)

CHAPTER II
RITE OF TEMPORARY PROFESSION DURING MASS
Introductory Rites (20)

Liturgy of the Word (22)

Religious Profession
Calling or Request (23-25)
Homily or Address (26)
Examination (27-28)
Prayer for God's Grace (29)
Profession (30)
Presentation of the Insignia of Religious Profession
Presentation of the Religious Habit (31)
Presentation of the Rule or Constitutions (32-35)
General Intercessions (36)

Liturgy of the Eucharist (37)

CHAPTER III
RITE OF PERPETUAL PROFESSION DURING MASS
Introductory Rites (51)

Liturgy of the Word (52)

Religious Profession

Renewal of Vows
Prayer for God's Grace (92)
Renewal of Profession (93)
General Intercessions (94)

Liturgy of the Eucharist (95)

CHAPTER V
OTHER TEXTS FOR THE RITES OF RELIGIOUS
PROFESSION

FOREWORD

On February 2, 1970, the Congregation for Divine Worship issued the Latin typical edition of *Ordo professionis religiosae*. An interim English translation was prepared by the International Commission on English in the Liturgy (ICEL) in 1971. A second revised edition was issued by ICEL in 1974.

On September 12, 1983, the Congregation for the Sacraments and Divine Worship published *Emendations in the Liturgical Books following upon the New Code of Canon Law*. This document indicates all the changes that are to be made in the liturgical books as a result of the promulgation of the revised *Code of Canon Law* of 1983. The most notable change made in the *Rite of Religious Profession* to conform it to the new *Code of Canon Law* is the deletion of the Rite of a Promise and of all references to it in the Introduction.

This revised edition of *The Rite of Religious Profession* contains all the changes mandated by the *Emendations*, as well as the 1982 revised translation of the Introduction to the rite, taken from *Documents on the Liturgy, 1963-1979: Conciliar, Papal, and Curial Texts*. In addition, the publication of this new edition has been the occasion for making several corrections in the text of the previous edition.

Secretariat for the Liturgy

National Conference of Catholic Bishops

SACRED CONGREGATION FOR DIVINE WORSHIP

Prot. n. 200/70

DECREE

The rite of profession by which religious, in commitment to the evangelical counsels, vow themselves to God, has been revised in accord with the intent of the *Constitution on the Liturgy*. The life dedicated to God by the bonds of religious life has always held a place of high honor in the eyes of the Church, which from the earliest centuries has surrounded the act of religious profession with liturgical rites. The Fathers of Vatican Council II directed that a rite of religious profession and renewal of vows be drawn up that would contribute to greater unity, simplicity, and dignity and that, apart from exceptions in particular law, it should be adopted by those who make their profession or renewal of vows within Mass (art. 80).

Carrying out this directive, the Consilium has composed the present rite of religious profession; Pope Paul VI by his apostolic authority has approved it and ordered that it be incorporated into the *Roman Ritual* and published. Consequently this Congregation for Divine Worship, at the explicit mandate of the Pope, promulgates this rite.

The conferences of bishops (where applicable, through the joint commission of nations of the same language) are to see to the careful vernacular translations of the rite, after consultation with the conferences of major religious superiors in each country.

The rite of profession must be an expression of the identity and spirit of the individual religious family. Therefore each religious institute should adapt this rite in such a way that the ritual clearly brings out the institute's special character, then send the rite to this Congregation as soon as possible for confirmation.

All things to the contrary notwithstanding.

From the Sacred Congregation for Divine Worship, 2 February 1970, the feast of the Presentation of the Lord.

+ Benno Cardinal Gut   A. Bugnini
Prefect   *Secretary*

INTRODUCTION*

I. NATURE AND IMPORT OF RELIGIOUS PROFESSION

1. In response to God's call many Christians dedicate themselves to his service and to the welfare of humanity through the sacred bonds of religious life and seek to follow Christ more closely through the evangelical counsels.[1] This leads to the grace of baptism achieving richer results in them.[2]

2. The Church has always esteemed the religious life, which, under the guidance of the Holy Spirit, has taken various forms in the course of history.[3] It has raised religious life to the rank of a canonical state and approved a great number of religious institutes and protected them by wise legislation.[4]

For it is the Church that receives the vows of those who make religious profession, begs God's grace for them by its public prayer, puts them in God's hands, blesses them, and unites their offering with the eucharistic sacrifice.[5]

II. RITES FOR THE DIFFERENT STAGES OF RELIGIOUS LIFE

3. The steps by which religious dedicate themselves to God and the Church are these: novitiate, first profession (or other sacred bonds), and final profession. The constitutions of religious institutes add to these a renewal of vows.

4. The novitiate, the beginning of life in the institute,[6] is a time of testing for both novice and community. Entry into the novitiate should be marked by a rite in which God's grace is sought for the special purpose of the period. This rite should, of its nature, be restrained and simple, celebrated in the presence only of the religious community. It should take place outside Mass.

5. First profession then follows. Through temporary vows before God and the Church the novices promise to observe the evangelical counsels. Such vows may be taken within Mass, but without special solemnity. The rite of first profession provides for the bestowal of insignia of the religious life and the habit, following the very ancient custom of giving the habit at the end of the period of probation, since the habit is a sign of consecration. [7]

6. After the period prescribed by law, final profession is made, by which religious bind themselves permanently to the service of God and the Church. Perpetual profession reflects the unbreakable union between Christ and his Bride, the Church.[8]

It is very fitting that the rite of final profession should take place within Mass, with due solemnity and in the presence of the religious community and the people.[9] The rite consists of these parts:

a. the calling or asking of those to be professed (this may be omitted if desired);

b. the homily or address, which reminds the people and those to be professed of the value of religious life;

c. the examination, by which the celebrant or superior asks those who are to be professed whether they are prepared to be consecrated to God and to follow the way of perfect charity, according to the rule of their religious family;

d. the litanies, in which prayer is offered to God the Father and the intercession of the Blessed Virgin Mary and all the saints is invoked;

e. the profession, made in the presence of the Church, the lawful superior of the institute, the witnesses, and the congregation;

f. the solemn blessing or consecration of the professed, by which the Church ratifies their profession through a liturgical consecration, asking the heavenly Father to pour forth upon them the gifts of the Holy Spirit;

g. the presentation of the insignia of profession, if this is the custom of the religious family, as outward signs of perpetual dedication to God.

7. In some religious communities vows are renewed at fixed times in accordance with the constitutions.

This renewal of vows may take place within Mass, but without solemnity, especially if renewal of vows is frequent or annual.

A liturgical rite has place only in the case of renewal of vows that has the force of law. In many religious communities, however, the custom of renewing vows has become established as an exercise of devotion. It may be carried out in many ways; but the practice of doing publicly within Mass what belongs to private devotion is not to be encouraged. If it seems appropriate to renew vows publicly on special anniversaries, for example, the twenty-fifth or fiftieth year of religious life, the rite for the renewal of vows may be used with the necessary adaptations.

8. Since all these rites have their own special character, each demands a celebration of its own. The celebration of several rites within the same liturgical service is to be absolutely excluded.

III. MASS FOR THE RITE OF RELIGIOUS PROFESSION

9. Whenever religious profession, and especially final profession, takes place within Mass, it is appropriate to choose one of the ritual Masses for the day of religious profession from the *Roman Missal* or from approved propers. In the case of a Sunday of Advent, Lent or Easter, of any solemnity, or of Ash Wednesday and all of Holy Week, the Mass is that of the day; but the special formularies for the professed during the eucharistic prayer and the final blessing may be retained.

10. Since the liturgy of the word for the rite of profession can be an important aid to bringing out the meaning of religious life and its responsibilities, it is lawful, when the Mass for the day of religious profession may not be used, to take one reading from the special list of readings for the rite of profession. But this may not be done during the Easter triduum, on the solemnities of Christmas, Epiphany, Ascension, Pentecost or Corpus Christi, or on other solemnities of obligation.

11. White vestments are worn for the ritual Mass for the day of religious profession.

IV. ADAPTATIONS TO BE MADE BY INDIVIDUAL INSTITUTES

12. The norms governing the rite of initiation (nos. 1-13 of the ritual) are not of obligation unless this is clearly stated (as in the prohibition of having the rite within Mass, no. 2) or the nature of the rite so demands (as in the rule that the rite should be restrained and simple, no. 3).

13. All who make or renew their religious profession within Mass must use the rites of temporary profession, final profession,

or renewal of vows, unless they possess a particular right in this matter.[10]

14. Religious families should adapt the rite so that it more closely reflects and manifests the character and spirit of each institute. For this purpose the faculty of adapting the rite is given to each institute; its decisions are then to be reviewed by the Apostolic See.

In making adaptations in the rite of profession, the following points should be especially respected:

a. The rite takes place immediately after the gospel.

b. The arrangement of parts must remain intact, but some parts may be omitted or others of a similar nature substituted.

c. A liturgical distinction between perpetual profession and temporary profession or renewal of vows must be strictly maintained. What is proper to one rite may not be inserted into another.

d. As is stated in the pertinent places, many formularies in the rite of profession may be changed, and in fact must be, to reflect more clearly the character and spirit of each institute. Where the *Roman Ritual* offers several optional formularies, particular rituals may add others of the same kind.

15. Profession in the presence of the blessed sacrament, prior to communion, is not in harmony with a true understanding of the liturgy. Henceforth, then, new religious communities are forbidden to adopt the practice. Institutes that follow this practice on the basis of a particular law are urged to discontinue it.

Similarly, all religious following a rite proper to them are instructed to embrace and follow authentic liturgical forms, putting aside anything in conflict with the principles of the liturgical reform. This is the way to achieve that simplicity, dignity, and closer unity that the Council has so strongly endorsed.[11]

PART I: RITE OF RELIGIOUS PROFESSION FOR MEN

CHAPTER I
NORMS FOR THE RITE OF INITIATION INTO THE RELIGIOUS LIFE

1. On the day when the canonical novitiate begins, it is fitting that there should be a ceremony to ask God's grace for achieving the special purpose of the novitiate.

2. It is forbidden to perform the rite of initiation during Mass.

3. The rite is to be very simple and direct, in the presence of the religious community only.

4. The texts for the rite must avoid anything that may seem to diminish the novices' freedom of choice or obscure the true meaning of a noviceship or time of testing.

5. The chapter hall or other similar room is an appropriate setting for the rite. If it seems necessary, however, the rite may take place in the chapel.

RITE OF INITIATION INTO THE RELIGIOUS LIFE

It is appropriate that the rite should take place during a special celebration of the word on the nature of the religious life and the spirit of the institute.

INTRODUCTORY RITES
GREETING OR SONG

6. The rite may appropriately begin with a greeting by the superior, or the singing of a psalm or other suitable hymn.

QUESTIONING OF THE POSTULANTS
OR REQUEST FOR ADMISSION

7. Then the superior questions the postulants in these or similar words:

Dear sons (brothers), what do you ask from us?

The postulants reply together in these or similar words:

We wish to try your way of life,
and are willing to be tested ourselves,
that we may follow Christ wholeheartedly
in this community of N.

The superior replies:
May the Lord grant you his help.
℟. Amen.

8. The questioning may be omitted, and the request for admission may take place as follows: one of the postulants, facing the superior and community, speaks in the name of all:
Drawn by God's mercy,
we have come here to learn your way of life.
We ask you to teach us to follow Christ crucified
and to live in poverty, obedience and chastity.
Teach us to persevere in prayer and penance,
in the service of the Church and of humankind.
Teach us to be one with you in heart and mind.
Help us to live out the Gospel every day of our lives.
Teach us your rule and help us to learn to love
our brothers as Christ commanded us.

Or he may use similar words, expressing the aspirations and thoughts of the postulants themselves.

The superior responds in these or similar words:
May God in his mercy be with you always
and may Christ our teacher grant light to us all.
℟. Amen.

OPENING PRAYER

9. After the questioning or request for admission, the superior says:
Let us pray.

Lord God,
you give us the desire to hear your call.
Listen favorably to the prayers of your servants N. and
**   N.,**

who, desiring to serve you more perfectly,
ask to join our community.
Grant that our life in common
may become a communion of love.

We ask this through Christ our Lord.
℟. Amen.

CELEBRATION OF THE WORD OF GOD

10. Suitable texts from holy Scripture are then read, with appropriate responsories (see nos. 91-136).

11. At their conclusion the superior addresses the religious community and the postulants on the meaning of the religious life and the spirit of the institute, or he reads an appropriate chapter of the rule.

CONCLUDING RITES

12. The rite fittingly concludes with the general intercessions (prayer of the faithful) and the Lord's Prayer, to which a suitable prayer may be added, such as:

Lord God,
you call us to your service
and inspire us to hear your call.
These brothers of ours
desire to test our way of life:
help them to know what you ask of them
and strengthen us all in your service.

We ask this through Christ our Lord.
℟. Amen.

13. After this the superior entrusts the newly admitted novices to the care of the novice master, and with his fellow religious greets them in the spirit of Christian love in the way customary in the religious community. Meanwhile, an appropriate song or canticle of praise is sung.

CHAPTER II
RITE OF TEMPORARY PROFESSION
DURING MASS

14. The rite described in this chapter takes place during Mass. It may be used only for those religious who make their first profession upon successful completion of the novitiate (see Introduction, no. 5).

15. The Mass may correspond to the liturgy of the day, or the ritual Mass for the day of first profession may be used, in accordance with the rubrics (see Introduction, nos. 9-11).

16. In clerical institutes it is proper for the superior who receives the profession to preside over the eucharistic sacrifice. In lay institutes a chair should be prepared in a convenient part of the sanctuary for the superior who is to receive the profession of the members of the institute.

17. The profession ordinarily takes place at the chair; if circumstances so dictate, the chair may be placed in front of the altar. Seats should be so arranged in the sanctuary for those making profession that the faithful have a complete view of the liturgical rites.

18. Enough bread and wine for consecration should be prepared for the ministers, those making their profession, and their parents, relatives, and fellow religious. If only one chalice is used, it should be sufficiently large.

19. In addition to what is needed for Mass, there should also be ready:

a) the ritual for religious profession;

b) the religious habit, if the religious institute has decided to present it on the occasion of first profession (see Introduction, no. 5);

c) the book of the rule or constitutions, and other insignia of religious profession which, according to law or custom, are to be presented.

RITE OF TEMPORARY PROFESSION DURING MASS

INTRODUCTORY RITES

20. When the people and the religious are assembled and everything is ready, the procession moves through the church to the altar in the usual way, while the choir and people sing the entrance song of the Mass. Those to be professed may fittingly join in the procession, accompanied by the novice master and, in lay institutes, the superior.

21. When they come to the sanctuary all make the customary reverence to the altar and go to their places; then Mass continues.

LITURGY OF THE WORD

22. The liturgy of the word takes place as usual, except for the following:

a) the readings may be taken from the Mass of the day or from the texts in nos. 91-136 (see Introduction, nos. 9-10);

b) the profession of faith may be omitted, even if prescribed by the rubrics of the day.

RELIGIOUS PROFESSION
CALLING OR REQUEST

23. After the gospel the celebrant and the people sit, but those to be professed stand. Then, according to choice or as circumstances demand, the deacon or the novice master calls those to be professed by name.

They answer:
Present,
or they make some other reply according to local usage or the custom of the religious community.

24. The celebrant then questions them in these or similar words:
My dear brothers (sons), what do you ask of God and of his holy Church?

The candidates reply together in these or similar words:
We ask for God's merciful love
and for the grace of serving him more perfectly
in your (this) religious community.

The celebrant and all the members of the religious community reply:
Thanks be to God,
or they express their approval in some other way.

25. The calling by name and the questioning by the celebrant may be omitted; a request by those to be professed may take their place. For example, one of those to be professed may stand facing the celebrant (or superior) and say, in the name of all, these or similar words:
With the help of God,
we (N. and N.) have studied your rule
and have lived among you as your brothers for the time
**   of probation.**
Father (Brother), we now ask to be allowed
to dedicate ourselves to God and his kingdom
by making profession in this religious community of N.

The celebrant and all the members of the religious community reply:
Thanks be to God,
or they express their approval in some other way.

HOMILY OR ADDRESS
26. Those to be professed then sit and listen to the homily or address which should develop the scriptural readings and the theme of religious profession as God's gift and call for the sanctification of those chosen and for the good of the Church and the whole human family.

EXAMINATION
27. After the homily or address, those to be professed stand, and the celebrant questions them on their readiness to dedicate themselves to God and to seek perfect charity, according to the rule or constitutions of the religious community. The questions may be changed or in part omitted, to suit the spirit and character of each religious institute.

The celebrant questions them, saying:
My dear sons (brothers),
by water and the Holy Spirit

you have already been consecrated to God's service:
are you resolved to unite yourselves more closely to him
by the new bond of religious profession?

They answer:

I am.

The celebrant continues:

**In your desire to follow Christ perfectly,
are you resolved to live in chastity
for the sake of the kingdom of heaven,
to choose a life of poverty,
and to offer the sacrifice of obedience?**

They answer:

I am.

28. Then the celebrant confirms their intention in these or similar words:

**May almighty God grant you his grace
to fulfill what you resolve.
℟. Amen.**

PRAYER FOR GOD'S GRACE

29. The celebrant then prays for God's help, saying:

Let us pray.

All pray for a while in silence. Then the celebrant says:

**Lord,
look upon these servants of yours
who are resolved to dedicate their lives to you
by making profession of the evangelical counsels
in the presence of your Church today.
Mercifully grant that their manner of life
may bring glory to your name
and further your loving plan of redemption.**

**We ask this through Christ our Lord.
℟. Amen.**

PROFESSION

30. After the prayer, if it is the custom of the religious community, two professed religious stand near the celebrant (or superior) to act as witnesses. Those to be professed come one by one to the celebrant (or superior) and read the formula of profession.

If there are very many religious making their profession, the formula of profession may be recited by all together. The concluding words, **This I promise . . .** or the like, must be said by each individually as a clear expression of his will. Then they return to their places and remain standing.

PRESENTATION OF THE INSIGNIA OF RELIGIOUS PROFESSION

PRESENTATION OF THE RELIGIOUS HABIT

31. After this the novice master and some members of the community present the religious habit to each of the newly professed to put on in the sanctuary or other suitable place. Meanwhile the choir may begin the antiphon:

**Lord, these are the men who long to see your face,
who seek the face of the God of Jacob (Psalm 24:6),**

with Psalm 24; or some other appropriate song may be sung. The antiphon is repeated after every two verses; at the end of the psalm **Glory to the Father** is not said but only the antiphon. If the presentation of the habits comes to an end before the whole psalm is sung, the psalm is interrupted and the antiphon repeated.

PRESENTATION OF THE RULE OR CONSTITUTIONS

32. Then, if customary, the newly professed, wearing the religious habit, come to the celebrant (or superior) who gives each the book of the rule or constitutions, saying these or similar words:

**Receive the rule of our (this) religious community.
By keeping it faithfully, may you arrive at the perfection of love.**

The professed replies:

Amen.

After receiving the book, he returns to his place and remains standing.

33. If the newly professed are numerous or there is some other reason, the celebrant (or superior) may present the rule and say the formula once only in these or similar words:

Receive the rule of our (this) religious community. By keeping it faithfully, may you arrive at the perfection of love.

The professed reply together:

Amen.

Then they come forward to the celebrant (superior) who gives each the book of the rule or constitutions. After receiving the book, they return to their places and remain standing.

34. If, in accordance with the rules or customs of the religious community, other insignia of religious profession are to be presented, this is done now in silence or with a suitable formula. In this matter a dignified simplicity should be observed.

35. An alternative way of presenting the insignia of profession is described in nos. 137-139.

GENERAL INTERCESSIONS

36. The rite fittingly concludes with the general intercessions (prayers of the faithful). For these, the formula given in nos. 140-142 may be used.

LITURGY OF THE EUCHARIST

37. During the offertory song, some of the newly professed religious may bring the bread, wine, and water to the altar for the eucharistic sacrifice.

38. If it seems opportune, the celebrant gives the sign of peace to each of the newly professed religious in the usual way or in accordance with the customs of the religious community or of the place.

39. After the celebrant has received the body and blood of Christ, the newly professed religious come to the altar to receive communion, which may be given to them under both kinds. Then

their parents, relatives, and fellow religious may receive communion in the same way.

CHAPTER III

RITE OF PERPETUAL PROFESSION DURING MASS

40. It is fitting that the rite of profession by which a religious binds himself to God for ever should take place on a Sunday or a solemnity of the Lord, of the Blessed Virgin Mary, or of a saint distinguished in the living of the religious life.

41. The rite of perpetual profession takes place separately from other rites of profession (see Introduction, no. 8).

42. Notice of the day and hour should be given to the faithful in good time so that they may attend in greater numbers.

43. The Mass is that of the liturgy of the day, or the ritual Mass for the day of perpetual profession may be used, in accordance with the rubrics (see Introduction, nos. 9-11).

44. Where possible and if the needs of the faithful do not demand individual celebration by the priests present, it is preferable that the Mass be concelebrated. If the superior who is to receive the profession is a priest, he should be the celebrant.

45. Profession ordinarily takes place in the church of the religious community. For pastoral reasons, however, or in order to promote esteem for the religious life, to give edification to the people of God, or to permit larger attendance, the rite may take place in the cathedral, parish church, or some other notable church, as may seem fitting.

46. Similarly, where religious from two or more institutes wish to celebrate their profession at the same eucharistic sacrifice, the rite of profession may suitably take place in the cathedral, a parish church, or some other notable church with the bishop presiding and the superiors of the institutes concelebrating. Those making their profession will pronounce their vows before their respective superiors.

47. As the nature of the rite demands, the whole liturgical service should be celebrated with fitting solemnity, but any appearance of lavishness unbecoming to religious poverty should be avoided.

48. The profession ordinarily takes place at the chair. To enable the faithful to take part more easily, the celebrant's chair may be placed in front of the altar. In lay institutes, a chair is to be prepared in a suitable part of the sanctuary for the superior who is to receive the profession of the members of the institute. Seats should be so arranged in the sanctuary for those making profession that the faithful may have a complete view of the liturgical rites.

49. Enough bread and wine for consecration should be prepared for the ministers, those making their profession, and their parents, relatives, and fellow religious. If only one chalice is used, it should be sufficiently large.

50. In addition to what is needed for Mass, there should also be ready:

a) the ritual for religious profession;

b) the insignia of religious profession, if these are to be presented in accordance with the rules or customs of the religious community.

RITE OF PERPETUAL PROFESSION DURING MASS

INTRODUCTORY RITES
51. When the people and the religious are assembled and everything is ready, the procession moves through the church to the altar in the usual way, while the choir and people sing the entrance song of the Mass. Those to be professed may fittingly join in the procession, accompanied by the novice master and, in lay institutes, the superior. When they come to the sanctuary, all make the customary reverence to the altar and go to their places; then Mass continues.

LITURGY OF THE WORD
52. The liturgy of the word takes place as usual, except for the following:

a) the reading may be taken from the Mass of the day or from the texts in nos. 91-136 (see Introduction, nos. 9-10);

b) the profession of faith may be omitted, even if prescribed by the rubrics of the day.

c) the general intercessions in the form customarily used during the celebration of Mass are omitted (see no. 62)

RELIGIOUS PROFESSION
CALLING OR REQUEST

53. After the gospel the celebrant and the people sit, but those to be professed stand. Then, according to choice or as circumstances demand, the deacon or the novice master calls those to be professed by name.

They answer:

Present,

or they make some other reply according to local usage or the custom of the religious community.

54. The celebrant then questions them in these or similar words:

My dear brothers (sons), what do you ask of God and of his holy Church?

The candidates reply together in these or similar words:

**We ask for perseverance in God's service
and in your (this) religious community
all the days of our lives.**

The celebrant and all the members of the religious community reply:

Thanks be to God,

or they express their approval in some other way.

55. The calling by name and the questioning by the celebrant may be omitted; a request by those to be professed may take their place. For example, one of those to be professed may stand facing the celebrant (or superior) and say, in the name of all, these or similar words:

**With the help of God,
we (N. and N.) have come to know
the life of religious dedication in your community.
Father (Brother), we now ask to be allowed to make**

**perpetual profession in this religious community of N.
for the glory of God and the service of the Church.**

The celebrant and all the members of the religious community
reply:
Thanks be to God,
or they express their approval in some other way.

HOMILY OR ADDRESS

56. Those to be professed then sit and listen to the homily or address which should develop the scriptural readings and the
theme of religious profession as God's gift and call for the sanctification of those chosen and for the good of the Church and the
whole human family.

EXAMINATION

57. After the homily or address, those to be professed stand, and
the celebrant questions them on their readiness to dedicate themselves to God and to seek perfect charity, according to the rule or
constitutions of the religious community. The questions may be
changed or in part omitted, to suit the spirit and character of
each religious institute.

The celebrant questions them, saying:
**Dear sons (brothers),
in baptism you have already died to sin
and been consecrated to God's service.
Are you now resolved to unite yourself more
    closely to God
by the bond of perpetual profession?**

They answer:
I am.

The celebrant continues:
**Are you resolved,
with the help of God,
to undertake that life of perfect chastity,
    obedience, and poverty
chosen for themselves by Christ our Lord**

and his Virgin Mother,
and to persevere in it for ever?

They answer:
I am.

The celebrant continues:
Are you resolved to strive steadfastly for perfection
in the love of God and of your neighbor
by living the Gospel with all your heart
and keeping the rule of this religious community?

They answer:
I am.

The celebrant continues:
Are you resolved,
with the help of the Holy Spirit,
to spend your whole life in the generous service
of God's people?

They answer:
I am.

58. In the case of religious communities wholly dedicated to the contemplative life, this may appropriately be added:

The celebrant asks:
Are you resolved to live for God alone,
in solitude and silence,
in persevering prayer and willing penance,
in humble work and holiness of life?

They answer:
I am.

59. At the end of the questions, the celebrant confirms the intention of those to be professed in these or similar words:

May God who has begun the good work in you
bring it to fulfillment
before the day of Christ Jesus.

All:
Amen.

LITANY

60. All then rise. The celebrant stands, with hands joined, and says, facing the people:

**Dear friends in Christ,
let us pray to God the almighty Father
for these servants of his
whom he has called to follow Christ in the religious life;
in his love may he bless them with his grace
and strengthen them in their holy purpose.**

61. The deacon gives the sign to kneel.

Let us kneel.

The celebrant kneels at his chair. Those to be professed prostrate themselves or kneel, according to the custom of the place or of the religious community. The rest kneel. During the Easter Season and on all Sundays, all stand except those to be professed.

62. Then the cantors sing the litany for the rite of religious profession, all making the responses. In this litany one or the other of the petitions marked with the same letter may be omitted. At the appropriate place there may be inserted invocations of saints especially venerated in the religious community or by the faithful; other petitions may be added to suit the occasion.

**Lord, have mercy   Lord, have mercy
Christ, have mercy   Christ, have mercy
Lord, have mercy   Lord, have mercy**

**Holy Mary, Mother of God   pray for us
Saint Michael   pray for us
Holy angels of God   pray for us
Saint John the Baptist   pray for us
Saint Joseph   pray for us
Saint Peter and Saint Paul   pray for us
Saint John   pray for us
Saint Mary Magdalene   pray for us
Saint Stephen and Saint Lawrence   pray for us
Saint Agnes   pray for us
Saint Basil   pray for us
Saint Augustine   pray for us
Saint Benedict   pray for us**

Saint Bernard   pray for us
Saint Francis and Saint Dominic   pray for us
Saint Ignatius of Loyola   pray for us
Saint Vincent de Paul   pray for us
Saint John Bosco   pray for us
Saint Catherine of Siena   pray for us
Saint Teresa of Jesus   pray for us
All holy men and women   pray for us.

Lord, be merciful   Lord, save your people
From all evil   Lord, save your people
From every sin   Lord, save your people
From everlasting death   Lord, save your people
By your coming as man   Lord, save your people
By your death and rising to new life   Lord, save your
   people
By your gift of the Holy Spirit   Lord, save your people

Be merciful to us sinners   Lord, hear our prayer

a) By the self-offering of your servants
and their apostolic work,
make the life of your Church ever more fruitful.
Lord, hear our prayer

a) Give in ever greater abundance
the gifts of the Holy Spirit
to your servant, Pope N.,
and to all his brother bishops.   Lord, hear our prayer.

b) By the life and labor of all religious
promote the welfare of all people.   Lord, hear our prayer

b) Lead all men and women
to the fullness of the Christian life.   Lord, hear our
   prayer

c) Grant that all religious communities
may live and grow
in the love of Christ
and the spirit of their founders.   Lord, hear our prayer

c) Give to all
who profess the Gospel counsels
a fuller share in the work
   of redemption.   Lord, hear our prayer

d) Reward a hundredfold
the parents of your servants
for the sacrifice they have made.   Lord, hear our prayer

d) Make these servants of yours
more and more like Christ,
the firstborn among many.   Lord, hear our prayer

e) Give these servants of yours
the grace of perseverance.   Lord, hear our prayer

e) Bless these brothers of ours,
   your servants,
make them holy,
and consecrate them to your service.   Lord, hear our
   prayer

Jesus, Son of the living God   Lord, hear our prayer
Christ, hear us   Christ, hear us
Lord Jesus, hear our prayer   Lord Jesus, hear our prayer

63. Then the celebrant alone rises and says, with hands joined:
Lord,
grant the prayers of your people.
Prepare the hearts of your servants
for consecration to your service.
By the grace of the Holy Spirit
purify them from all sin
and set them on fire with your love.

We ask this through Christ our Lord.
℟. Amen.

The deacon then says:
Let us rise.

All stand.

PROFESSION

64. After the litany, if it is the custom of the religious community, two professed religious stand near the celebrant (or superior) to act as witnesses. Those to be professed come, one by one, to the celebrant (or superior) and read the formula of profession, which they themselves have written out beforehand.

65. Then the newly professed may fittingly go to the altar, one by one, to place on it the formula of profession; if it can be done conveniently, each of them should sign the document of profession upon the altar itself. After this, each goes back to his place.

66. Afterward, if this is the practice of the community, the newly professed may stand and sing an antiphon or other song expressing the spirit of self-giving and joy, for example:

Uphold me, Lord, according to your promise
and I shall live;
and do not bring to nothing all my hope (Psalm 119:116).

SOLEMN BLESSING OR CONSECRATION
OF THE PROFESSED

67. Then the newly professed kneel; the celebrant with hands extended over them says the prayer of blessing **Father in heaven, source of all holiness,** in which the words in brackets may, to suit the occasion, be omitted, or else the prayer **Lord God, source of holiness and growth in your Church,** which is found in no. 143.

Father in heaven,
source of all holiness,
creator of the human race,
your love for us was so great
that you gave us a share in your own divine life.
Neither the sin of Adam
nor even the sins of the whole world
could alter your loving purpose.

In the dawn of history
you gave us Abel as an example of holiness.
Later, from your beloved Hebrew people
you raised up men and women graced with every virtue.

Foremost among them all stands Mary,
the ever-virgin daughter of Zion.
From her pure womb was born Jesus Christ,
your eternal Word,
the Savior of the world.

You sent him, Father, as our pattern of holiness.
He became poor to make us rich,
a slave to set us free.
With love no words can tell
he redeemed the world by his paschal mystery
and won from you the gifts of the Spirit
to sanctify his Church.

The voice of the Spirit has drawn
countless numbers of your children
to follow in the footsteps of your Son.
They leave all things
to be one with you in the bonds of love
and give themselves wholly to your service
and the service of all your people.

Look with favor, then,
on these who have heard your call.
Send them the Spirit of holiness;
help them to fulfill in faith
what you have enabled them to promise in joy.
Keep always before their eyes Christ, the divine teacher.

[Give them perfect chastity,
ungrudging poverty
and wholehearted obedience.
May they glorify you by their humility,
serve you with docility,
and be one with you in fervent love.]

May they build up the Church by the holiness of their
    lives,
advance the salvation of the world,
and stand as a sign of the blessings that are to come.

Lord, protect and guide these servants of yours.
At the judgment seat of your Son
be yourself their great reward.
Give them the joy of vows fulfilled.
Made perfect in your love,
may they rejoice in the communion of your saints
and praise you for ever in their company.

We ask this through Christ our Lord.
R̂. Amen.

PRESENTATION OF THE INSIGNIA OF PROFESSION

68. After the blessing of the professed, if it is the custom of the religious community to present insignia of religious profession, the newly professed rise and come before the celebrant, who presents the insignia to each in silence or with a suitable formula.

69. Meanwhile the choir and people together sing the antiphon:
How happy, Lord, are those who dwell in your house,
who sing your praise for ever (*Psalm 84:5*),

with Psalm 84; or some other appropriate song may be sung. The antiphon is repeated after every two verses; at the end of the psalm **Glory to the Father** is not said but only the antiphon. If the presentation of the insignia comes to an end before the whole psalm is sung, the psalm is interrupted and the antiphon repeated.

STATEMENT OF ADMISSION OR SIGN OF PEACE

70. When the presentation of the insignia is completed, or after the prayer of solemn blessing, if it is customary or seems opportune, there may be a ceremony to mark the fact that the newly professed religious have been admitted as lifelong members of the institute or religious family. This can take the form of a suitable statement by the celebrant (or superior) or of the sign of peace. For example:

a) The celebrant (or superior) says these or similar words:
We confirm that you are now one with us
as members of this religious community of N.,

**sharing all things in common with us
now and in the future.**

He may add:

**Be faithful to the ministry the Church entrusts to you
to be carried out in its name.**

The members of the community manifest their assent, saying:

Amen.

b) The above may be omitted and the celebrant (or superior) and members of the community may give the sign of peace to the newly professed in the usual way or according to the custom of the place. Meanwhile the choir and the people sing the antiphon:

**See how good it is, how pleasant,
that brothers live in unity (*Psalm 133:1*),**

with Psalm 133; or some other appropriate song may be sung.

71. The newly professed religious return after this to their places. The Mass continues.

LITURGY OF THE EUCHARIST

72. During the offertory song, some of the newly professed may bring to the altar the bread, wine, and water for the eucharistic sacrifice.

73. In the eucharistic prayers, the offering of the professed may be mentioned according to the text below:

a) In Eucharistic Prayer I, the special form of **Father, accept this offering** is said:

**Father, accept and sanctify this offering
from your whole family and from these your servants
which we make to you on the day of their profession.
By your grace
they have dedicated their lives to you today.
When your Son returns in glory,
may they share the joy of the unending paschal feast.**

[Through Christ our Lord. Amen.]

b) In the intercessions of Eucharistic Prayer II, after the words **and all the clergy**, there is added:

Lord, remember also these your brothers
who have today dedicated themselves to serve
  you always.
Grant that they may always raise their minds and hearts
  to you
and glorify your name.

c) In the intercessions of Eucharistic Prayer II, after the words
your Son has gained for you, there is added:
Strengthen also these your servants in their holy purpose,
for they have dedicated themselves
by the bonds of religious consecration to serve
  you always.
Grant that they may give witness in your Church
to the new and eternal life won by Christ's redemption.

d) In the intercessions of Eucharistic Prayer IV, the professed
may be mentioned in this way:
. . . bishop, and bishops and clergy everywhere.
Remember these our brothers
who unite themselves more closely to you today
by their perpetual profession.
Remember those who take part in this offering . . .

74. The celebrant gives the sign of peace to each of the newly professed in the usual way, or according to the custom of the place
or of the religious community.

75. After the celebrant has received the body and blood of Christ,
the newly professed religious come to the altar to receive communion which may be given to them under both kinds. Then
their parents, relatives, and fellow religious may receive communion in the same way.

CONCLUDING RITE
SOLEMN BLESSING
76. When the prayer after communion has been said, the newly
consecrated religious stand before the altar, and the celebrant,
facing them, may say:
God inspires all holy desires and brings them
  to fulfillment.

May he protect you always by his grace
so that you may fulfill the duties of your vocation
with a faithful heart.
℟. Amen.

May he make each of you a witness
and sign of his love for all people.
℟. Amen.

May he make those bonds,
with which he has bound you to Christ on earth,
endure for ever in heavenly love.
℟. Amen.

Another form of the blessing may be found in no. 144.

77. Finally, the celebrant blesses the whole congregation:
May almighty God,
the Father, and the Son,   ✠   and the Holy Spirit,
bless all of you who have taken part in this celebration.
℟. Amen.

CHAPTER IV
RITE FOR RENEWAL OF VOWS DURING MASS

78. Renewal of vows, which is governed by the general law of the Church or by a particular ruling of the constitutions, may take place during Mass if the religious community thinks it appropriate.

79. The rite for the renewal of vows should be conducted with the greatest simplicity, especially if, in accordance with the constitutions of the religious institute, vows are renewed frequently or annually.

80. Either the Mass corresponding to the liturgy of the day or the ritual Mass for the day of the renewal of vows is used, in accordance with the rubrics (see Introduction, no. 9).

81. In clerical institutes it is proper for the superior who receives the renewal of vows to preside over the eucharistic sacrifice. In lay institutes a chair should be prepared in a convenient part of the sanctuary for the superior who is to receive the profession of his fellow religious.

82. Religious who renew their profession may receive communion under both kinds. If only one chalice is used, it should be sufficiently large.

LITURGY OF THE WORD

83. In the liturgy of the word, all takes place as usual except for the following:

a) the readings may be taken from the Mass of the day or from the texts set out in nos. 91-136 (see Introduction, nos. 9-10);

b) the profession of faith may be omitted, even if prescribed by the rubrics of the day.

84. After the gospel a homily which uses the readings from Scripture to emphasize the meaning and the value of religious life is given.

RENEWAL OF VOWS
PRAYER FOR GOD'S GRACE
85. After the homily the celebrant prays for God's help, saying:

God our Father gives us the grace
   to persevere in our resolutions.
Let us pray to him for these servants of his
who are resolved to renew their vows today
   in the presence of the Church.

All pray for a time in silence. Then the celebrant says:

Lord,
in your providence
you have called these servants of yours
to be perfect as the Gospel teaches.
In your mercy grant that they may persevere to the end
along the way of your love
on which they have set out with such joy.

We ask this through Christ our Lord.
℟. Amen.

RENEWAL OF PROFESSION
86. After the prayer, if it is the custom of the religious community, two professed members of the community stand near the celebrant (or superior) to act as witnesses. Those who are to renew their profession come, one by one, to the celebrant (or superior) and read the formula of profession.

If there is a large number renewing their vows, the formula of profession may be recited by all. The concluding words, **This I promise...** or the like, must be said by each individually, as a clear expression of his will.

GENERAL INTERCESSIONS
87. The rite fittingly concludes with the recitation of the general intercessions (prayer of the faithful); for these the formula set out in nos. 140-142 may be used.

LITURGY OF THE EUCHARIST

88. During the offertory song some of the religious who have renewed their vows may bring the bread, wine, and water to the altar for the eucharistic sacrifice.

89. The celebrant, after saying, **"The peace of the Lord,"** gives to each of the religious who have renewed their vows the sign of peace in the usual way or in accordance with the custom of the place or of the religious community. If there are many, he gives the sign of peace to the first, who gives it to the rest.

90. After the celebrant has received the body and blood of Christ, the religious who have renewed their profession come to the altar to receive communion under both kinds.

Chapter V

OTHER TEXTS FOR THE RITES OF RELIGIOUS PROFESSION

I. BIBLICAL READINGS

READINGS FROM THE OLD TESTAMENT

91. Genesis 12:1-4a
Leave your country, your family, and come.

92. 1 Samuel 3:1-10
Speak, Lord, your servant is listening.

93. 1 Kings 19:4-9a, 11-15a
Go out and stand on the mountain
before the Lord.

94. 1 Kings 19:16b, 19-21
Elisha left and followed Elijah.

READINGS FROM THE NEW TESTAMENT

95. Acts 2:42-47
All those who believed were equal and held everything in common.

96. Acts 4:32-35
One heart and one soul.

97. Romans 6:3-11
Let us walk in newness of life.

98. Romans 12:1-13
Offer your bodies as a living, holy sacrifice,
truly pleasing to God.

99. 1 Corinthians 1:22-31
To many, preaching a crucified Christ is madness;
to us it is the power of God.

100. Ephesians 1:3-14
The Father chose us in Christ to be holy and spotless in love.

101. Philippians 2:1-4
Be united in your convictions and in your love.

102. Philippians 3:8-14
I look on everything as useless if only I can know Christ.

103. Colossians 3:1-4
Let your thoughts be on heavenly things, not on the things that
  are on the earth.

104. Colossians 3:12-17
Above everything, have love for each other because that is the
  bond of perfection.

105. 1 Thessalonians 4:1-3a, 7-12
What God wants is for you to be holy.

106. 1 Peter 1:3-9
You have not seen the Christ, yet you love him.

107. 1 John 4:7-16
As long as we love one another God will live in us.

108. Revelation 3:14b, 20-22
I shall share a meal side by side with him.

109. Revelation 22:12-14, 16-17, 20
Come, Lord Jesus!

RESPONSORIAL PSALMS
110. Psalm 24:1-2, 3-4ab, 5-6,
℟. (6): **Lord, this is the people
that longs to see your face.**

111. Psalm 27:1, 4, 5, 8b-9abc, 9d and 11
℟. (8b): **I long to see your face, O Lord.**

112. Psalm 33:2-3, 4-5, 11-12, 13-14, 18-19, 20-21
℟. (12b): **Happy the people the Lord has chosen to be his
own.**

113. Psalm 34:2-3, 4-5, 6-7, 8-9 or 10-11, 12-13, 14-15, 17 and 19
℟. (2a): **I will bless the Lord at all times.**
or (9a): **Taste and see the goodness of the Lord.**

114. Psalm 40:2 and 4ab, 7-8a, 8b-9, 10, 12
℟. (8a and 9a): **Here am I, Lord; I come to do your will.**

115. Psalm 63:2, 3-4, 5-6, 8-9
℟. (2b): **My soul is thirsting for you, O Lord my God.**

116. Psalm 84:3, 4, 5-6a and 8a, 11, 12
℟. (2): **How lovely is your dwelling place, Lord, mighty God!**

117. Psalm 100:2, 3, 4, 5
℟. (2c): **Come with joy into the presence of the Lord.**

ALLELUIA VERSE AND VERSE BEFORE THE GOSPEL
118. Psalm 133:1
See how good it is, how pleasant, that brothers and sisters live in unity.
119. Matthew 11:25
Blessed are you, Father, Lord of heaven and earth;
you have revealed to little ones the mysteries
of the kingdom.
120. John 13:34
I give you a new commandment:
love one another as I have loved you.
121. John 15:5
I am the vine and you are the branches, says the Lord:
those who live in me, and I in them, will bear much fruit.
122. 2 Corinthians 8:9
Jesus Christ was rich but he became poor
to make you rich out of his poverty.
123. Galatians 6:14
My only glory is the cross of our Lord Jesus Christ,
which crucifies the world to me and me to the world.
124. Philippians 3:8-9
I count all things worthless but this:
to gain Jesus Christ and to be found in him.

GOSPEL

125. Matthew 11:25-30
You have hidden these things from the learned and clever
    and revealed them to little children.

126. Matthew 16:24-27

Any who lose their life for my sake will find it.

127. Matthew 19:3-12
There are some persons who choose to remain unmarried for the
sake of the kingdom of heaven.

128. Matthew 19:16-26
If you wish to be perfect, go and sell everything you have and
come, follow me.

129. Mark 3:31-35
Whoever does the will of God is my brother, my sister,
and my mother.

130. Mark 10:24b-30
We have left everything and have followed you.

131. Luke 9:57-62
Once the hand is laid on the plow, no one who looks back is fit
for the kingdom of God.

132. Luke 11:27-28
Happy are they who hear the word of God and keep it.

133. John 12:24-26
If a grain of wheat falls on the ground and dies, it yields
a rich harvest.

134. John 15:1-8
Those who live in me, and I in them, will bear much fruit.

135. John 15:9-17
You are friends if you do what I command you.

136. John 17:20-26
I want those you have given me to be with me where I am.

II. ANOTHER FORM FOR PRESENTING
THE INSIGNIA OF FIRST PROFESSION
PRESENTATION OF THE HABIT
137. After the profession the celebrant (or superior) assisted by
the novice master gives the religious habit to each of the professed with these or similar words:

Receive this habit as a sign of your consecration. May you be as closely united to the Lord in your heart as it proclaims you to be.

The professed replies:

Amen.

They put on the habit in some convenient place. After one or two have received the habit the choir may begin the antiphon:

Lord, these are the men who long to see your face, who seek the face of the God of Jacob (Psalm 24:6),

with Psalm 24 or some other appropriate song may be sung. The antiphon is repeated after every two verses; at the end of the psalm **Glory to the Father** is not said but only the antiphon. If the presentation of the insignia comes to an end before the whole psalm is sung, the psalm is interrupted and the antiphon repeated.

PRESENTATION OF THE RULE
OR CONSTITUTIONS

138. Then, if customary, the newly professed, wearing the religious habit, come to the celebrant (or superior) one by one. He gives the book of the rule or constitutions to each of them, saying these or similar words:

Receive the rule of our (this) religious community. By keeping it faithfully, may you arrive at the perfection of love.

The professed replies:

Amen.

After receiving the book, he returns to his place and remains standing.

139. If the newly professed are numerous, or there is some other reason, the celebrant (or superior) may present each of them with the rule and habit and say the formula once for all.

If, in accordance with the rules or customs of the religious community, other signs of religious profession are to be presented, this is done now in silence or with a suitable formula. In this matter a dignified simplicity should be observed.

III. OPTIONAL GENERAL INTERCESSIONS
INTRODUCTION
140. a) In the Mass of first profession:

Dear friends (brothers),
today our community rejoices in the Lord,
because these servants of his desire by their
    religious profession
to be more generous
in their service of God and of his Church.
Let us in unity of heart pray to God our Father
who gives to each the grace of his vocation.

b) In the Mass of the renewal of vows:

Dear friends (brothers),
let us pray to God our Father for his Church,
for the peace and salvation of the world,
for our own community,
and especially for our brothers who have renewed their
    vows today.

INTENTIONS
141.
I. a) For the holy Church of God,
that adorned by the virtues of her children
she may shine ever more brightly for Christ, her
    Bridegroom:
let us pray to the Lord.

b) For our holy father the Pope and the other bishops,
that by sound teaching and loving care
they may be faithful shepherds of God's holy people:
let us pray to the Lord.

II. a) For the peace and salvation of the world,
that all religious may be messengers and servants of the
peace of Christ:
let us pray to the Lord.

b) For the good of all people,
that those who are dedicated to the Lord's service

may pursue the things of heaven
and spend their days in the service of others:
let us pray to the Lord.

c) For all who believe in Christ,
that they may listen attentively to the secret voice of God
as he invites them all to a life of holiness:
let us pray to the Lord.

d) For the poor and suffering,
that Christ's example may always inspire religious
to bring the good news to the poor,
to care for the sick and to comfort the afflicted:
let us pray to the Lord.

III. a)
For all religious,
that their way of life
may be a sign to all of the future world to come:
let us pray to the Lord.

b) For those who follow the evangelical counsels,
that the law of love may shine in their lives,
and that like the first disciples
they may be one in heart and mind:
let us pray to the Lord.

c) For all religious,
that each one, according to the call of God,
may increase the holiness of the Church
and work to spread God's kingdom:
let us pray to the Lord.

IV. a) For these brothers of ours
who have today bound themselves more closely to God
by religious profession,
that in his goodness he may give them a love of prayer,
a spirit of penance,
and zeal in the apostolate:
let us pray to the Lord.

b) For these brothers of ours
who have today
bound themselves more closely to God's service,
that their hearts may be filled
with generous love for all:
let us pray to the Lord.

c) For those who today make profession of the
evangelical counsels,
that religious consecration may increase the holiness to
which baptism has called them:
let us pray to the Lord.

d) For those who seek to follow Christ
more closely by religious profession,
that their chastity may show the fruitfulness of the
    Church,
their poverty serve those in need,
and their obedience lead the rebellious
to accept the gentle rule of Christ:
let us pray to the Lord.

e) For all Christ's faithful people,
that the whole Church
may be the light of the world
and the leaven in its midst
to renew society by holy living and hidden prayer:
let us pray to the Lord.

f) For all here present,
that we may be faithful to Christ's teaching
as he calls us to be perfect,
and that we may bear fruit in holiness,
grow into the fullness of Christ,
and meet together in the heavenly city of peace:
let us pray to the Lord.

CONCLUDING PRAYER
142. a) In the Mass of the first profession:

Lord,
hear the prayers of your people.
In your goodness you called these servants of yours
to follow Christ and to be perfect.
Through the intercession of the Blessed Virgin Mary,
the mother of the Church,
pour forth your Holy Spirit upon them
so that they may fulfill in their whole lives
the promise they have made today.

We ask this through Christ our Lord.
℟. Amen.

b) In the Mass of renewal of vows:
Lord God,
all holiness is from you.
In your goodness hear the prayers of your family,
and by the intercession of Blessed Mary, your handmaid,
pour forth your blessings in abundance upon these
servants of yours,
so that by your continued help
they may fulfill the vows
your love has inspired them to renew.

We ask this through Christ our Lord.
℟. Amen.

IV. ANOTHER SOLEMN PRAYER OF BLESSING OR CONSECRATION OF THE PROFESSED

143. Lord God,
source of holiness and growth in your Church,
all creation owes you its debt of praise.
In the beginning of time
you created the world to share your joy.
When it lay broken by Adam's sin,
you promised a new heaven and a new earth.
You entrusted the earth to the care of men and women
to be made fruitful by their work.
Living in this world they were to direct their steps

to the heavenly city.
By your sacraments
you make us your children
and welcome us into your Church;
you distribute among us
the many gifts of your Spirit.
Some serve you in chaste marriage;
others forego marriage for the sake of your kingdom.
Sharing all things in common,
with one heart and mind in the bond of love,
they become a sign of the communion of heaven.

Father, we pray now,
send your Spirit upon these servants of yours
who have committed themselves
with steadfast faith
to the words of Christ your Son.
Strengthen their understanding
and direct their lives by the teaching of the Gospel.
May the law of love rule in their hearts,
and concern for others distinguish their lives,
so that they may bear witness to you, the one true God,
and to your infinite love for all people.
By their courage in daily trials
may they receive, even in this life,
your promised hundredfold,
and at the end an everlasting reward in heaven.

We ask this through Christ our Lord.
℟. Amen.

V. ANOTHER FORM OF BLESSING AT THE END
OF THE MASS OF PERPETUAL PROFESSION
144. May God, who is the source of all good intentions,
enlighten your minds and strengthen your hearts.
May he help you to fulfill with steadfast faith
all you have promised.
℟. Amen.

May the Lord enable you to travel in the joy of Christ
as you follow along his way,
and may you gladly share each other's burdens.
℟. Amen.

May the love of God unite you and make you a true family praising his name and showing forth Christ's love.
℟. Amen.

May almighty God,
the Father, and the Son, ✠ and the Holy Spirit,
bless all of you who have taken part in these
    sacred celebrations.
℟. Amen.

PART II: RITE OF RELIGIOUS PROFES-SION FOR WOMEN

Chapter I
NORMS FOR THE RITE OF INITIATION INTO THE RELIGIOUS LIFE

1. On the day when the canonical novitiate begins, it is fitting that there should be a ceremony to ask God's grace for achieving the special purpose of the novitiate.

2. It is forbidden to perform the rite of initiation during Mass.

3. The rite is to be very simple and direct, in the presence of the religious community only.

4. The texts for the rite must avoid anything that may seem to diminish the novices' freedom of choice or obscure the true meaning of a noviceship or time of testing.

5. The chapter hall or other similar room is an appropriate setting for the rite. If it seems necessary, however, the rite may take place in the chapel.

RITE OF INITIATION INTO THE RELIGIOUS LIFE

It is appropriate that the rite should take place during a special celebration of the word on the nature of the religious life and the spirit of the institute

INTRODUCTORY RITES
GREETING OR SONG
6. The rite may appropriately begin with a greeting by the superior, or the singing of a psalm or other suitable hymn.

QUESTIONING OF THE POSTULANTS
OR REQUEST FOR ADMISSION
7. Then the superior questions the postulants in these or similar words:

Dear daughters (sisters), what do you ask from us?

The postulants reply together in these or similar words:

We wish to try your way of life,
and are willing to be tested ourselves,
that we may follow Christ wholeheartedly
in this community of N.

The superior replies:
May the Lord grant you his help.
℟. Amen.

8. The questioning may be omitted, and the request for admission takes place as follows: one of the postulants, facing the superior and community, speaks in the name of all:
Drawn by God's mercy,
we have come here to learn your way of life.
We ask you to teach us to follow Christ crucified
and to live in poverty, obedience and chastity.
Teach us to persevere in prayer and penance,
in the service of the Church and of humankind.
Teach us to be one with you in heart and mind.
Help us to live out the Gospel every day of our lives.
Teach us your rule and help us to learn to love
our sisters as Christ commanded us.

Or she may use similar words, expressing the aspirations and thoughts of the postulants themselves.

The superior responds in these or similar words:
May God in his mercy be with you always,
and may Christ our teacher grant light to us all.
℟. Amen.

9. After the questioning or request for admission, the superior says:

Let us pray.
Lord God,
you give us the desire to hear your call.
Listen favorably to the prayers of your servants N.
    and N.,
who, desiring to serve you more perfectly,
ask to join our community.

Grant that our life in common
may become a communion of love.

We ask this through Christ our Lord.
℟. Amen.

CELEBRATION OF THE WORD OF GOD
10. Suitable texts from holy Scripture are then read, with appropriate responsories (see nos. 98-152).

11. At their conclusion the superior addresses the religious community and the postulants on the meaning of the religious life and the spirit of the institute, or she reads an appropriate chapter of the rule.

CONCLUDING RITES
12. The rite fittingly concludes with the general intercessions (prayer of the faithful) and the Lord's Prayer, to which a suitable prayer may be added, such as:

God our Father,
it is you who have called us.
Hear our prayers and bless these sisters of ours
who wish to follow your Son in religious life.
Help us all to do what you ask of us
so that your plans for them may be fulfilled.

We ask this through Christ our Lord.
℟. Amen.

13. After this the superior entrusts the newly admitted novices to the care of the novice mistress, and with her fellow religious greets them in the spirit of Christian love in the way customary in the religious community. Meanwhile, an appropriate song or a canticle of praise is sung.

CHAPTER II

RITE OF TEMPORARY PROFESSION

DURING MASS

14. The rite described in this chapter takes place during Mass. It may be used only for those religious who make their first profession upon successful completion of the novitiate (see Introduction, no. 5).

BLESSING OF THE HABIT
ON THE DAY BEFORE PROFESSION
15. It is appropriate to give the religious habit, with the exception of the veil, to the novices the day before their first profession.

16. The habits, but not the veils, are blessed by a priest or other competent minister, using this or similar prayer:
V. Our help is in the name of the Lord.
Who made heaven and earth.

V. The Lord be with you.
And also with you.

Let us pray.

God, you clothed your Son with our mortal flesh
in the chaste womb of the Virgin Mary;
give a rich blessing to these habits,
and grant that your servants who wear them on earth
may be a sign of the resurrection to come
and be clothed in the glory of eternal life.

We ask this through Christ our Lord.
R̦. Amen.

The habits may then be sprinkled with holy water.

17. At an appropriate time, the superior assembles the community and the novices; in a brief address she prepares the minds of all for the rite of profession to take place the following day. Then she gives the religious habit, with the exception of the veil, to each novice so that she may wear it for the entrance procession at the beginning of Mass.

18. The Mass may correspond to the liturgy of the day, or the ritual Mass for the day of first profession may be used, in accordance with the rubrics (see Introduction, nos. 9-11).

19. The profession ordinarily takes place at the chair. A chair for the superior who is to receive the sisters' profession should be prepared in a suitable place in the sanctuary. Seats should be so arranged in the sanctuary for those making profession that the faithful may have a complete view of the liturgical rites.

20. Religious bound by the law of enclosure may make their temporary profession in the sanctuary, with due respect for the general laws of the Church and the particular occasion.

21. Enough bread and wine for consecration should be prepared for the ministers, those making their profession, and their parents, relatives, and fellow religious. If only one chalice is used, it should be sufficiently large.

22. In addition to what is needed for Mass, there should also be ready:

a) the ritual for religious profession;

b) the religious veils, if the religious institute has decided to present them on the occasion of first profession (see Introduction, no. 5);

c) the book of the rule or constitutions, and other insignia of religious profession which, according to law or custom, are to be presented.

RITE OF TEMPORARY PROFESSION DURING MASS

INTRODUCTORY RITES

23. When the people and the religious are assembled and everything is ready, the procession moves through the church to the altar in the usual way, while the choir and people sing the entrance song of the Mass. Those to be professed may fittingly join in the procession, accompanied by the superior and the novice mistress.

24. When they come to the sanctuary all make the customary reverence to the altar and go to their places; then Mass continues.

LITURGY OF THE WORD

25. The liturgy of the word takes place as usual, except for the following:

    a) the readings may be taken from the Mass of the day or from the texts in nos. 98-152 (see Introduction, nos. 9-10);

    b) the profession of faith may be omitted, even if prescribed by the rubrics of the day.

RELIGIOUS PROFESSION

CALLING OR REQUEST

26. After the gospel the celebrant and the people sit, but those to be professed stand. Then, according to choice or as circumstances demand, the deacon or the novice mistress calls those to be professed by name.

They answer:

Lord, you have called me; here I am,

or they make some other reply according to local usage or the custom of the religious community.

27. The celebrant then questions them in these or similar words:

My dear sisters (daughters), what do you ask of God and of his holy Church?

The candidates reply together in these or similar words:

We ask for God's merciful love
and a share in the life of this religious community of N.

The celebrant and all the members of the religious community reply:

Thanks be to God,

or they express their approval in some other way.

28. The calling by name and the questioning by the celebrant may be omitted; a request by those to be professed may take their place. For example, one of those to be professed may stand facing the superior and say, in the name of all, these or similar words:

With the help of God,
we (N. and N.) have studied your rule
and have lived among you as your sisters

for the time of probation.
Mother (Sister), we now ask to be allowed
to dedicate ourselves to God and his kingdom
by making profession in this religious community of N.

The superior and all the members of the religious community
reply:
Thanks be to God,
or they express their approval in some other way.

HOMILY OR ADDRESS
29. Those to be professed then sit and listen to the homily or address which should develop the scriptural readings and the
theme of religious profession as God's gift and call for the sanctification of those chosen and for the good of the Church and the
whole human family.

EXAMINATION
30. After the homily or address, those to be professed stand, and
the celebrant questions them on their readiness to dedicate themselves to God and to seek perfect charity, according to the rule or
constitutions of the religious community. The questions may be
changed or in part omitted, to suit the spirit and character of
each religious institute.

My dear sisters (daughters),
by water and the Holy Spirit
you have already been consecrated to God's service:
are you resolved to unite yourselves more closely to him
by the new bond of religious profession?

They answer:
I am.

The celebrant continues:
In your desire to follow Christ perfectly,
are you resolved to live in chastity
for the sake of the kingdom of heaven,
to choose a life of poverty,
and to offer the sacrifice of obedience?

They answer:
I am.

31. Then the celebrant confirms their intention in these or similar words:
May almighty God grant you his grace
to fulfill what you resolve.
R̰. Amen.

PRAYER FOR GOD'S GRACE
32. The celebrant then prays for God's help, saying:
Let us pray.

All pray for a while in silence. Then the celebrant says:
Lord,
look upon these servants of yours
who are resolved to dedicate their lives to you
by making profession of the evangelical counsels
in the presence of your Church today.
Mercifully grant that their manner of life
may bring glory to your name
and further your loving plan of redemption.

We ask this through Christ our Lord.
R̰. Amen.

PROFESSION
33. After the prayer, if it is the custom of the religious community, two professed religious stand near the superior to act as witnesses. Those to be professed come, one by one, to the superior and read the formula of profession.

If there are very many religious making their profession, the formula of profession may be recited by all together. The concluding words, **This I promise . . .** or the like, must be said by each individually as a clear expression of her will.

After the profession, they return to their places and remain standing.

PRESENTATION OF THE INSIGNIA OF RELIGIOUS PROFESSION

PRESENTATION OF THE VEIL

34. After this, if the veil is to be presented, the celebrant, with the assistance of the superior and the mistress of novices, clothes each one with the veil, saying, for example:

Receive this veil
which proclaims
that you belong entirely to Christ the Lord
and are dedicated to the service of the Church.
℟. **Amen.**

PRESENTATION OF THE RULE OR CONSTITUTIONS

35. Then, where it is the custom, the celebrant gives her the books of the rule or constitutions, using this or a similar formula:

Receive the rule of this religious community,
and show in your whole life
what you have faithfully learned.

The professed replies:
℟. **Amen.**

After receiving the book, she returns to her place.

36. After the first or second of the professed has received the veil and rule, the choir intones the antiphon:

I have sought the Lord whom I love with all my heart
(Song of Songs 3:4),

with Psalm 45; or some other appropriate song may be sung. The antiphon is repeated after every two verses; at the end of the psalm, **Glory to the Father** is not said but only the antiphon. If the presentation of the insignia comes to an end before the whole psalm is sung, the psalm is interrupted and the antiphon repeated.

37. If, in accordance with the rules or customs of the religious community, other insignia of religious profession are to be presented, this is done now in silence or with a suitable formula. In this matter a dignified simplicity should be observed.

38. An alternative way of presenting the insignia of profession is described in nos. 153-155.

GENERAL INTERCESSIONS

39. The rite fittingly concludes with the general intercessions (prayers of the faithful). For these, the formula given in nos. 156-158 may be used.

LITURGY OF THE EUCHARIST

40. During the offertory song, some of the newly professed religious may bring the bread, wine, and water to the altar for the eucharistic sacrifice.

41. The celebrant, after saying, **"The peace of the Lord,"** gives the sign of peace in some suitable way to the newly professed religious and all those present.

42. After the celebrant has received the body and blood of Christ, the newly professed religious come to the altar to receive communion, which may be given to them under both kinds. Then their parents, relatives, and fellow religious may receive communion in the same way.

CHAPTER III
RITE OF PERPETUAL PROFESSION DURING MASS

43. It is fitting that the rite of profession by which a religious binds herself to God for ever should take place on a Sunday or a solemnity of the Lord, of the Blessed Virgin Mary, or of a saint distinguished in the living of the religious life.

44. The rite of perpetual profession takes place separately from other rites of profession (see Introduction, no. 8).

45. Notice of the day and hour should be given to the faithful in good time so that they may attend in greater numbers.

46. The Mass is that of the liturgy for the day, or the ritual Mass for the day of perpetual profession may be used, in accordance with the rubrics (see Introduction, nos. 9-11).

47. Where possible and if the needs of the faithful do not demand individual celebration by the priests present, it is preferable that the Mass be concelebrated.

48. The profession ordinarily takes place at the chair. A chair for the superior who is to receive the profession of the sisters should be prepared in a suitable place in the sanctuary. Seats should be so arranged in the sanctuary for those making profession that the faithful may have a complete view of the liturgical rites.

49. It is fitting that religious bound by the law of enclosure also make their perpetual profession in the sanctuary.

50. Profession ordinarily takes place in the church of the religious community. For pastoral reasons, however, or in order to promote esteem for the religious life, to give edification to the people of God, or to permit larger attendance, the rite may take place in the cathedral, parish church, or some other notable church, as may seem fitting.

51. Similarly, where religious from two or more institutes wish to celebrate their profession at the same eucharistic sacrifice, the rite of profession may suitably take place in the cathedral, a parish church, or some other notable church with the bishop presid-

ing. Those making their profession will pronounce their vows before their respective superiors.

Enclosed religious, however, are to observe carefully the laws of their enclosure in this matter.

52. As the nature of the rite demands, the whole liturgical service should be celebrated with fitting solemnity, but any appearance of lavishness unbecoming to religious poverty should be avoided.

53. Enough bread and wine for consecration should be prepared for the ministers, those making their profession, and their parents, relatives, and fellow religious. If only one chalice is used, it should be sufficiently large.

54. In addition to what is needed for Mass, there should also be ready:

a) the ritual for religious profession;

b) the rings and other insignia of religious profession, if these are to be presented in accordance with the rules or customs of the religious community.

RITE OF PERPETUAL PROFESSION DURING MASS

INTRODUCTORY RITES
55. When the people and the religious are assembled and everything is ready, the procession moves through the church to the altar in the usual way, while the choir and people sing the entrance song of the Mass. Those to be professed may join in the procession, accompanied by the superior and the novice mistress.

56. When they come to the sanctuary, all make the customary reverence to the altar and go to their places; then Mass continues.

LITURGY OF THE WORD
57. The liturgy of the word takes place as usual, except for the following:

a) the readings may be taken from the Mass of the day or from the texts in nos. 98-152 (see Introduction, nos. 9-10);

b) the profession of faith may be omitted, even if prescribed by the rubrics of the day.

c) the general intercessions in the form customarily used
during the celebration of Mass are omitted (see no. 67).

RELIGIOUS PROFESSION
CALLING OR REQUEST
58. After the gospel the celebrant and the people sit, but those to
be professed stand. Then, according to choice or as circumstances demand, the deacon or the novice mistress calls those to
be professed by name.

They answer:
Lord, you have called me; here I am,
or they make some other reply according to local usage or the
custom of the religious community.

59. The celebrant then questions them in these or similar words:
**My dear sisters (daughters), what do you ask of God and
of his holy Church?**

The candidates reply together in these or similar words:
**We ask for perseverance
in following Christ our Bridegroom
in this religious community
all the days of our lives.**

The celebrant, superior, and all the members of the religious community reply:
Thanks be to God,

or they express their approval in some other way.

60. The calling by name and the questioning by the celebrant
may be omitted; a request by those to be professed may take
their place. For example, one of those to be professed may stand
facing the superior and say, in the name of all, these or similar
words:
**With the help of God,
we (N. and N.) have come to know
in your religious community
the difficulty and the joy of a life
completely dedicated to him.
Mother (Sister), we now ask to be allowed**

to make perpetual profession in this community of N.
for the glory of God and the service of the Church.

The superior and all the members of the religious community reply:
Thanks be to God,

or they express their approval in some other way.

HOMILY OR ADDRESS

61. Those to be professed then sit and listen to the homily or address which should develop the scriptural readings and the theme of religious profession as God's gift and call for the sanctification of those chosen and for the good of the Church and the whole human family.

EXAMINATION

62. After the homily or address, those to be professed stand, and the celebrant questions them on their readiness to dedicate themselves to God and to seek perfect charity, according to the rule or constitutions of the religious community. The questions may be changed or in part omitted, to suit the spirit and character of each religious institute.

Dear sisters (daughters),
in baptism you have already died to sin
and have been set aside for God's service.
Are you now resolved to unite yourself more
    closely to God
by the bond of perpetual profession?

They answer:
I am.

The celebrant continues:
Are you resolved,
with the help of God,
to undertake that life of perfect chastity, obedience,
    and poverty
chosen for themselves by Christ our Lord
    and his Virgin Mother,
and to persevere in it for ever?

They answer:

I am.

The celebrant continues:

**Are you resolved to strive steadfastly for perfection
in the love of God and of your neighbor
by living the Gospel with all your heart
and keeping the rule of this religious community?**

They answer:

I am.

The celebrant continues:

**Are you resolved,
with the help of the Holy Spirit,
to spend your whole life in the generous
  service of God's people?**

They answer:

I am.

63. In the case of religious communities wholly dedicated to the contemplative life, this may appropriately be added:

The celebrant asks:

**Are you resolved to live for God alone,
in solitude and silence,
in persevering prayer and willing penance,
in humble work and holiness of life?**

They answer:

I am.

64. At the end of the questions, the celebrant confirms the intention of those to be professed in these or similar words:

**May God who has begun the good work in you
bring it to fulfillment
before the day of Christ Jesus.**

All:

Amen.

LITANY

65. All then rise. The celebrant stands, with hands joined, and says facing the people:

**Dear friends in Christ,
let us pray to God the almighty Father
who gives us everything that is good:
in his mercy may he strengthen his servants
in the purpose he has inspired in them.**

66. The deacon gives the sign to kneel.

Let us kneel.

The celebrant, at his chair, the ministers, those to be professed and the people kneel. Where there is the custom of prostration of those to be professed, this may be kept. During the Easter Season and on all Sundays, all stand except those to be professed.

67. Then the cantors sing the litany for the rite of religious profession, all making the responses. In this litany one or the other of the petitions marked with the same letter may be omitted. At the appropriate place there may be inserted invocations of saints especially venerated in the religious community or by the faithful; other petitions may be added to suit the occasion.

**Lord, have mercy   Lord, have mercy
Christ, have mercy   Christ, have mercy
Lord, have mercy   Lord, have mercy**

**Holy Mary, Mother of God   pray for us
Saint Michael   pray for us
Holy angels of God   pray for us
Saint John the Baptist   pray for us
Saint Joseph   pray for us
Saint Peter and Saint Paul   pray for us
Saint John   pray for us
Saint Mary Magdalene   pray for us
Saint Stephen and Saint Lawrence   pray for us
Saint Agnes   pray for us
Saint Basil   pray for us
Saint Augustine   pray for us
Saint Benedict   pray for us
Saint Bernard   pray for us**

Saint Francis and Saint Dominic   pray for us
Saint Macrina   pray for us
Saint Scholastica   pray for us
Saint Clare and Saint Catherine   pray for us
Saint Teresa of Jesus   pray for us
Saint Rose of Lima   pray for us
Saint Jane Frances de Chantal   pray for us
Saint Louise de Marillac   pray for us
All holy men and women   pray for us

Lord, be merciful   Lord, save your people
From all evil   Lord, save your people
From every sin   Lord, save your people
From everlasting death   Lord, save your people
By your coming as man   Lord, save your people
By your death and rising to new life   Lord, save your people
By your gift of the Holy Spirit   Lord, save your people

Be merciful to us sinners   Lord, hear our prayer

a) By the self-offering of your servants
and their apostolic work,
make the life of your Church
ever more fruitful.   Lord, hear our prayer

a) Give in ever greater abundance
the gifts of the Holy Spirit
to your servant, Pope N.,
and to all his brother bishops.   Lord, hear our prayer

b) By the life and labor of all religious
promote the welfare of all people.   Lord, hear our prayer

b) Lead all men and women
to the fullness of the Christian life.   Lord, hear our prayer

c) Grant that all religious families
may live and grow

in the love of Christ
and the spirit of their founders.   Lord, hear our prayer.

c) Give to all
who profess the Gospel counsels
a fuller share in the work of
    redemption.   Lord, hear our prayer

d) Reward a hundredfold
the parents of your servants
for the sacrifice they have made.   Lord, hear our prayer

d) Make these servants of yours
more and more like Christ,
the firstborn among many.   Lord, hear our prayer

e) Give these servants of yours
the grace of perseverance.   Lord, hear our prayer

e) Bless these sisters of ours,
 your servants,
make them holy,
and consecrate them to your service.   Lord, hear our
    prayer

Jesus, Son of the living God   Lord, hear our prayer
Christ, hear us   Christ, hear us
Lord Jesus, hear our prayer   Lord Jesus, hear our prayer

68. Then the celebrant alone rises and says, with hands joined:
Lord,
grant the prayers of your people.
Prepare the hearts of your servants
for consecration to your service.
By the grace of the Holy Spirit
purify them from all sin
and set them on fire with your love.

We ask this through Christ our Lord.
℟. Amen.

The deacon then says:

Let us rise.

All stand.

PROFESSION

69. After the litany, if it is the custom of the religious community, two professed members of the community come to the chair of the superior and, standing, act as witnesses. Those to be professed come, one by one, to the superior and read the formula of profession, which they themselves have written out beforehand.

70. Then the newly professed may fittingly go to the altar, one by one, to place on it the formula of profession; if it can be done conveniently, each of them should sign the document of profession upon the altar itself. After this, each goes back to her place.

71. Afterward, if this is the practice of the community, the newly professed may stand and sing an antiphon or other song expressing the spirit of self-giving and joy, for example:

Uphold me, Lord, according to your promise
and I shall live;
and do not bring to nothing all my hope (Psalm 119:116).

SOLEMN BLESSING OR CONSECRATION
OF THE PROFESSED

72. Then the newly professed kneel; the celebrant with hands extended over them says the prayer of blessing **Father in heaven, our desire to serve you,** in which the words in brackets may, to suit the occasion, be omitted, or else the prayer **Lord God, creator of the world and Father of mankind,** which is found in no. 159.

Father in heaven,
our desire to serve you is itself your gift
and our perseverance needs your guiding hand.
How right it is that we should sing your praise.

With boundless love
you created the human family
through your Word, in the Holy Spirit,
and lifted it up into communion with yourself;

you make the human family your bride
radiant with your own likeness,
adorned with the gift of everlasting life.

When your bride, deceived by the evil one,
broke faith with you,
you did not abandon her.
With everlasting love you renewed with your servant
  Noah
the covenant you made with Adam.
[Then you chose Abraham, the man of faith,
to be the father of a people
more numerous than the stars of heaven.
By the hand of Moses
you sealed a covenant with them in the tables of the law.
Throughout the ages
there arose from this favored people
holy women renowned for devotion and courage,
  justice and faith.]

In the fullness of time
you raised up the Holy Virgin from the stock of Jesse.
The Holy Spirit was to come upon her,
and your power was to overshadow her,
making her the immaculate Mother of the world's
  Redeemer.

He became poor, humble, and obedient
the source and pattern of all holiness.
He formed the Church into his bride,
loving it with love so great
that he gave himself up for it
and sanctified it in his blood.

Father, in your loving wisdom
you have singled out many of your daughters
to be disciples espoused to Christ
and to receive the honor of his love.
[Holy Church shines with their rich variety,
a bride adorned with jewels,

a queen robed in grace,
a mother rejoicing in her children.]

Father, we earnestly pray you:
send the fire of the Holy Spirit
into the hearts of your daughters
to keep alive within them
the holy desire he has given them.

Lord, may the glory of baptism and holiness of life
shine in their hearts.
Strengthened by the vows of their consecration,
may they be always one with you
in loving fidelity to Christ, their only Bridegroom.
May they cherish the Church as their mother
and love the whole world as God's creation,
teaching all people to look forward in joy and hope
to the good things of heaven.

Lord, holy Father,
guide the steps of your servants
and guard them on their pilgrimage through life.
When they come at last to the throne of Christ the King,
may they not fear him as their judge,
but hear the voice of their Bridegroom
lovingly inviting them to the wedding feast of heaven.

We ask this through Christ our Lord.
℟. Amen.

PRESENTATION OF THE INSIGNIA
OF PROFESSION
73. After the blessing of the professed, the celebrant and the people sit; if rings are to be presented, the newly professed rise and come to the celebrant, who gives the ring to each, saying, for example:

Receive this ring,
for you are betrothed to the eternal King;
keep faith with your Bridegroom
so that you may come to the wedding feast of eternal joy.

The professed replies:

Amen.

Then she returns to her place.

74. If there are several newly professed, or if there is any other good reason, the celebrant may use one formula for presenting the rings to all:

Receive this ring,
for you are betrothed to the eternal King;
keep faith with your Bridegroom
so that you may come to the wedding feast of eternal joy.

They reply:

Amen.

Then they go to the celebrant to receive the rings.

75. Meanwhile the choir and people together sing this or some other suitable antiphon:

I am betrothed to the Son of the eternal Father,
to him who was born of the Virgin Mother
to be the Savior of all the world,

with Psalm 45; or some other appropriate song may be sung. The antiphon is repeated after every two verses; at the end of the psalm **Glory to the Father** is not said but only the antiphon. If the presentation of the insignia comes to an end before the whole psalm is sung, the psalm is interrupted and the antiphon repeated.

76. If, in accordance with the laws or customs of the religious community, other insignia of religious profession are to be presented, this is done now, in silence or with a suitable formula. In this matter a dignified simplicity should be observed.

STATEMENT OF ADMISSION OR SIGN OF PEACE

77. After this, if it is customary or seems opportune, there may be a ceremony to mark the fact that the newly professed religious have been admitted as lifelong members of the religious family. This can take the form of a suitable statement by the superior or of the sign of peace. For example:

a) The superior says these or similar words:

We confirm that you are now one with us
as members of this religious community of N.,
sharing all things in common with us
now and in the future.

She may add:
Be faithful to the ministry the Church entrusts to you
to be carried out in its name.

The members of the community manifest their assent, saying:
Amen.

b) The above may be omitted and the celebrant may give the
sign of peace. The superior and the members of the community
express fraternal love for the newly professed by the sign of
peace or in another way, according to the custom of the religious
community. Meanwhile the choir and the people sing the antiphon:
How lovely is your dwelling place, Lord, mighty God!
My soul is longing and fainting for the courts of the
Lord (Psalm 84:2-3),

with Psalm 84; or some other appropriate song may be sung.

78. The newly professed religious return after this to their places.
The Mass continues.

LITURGY OF THE EUCHARIST

79. During the offertory song, some of the newly professed may
bring to the altar the bread, wine, and water for the eucharistic
sacrifice.

80. In the eucharistic prayers, the offering of the professed may
be mentioned according to the texts below:

a) In Eucharistic Prayer I, the special form of **Father, accept this**
offering is said:
Father, accept and sanctify this offering
from your whole family and from these your servants
which we make to you on the day of their consecration.
By your grace
they join themselves more closely to your Son today.

When he comes in glory at the end of time,
may they joyfully meet him.

[Through Christ our Lord. Amen.]

b) In the intercessions of Eucharistic Prayer III, after the words and all the clergy, there is added:

Remember all these sisters of ours
who have left all things for your sake,
so that they may find you in all things
and by forgetting self serve the needs of all.

c) In the intercessions of Eucharistic Prayer III, after the words your Son has gained for you, there is added:

Lord, strengthen these servants of yours in their holy
purpose,
as they strive to follow Christ your Son in consecrated
holiness
by giving witness to his love in their religious life.

d) In the intercessions of Eucharistic Prayer IV, the professed may be mentioned in this way:

... bishop, and bishops and clergy everywhere.
Remember our sisters who have consecrated themselves
to you today
by the bond of religious profession.
Remember those who take part in this offering ...

81. The celebrant gives the sign of peace in some suitable form to the newly professed religious and to all those present.

82. After the celebrant has received the body and blood of Christ, the newly professed religious come to the altar to receive communion which may be given to them under both kinds. Then their parents, relatives, and fellow religious may receive communion in the same way.

CONCLUDING RITE
SOLEMN BLESSING

83. When the prayer after communion has been said, the newly consecrated religious stand before the altar, and the celebrant, facing them, may say:

God inspires all holy desires and brings them to fulfillment. May he protect you always by his grace
so that you may fulfill the duties of your vocation
with a faithful heart.
℟. Amen.

May he make each of you a witness
and sign of his love for all people.
℟. Amen.

May he make those bonds,
with which he has bound you to Christ on earth,
endure for ever in heavenly love.
℟. Amen.

Another form of the blessing may be found in no. 160.

84. Finally, the celebrant blesses the whole congregation:
May almighty God,
the Father, and the Son, ✠ and the Holy Spirit,
bless all of you who have taken part in this celebration.
℟. Amen.

CHAPTER IV

RITE FOR RENEWAL OF VOWS DURING MASS

85. Renewal of vows, which is governed by the general law of the Church or by a particular ruling of the constitutions, may take place during Mass if the religious community thinks it appropriate.

86. The rite for the renewal of vows should be conducted with the greatest simplicity, especially if, in accordance with the constitutions of the religious institute, vows are renewed frequently or annually.

87. Either the Mass corresponding to the liturgy of the day or the ritual Mass for the day of the renewal of vows is used, in accordance with the rubrics (see Introduction, nos. 9-10).

88. The renewal of vows customarily takes place before the superior, whose chair may be placed in a suitable place in the sanctuary.

89. Religious who renew their profession may receive communion under both kinds. If only one chalice is used, it should be sufficiently large.

LITURGY OF THE WORD
90. In the liturgy of the word, all takes place as usual except for the following:

> a) the readings may be taken from the Mass of the day or from the texts set out in nos. 98-152 (see Introduction, nos. 9-10);

> b) the profession of faith may be omitted, even if prescribed by the rubrics of the day.

91. After the gospel a homily which uses the readings from Scripture to emphasize the meaning and the value of religious life is given.

RENEWAL OF VOWS
PRAYER FOR GOD'S GRACE
92. After the homily the celebrant prays for God's help, saying:

God our Father gives us the grace
to persevere in our resolutions.
Let us pray to him for these servants of his
who are resolved to renew their vows today
in the presence of the Church.

All pray for a time in silence. Then the celebrant says:

Lord,
in your providence
you have called these servants of yours
to follow your Son more closely.
Mercifully grant that they may persevere to the end
along the way of your love
on which they have set out with such joy.

We ask this through Christ our Lord.
R̊. Amen.

RENEWAL OF PROFESSION

93. After the prayer, if it is the custom of the religious community, two professed sisters stand near the superior to act as witnesses.

Those who are to renew their profession come, one by one, to the superior and read the formula of profession. If there is a large number renewing their vows, the formula of profession may be recited by all. The concluding words, **This I promise . . .** or the like, must be said by each individually, as a clear expression of her will.

Where profession is renewed by all each year, in accordance with the constitutions of the institute, the superior and all the sisters should recite the formula of profession together.

GENERAL INTERCESSIONS

94. The rite fittingly concludes with the recitation of the general intercessions (prayer of the faithful); for these the formula set out in nos. 156-158 may be used.

LITURGY OF THE EUCHARIST

95. During the offertory song some of the religious who have renewed their vows may bring the bread, wine, and water to the altar for the eucharistic sacrifice.

96. The celebrant, after saying, **"The peace of the Lord,"** gives the sign of peace in a suitable way to the religious who have just renewed their profession and to all those present.

97. After the celebrant has received the body and blood of Christ, the religious who have renewed their profession come to the altar to receive communion under both kinds.

CHAPTER V
OTHER TEXTS FOR THE RITES OF RELI-
GIOUS PROFESSION

I. BIBLICAL READINGS

READINGS FROM THE OLD TESTAMENT

98. Genesis 12:1-4a
Leave your country, your family, and come.

99. 1 Samuel 3:1-10
Speak, Lord, your servant is listening.

100. 1 Kings 19:4-9a, 11-15a
Go out and stand on the mountain before the Lord.

101. 1 Kings 19:16b, 19-21
Elisha left and followed Elijah.

102. Song of Songs 2:8-14
Rise, my love, and come.

103. Song of Songs 8:6-7
Love is strong as death.

104. Isaiah 61:9-11
I exult for joy in the Lord.

105. Hosea 2:14, 19-20 (Hebrew 16, 21-22):
I will betroth you to myself for ever

READINGS FROM THE NEW TESTAMENT

106. Acts 2:42-47
All those who believed were equal and held everything
  in common.

107. Acts 4:32-35
One heart and one soul.

108. Romans 6:3-11
Let us walk in newness of life.

109. Romans 12:1-13
Offer your bodies as a living, holy sacrifice,
  truly pleasing to God.

110. 1 Corinthians 1:22-31
To many, preaching a crucified Christ is madness;
   to us it is the power of God.

111. 1 Corinthians 7:25-35
An unmarried woman can devote herself to the Lord's work.

112. Ephesians 1:3-14
The Father chose us in Christ to be holy and spotless in love.

113. Philippians 2:1-4
Be united in your convictions and in your love.

114. Philippians 3:8-14
I look on everything as useless if only I can know Christ.

115. Colossians 3:1-4
Let your thought be on heavenly things, not on the things that
   are on the earth.

116. Colossians 3:12-17
Above everything, have love for each other because that is the
   bond of perfection.

117. 1 Thessalonians 4:1-3a, 7-12
What God wants is for you to be holy.

118. 1 Peter 1:3-9
You have not seen the Christ, yet you love him.

119. 1 John 4:7-16
As long as we love one another God will live in us.

120. Revelation 3:14b, 20-22
I shall share a meal side by side with him.

121. Revelation 22:12-14, 16-17, 20
Come, Lord Jesus!

RESPONSORIAL PSALMS
122. Psalm 24:1-2, 3-4ab, 5-6
℟. (6): **Lord, this is the people that longs to see your face.**

123. Psalm 27:1, 4, 5, 8bc-9abc and 11
℟. (8b): **I long to see your face, O Lord.**

124. Psalm 33:2-3, 4-5, 11-12, 13-14, 18-19, 20-21
℟. (12b): **Happy the people the Lord has chosen to be his own.**

125. Psalm 34:2-3, 4-5, 6-7, 8-9 or 10-11, 12-13, 14-15, 17 and 19
℞. (2a): I will bless the Lord at all times.
or (9a): Taste and see the goodness of the Lord.

126. Psalm 40:2 and 4ab, 7-8a, 8b-9, 10, 12
℞. (8a and 9a): Here am I, Lord; I come to do your will.

127. Psalm 45:11-12, 14-15, 16-17
℞. (Matthew 25:6): The Bridegroom is here; let us go out to meet Christ the Lord.

128. Psalm 63:2, 3-4, 5-6, 8-9
℞. (2b): My soul is thirsting for you, O Lord my God.

129. Psalm 84:3, 4, 5-6a and 8a, 11, 12
℞. (2): How lovely is your dwelling place, Lord, mighty God!

130. Psalm 100:2, 3, 4, 5
℞. (2c): Come with joy into the presence of the Lord.

ALLELUIA VERSE AND VERSE BEFORE THE GOSPEL
131. Psalm 133:1
See how good it is, how pleasant,
that brothers and sisters live in unity.

132. Matthew 11:25
Blessed are you, Father, Lord of heaven and earth;
you have revealed to little ones the mysteries of the kingdom.

133. John 13:34
I give you a new commandment:
love one another as I have loved you.

134. John 15:5
I am the vine and you are the branches, says the Lord:
those who live in me, and I in them, will bear much fruit.

135. 2 Corinthians 8:9
Jesus Christ was rich but he became poor
to make you rich out of his poverty.

136. Galatians 6:14

**My only glory is the cross of our Lord Jesus Christ,
which crucifies the world to me and me to the world.**

137. Philippians 3:8-9

**I count all things worthless but this:
to gain Jesus Christ and to be found in him.**

GOSPEL

138. Matthew 11:25-30
You have hidden these things from the learned
   and clever and revealed them to little children.

139. Matthew 16:24-27
Any who lose their life for my sake will find it.

140. Matthew 19:3-12
There are some persons who choose to remain unmarried for the
   sake of the kingdom of heaven.

141. Matthew 19:16-26
If you wish to be perfect, go and sell everything you have and
   come, follow me.

142. Matthew 25:1-13
Look, the Bridegroom is coming; go out and meet him.

143. Mark 3:31-35
Whoever does the will of God is my brother, my sister,
   and my mother.

144. Mark 10:24b-30
We have left everything and have followed you.

145. Luke 1:26-38
I am the handmaid of the Lord.

146. Luke 9:57-62
Once the hand is laid on the plow, no one who looks back is fit
   for the kingdom of God.

147. Luke 10:38-42
Jesus accepts the hospitality of Martha and praises
   the attentiveness of Mary.

148. Luke 11:27-28

Happy are they who hear the word of God and keep it.

149. John 12:24-26

If a grain of wheat falls on the ground and dies, it yields
a rich harvest.

150. John 15:1-8

Those who live in me, and I in them, will bear much fruit.

151. John 15:9-17

You are friends if you do what I command you.

152. John 17:20-26

I want those you have given me to be with me where I am.

II. ANOTHER FORM FOR PRESENTING THE INSIGNIA OF FIRST PROFESSION

PRESENTATION OF THE VEIL AND RULE

153. If there are many newly professed religious, or if there is
any other good reason, the celebrant presenting the insignia of
profession uses this formula once for all:

Receive, dear sisters,
this veil and rule
which are the signs of your profession.
Give yourselves wholeheartedly to Christ the Lord,
and show in your whole life
what you have faithfully learned.

The professed reply:

Amen.

They come to the celebrant who, with the assistance of the superior and the mistress of novices, gives to each of them the veil
and the book of the rule.

When they have received them they return to their places.

154. Meanwhile, the choir intones the antiphon:

I have sought the Lord whom I love with all my heart
(Song of Songs 3:4),

with Psalm 45; or some other appropriate song may be sung. At
the end of the psalm **Glory to the Father** is not said but only the

antiphon. If the presentation of the insignia comes to an end before the whole psalm is sung, the psalm is interrupted and the antiphon repeated.

155. If, in accordance with the rules or customs of the religious community, other insignia of religious profession are to be presented, this is done now in silence or with a suitable formula. In this matter a dignified simplicity should be observed.

III. OPTIONAL GENERAL INTERCESSIONS
INTRODUCTION
156. a) In the Mass of first profession:

Dear friends,
as we celebrate the paschal mystery of Christ
and the first profession of these sisters,
let us pray together to God the almighty Father,
through Jesus Christ, the inspiration of religious life.

b) In the Mass of renewal of vows:

Dear friends,
Christ our Lord has told us,
"Without me you can do nothing."
Let us pray through him to the Father of all mercies
for the salvation of all people,
for peace in our time,
and for these sisters of ours who renew their vows today.

INTENTIONS
157. *I. a)* **For the holy Church of God,**
that adorned by the virtues of her children
she may shine ever more brightly for Christ,
    her Bridegroom:
let us pray to the Lord.

b) **For our holy father the Pope and the other bishops,**
that the Holy Spirit who filled the apostles
may pour out his grace unceasingly upon
    their successors:
let us pray to the Lord.

c) For all those who minister to the Church,
that by word and work
they may lead to salvation
the people entrusted to their care:
let us pray to the Lord.

II. a) For the peace and salvation of the world,
that all religious may be messengers and servants
    of the peace of Christ:
let us pray to the Lord.

b) For the good of all people,
that those who are dedicated to the Lord's service
may pursue the things of heaven
and spend their days in the service of others:
let us pray to the Lord.

c) For all who believe in Christ,
that they may listen attentively to the secret
    voice of God
as he invites them all to a life of holiness:
let us pray to the Lord.

III. a) For all religious,
that they may offer
spiritual sacrifices to God with heart and tongue,
with hand and mind,
in labor and suffering:
let us pray to the Lord.

b) For those who follow the evangelical counsels,
that the law of love may shine in their lives,
and that like the first disciples
they may be one in heart and mind:
let us pray to the Lord.

c) For all who are consecrated to God in religion
that they may share in the life of the Church
and cooperate fully in all her works and hopes:
let us pray to the Lord.

d) For all religious,
that each one, according to the call of God,
may increase the holiness of the Church
and work to spread God's kingdom:
let us pray to the Lord.

IV. *a)* For these sisters of ours
who have today bound themselves more closely to God
by religious profession,
that in his goodness he may give them a love of prayer,
a spirit of penance,
and zeal in the apostolate:
let us pray to the Lord.

b) For these sisters of ours
who have today
bound themselves more closely to God's service,
that their hearts may be filled
with generous love for all:
let us pray to the Lord.

c) For these sisters of ours
who have today dedicated themselves
to Christ the Lord,
that, like the wise virgins,
they may keep alight the lamp of faith and love:
let us pray to the Lord.

d) For these religious
who have today sealed their desire for holiness,
that they may keep watch for the Bridegroom,
and so enter the wedding feast of heaven:
let us pray to the Lord.

e) For those who today make profession of
   the evangelical counsels,
that religious consecration may increase the holiness
to which baptism has called them:
let us pray to the Lord.

f) For all here present,
that we may be faithful to Christ's teaching
as he calls us to be perfect,
and that we may bear fruit in holiness,
grow into the fullness of Christ,
and meet together in the heavenly city of peace:
let us pray to the Lord.

CONCLUDING PRAYER

158. a) In the Mass of the first profession:

Lord, protect your family,
and in your goodness grant our prayers
for these sisters of ours
as they offer you the first fruits
of their consecrated lives.

We ask this through Christ our Lord.
℟. Amen.

b) In the Mass of renewal of vows:

Lord God,
you are the source of truth and mercy.
Hear the prayers of your people,
and by the intercession of the Blessed Virgin Mary,
    Mother of God,
pour into these your servants
the strength to persevere,
so that by following you faithfully
they may fulfill the vows which they now renew.

We ask this through Christ our Lord.
℟. Amen.

IV. ANOTHER SOLEMN PRAYER OF BLESSING
OR CONSECRATION OF THE PROFESSED

159. Lord God, creator of the world and Father of
    humankind,
we honor you with praise and thanksgiving,
for you chose a people from the stock of Abraham

and consecrated them to yourself,
calling them by your name.
While they wandered in the wilderness
your word gave them comfort
and your right hand protection.

When they were poor and despised,
you united them to yourself in a covenant of love.
When they strayed from your friendship your mercy
led them back to the right way.
When they sought you,
your fatherly care looked after them
until they came to dwell in the land of freedom.

But above all, Father, we thank you
for revealing the knowledge of your truth
through Jesus Christ, your Son, our brother.

Born of the Blessed Virgin,
by dying he ransomed your people from sin,
and by rising again he showed them the glory
that would one day be their own.

When he took his place at your right hand,
he sent the Holy Spirit to call countless disciples
to follow the evangelical counsels
and consecrate their lives to the glory of your name
and the salvation of all.

Today it is right
that your house should echo with a new song
    of thanksgiving
for these sisters of ours
who have listened to your voice
and made themselves over to your holy service.

Lord, send the gift of your Holy Spirit upon
    your servants
who have left all things for your sake.
Father, may their lives reveal the face of Christ your Son,

so that all who see them may come to know
that he is always present in your Church.

We pray that in the freedom of their hearts
they may free from care the hearts of others;
in helping the afflicted, may they bring comfort to Christ
suffering in his brothers and sisters;
may they look upon the world
and see it ruled by your loving wisdom.
May the gift they make of themselves
hasten the coming of your kingdom,
and make them one at last with your saints in heaven.

We ask this through Christ our Lord.
℟. **Amen.**

V. ANOTHER FORM OF BLESSING AT THE END
OF THE MASS OF PERPETUAL PROFESSION

160. May the almighty Father make you firm in faith,
innocent in the midst of evil,
and wise in the pursuit of goodness.
℟. **Amen.**

May the Lord Jesus, whom you follow,
enable you to live out the mystery
of his death and resurrection in your own life.
℟. **Amen.**

May the fire of the Holy Spirit
cleanse your hearts from all sin
and set them on fire with his love.
℟. **Amen.**

May almighty God,
the Father, and the Son, ✚ and the Holy Spirit,
bless all of you who have taken part in these sacred
    celebrations.
℟. **Amen.**

APPENDIX

I. A SAMPLE FORMULA OF PROFESSION

Each religious community may compose a formula of profession, to be approved by the Sacred Congregation for Religious and for Secular Institutes. For the convenience of religious institutes the following example is given.

1. Candidates for profession:

I, N.,
for the glory of God,
and intending to consecrate myself more closely to him
and to follow Christ more generously all my life,
with (Bishop N., and) my brothers (sisters) as witnesses
and in your presence, N.,[1]
vow perpetual[2] chastity, poverty, and obedience
according to the (rule and) constitutions of N.[3]
With my whole heart I give myself
to this religious community, to seek perfect charity
in the service of God and the Church,
by the grace of the Holy Spirit
and the prayers of the Blessed Virgin Mary.

2. The person who receives the vows may at a suitable point in the rite (see Part I, no. 70; Part II, no. 77) say the following:

By the authority entrusted to me,
and in the name of the Church,
I receive the vows you have taken
in the community of N.[3]
I earnestly commend you to God,
that your gift of self,
made one with the sacrifice of the Eucharist,
may be brought to perfection.

NOTES

[1] Here are mentioned the name and office of the superior receiving the profession.

[2] Or the period of temporary profession.

[3] The name of the religious community is mentioned.

II. TEXTS FOR MASS

This Mass may be said on any day except the Sundays of Advent, Lent and Easter, solemnities, Ash Wednesday and the weekdays of Holy Week. White vestments may be worn.

1. FIRST RELIGIOUS PROFESSION

Introductory Rites Here am I, Lord; I come to do your will.
Your law is written on my heart (Psalm 40:8-9).

OPENING PRAYER

Lord,
you have inspired our brothers (sisters)
with the resolve to follow Christ more closely.
Grant a blessed ending to the journey
on which they have set out,
so that they may be able to offer you
the perfect gift of their loving service.

We ask this through our Lord Jesus Christ, your Son,
who lives and reigns with you and the Holy Spirit,
one God, for ever and ever.

See **Lectionary for Mass**, nos. 784-788.

PRAYER OVER THE GIFTS

Pray, brethren . . .

Lord,
receive the gifts and prayers which we offer to you
as we celebrate the beginning of this religious
  profession.
Grant that these first fruits of your servants
may be nourished by your grace
and be the promise of a richer harvest.

We ask this through Christ our Lord.

Preface of Religious Profession, page 295; intercessions of the eucharistic prayers, pages 289-290.

Communion Rite Whoever does the will of God is my brother, my sister, and my mother (Mark 3:35).

PRAYER AFTER COMMUNION

Let us pray.

Pause for silent prayer, if this has not preceded.

Lord,
may the sacred mysteries we have shared bring us joy.
By their power grant that your servants
may constantly fulfill the religious duties
   they now take up
and freely give their service to you.

We ask this through Christ our Lord.

2. PERPETUAL PROFESSION

A

Introductory Rites I rejoiced when I heard them say: let us go to the house of the Lord. Jerusalem, we stand as pilgrims in your court! (Psalm 122:1-2)

OPENING PRAYER

God our Father,
you have caused the grace of baptism
to bear such fruit in your servants
that they now strive to follow your Son more closely.
Let them rightly aim at true evangelical perfection
and increase the holiness and apostolic zeal
   of your Church.

We ask this through our Lord Jesus Christ, your Son,
who lives and reigns wth you and the Holy Spirit,
one God, for ever and ever.

See **Lectionary for Mass,** nos. 784-788.

PRAYER OVER THE GIFTS

Pray, brethren . . .

Lord,
accept the gifts and the vows of your servants.
Strengthen them by your love
  as they profess the evangelical counsels.

We ask this through Christ our Lord.

Preface of Religious Profession, page 294.

In the eucharistic prayers, the offering of the professed may be mentioned according to the texts below:

I. FOR MEN

a) In Eucharistic Prayer I, the special form of **Father, accept this offering** is said:

Father, accept and sanctify this offering
from your whole family and from these your servants
which we make to you on the day of their profession.
By your grace
they have dedicated their lives to you today.
When your Son returns in glory,
may they share in the joy of unending paschal feast.

[Through Christ our Lord. Amen.]

b) In the intercessions of Eucharistic Prayer II, after the words **and all the clergy,** there is added:

Lord, remember also these our brothers
who have today dedicated themselves to serve
  you always.
Grant that they may always raise their minds and hearts
  to you
and glorify your name.

c) In the intercessions of Eucharistic Prayer III, after the words **your Son has gained for you,** there is added:

Strengthen also these servants of yours in their holy pur-
pose, for they have dedicated themselves
by the bonds of religious consecration to serve
  you always.

Grant that they may give witness in your Church
to the new and eternal life won by Christ's redemption.

d) In the intercessions of Eucharistic Prayer IV, the professed
may be mentioned in this way:

... bishop, and bishops and clergy everywhere.
Remember these our brothers
who unite themselves more closely to you today
by their perpetual profession.
Remember those who take part in this offering ...

II. FOR WOMEN

a) In Eucharistic Prayer I, the special form of **Father, accept this
offering** is said:

Father, accept and sanctify this offering
from your whole family and from these your servants
which we make to you on the day of their consecration.
By your grace
they join themselves more closely to your Son today.
When he comes in glory at the end of time,
may they joyfully meet him.

[Through Christ our Lord. Amen.]

b) In the intercessions of Eucharistic Prayer II, after the words
and all the clergy, there is added:

Remember all these sisters of ours
who have left all things for your sake
so that they might find you in all things
and by forgetting self serve the needs of all.

c) In the intercessions of Eucharistic Prayer III, after the words
your Son has gained for you, there is added:

Lord, strengthen these servants of yours in their holy
purpose as they strive to follow Christ your Son in consecrated holiness by giving witness to his love in their religious life.

d) In the intercessions of Eucharistic Prayer IV, the professed
may be mentioned in this way:

... bishop, and bishops and clergy everywhere.
Remember our sisters who have consecrated themselves
    to you today
by the bond of religious profession.
Remember those who take part in this offering ...

Communion Rite   I am nailed with Christ to the cross; I am
    alive, not by my own life but by Christ's life within me
    (Galatians 2:19-20).

PRAYER AFTER COMMUNION
Let us pray.

Pause for silent prayer, if this has not preceded.

Lord,
as we share these sacred mysteries,
we pray for these your servants
who are bound to you by their holy offering.
Increase in them the fire of your Holy Spirit
and unite them in eternal fellowship with your Son,
who is Lord for ever and ever.

SOLEMN BLESSING
May God who is the source of all good intentions
enlighten your minds and strengthen your hearts.
May he help you to fulfill with steadfast faith all you
    have promised.
℟. Amen.

May the Lord enable you to travel in the joy of Christ
as you follow along his way,
and may you gladly share each other's burdens.
℟. Amen.

May the love of God unite you and make
    you a true family,
praising his name and showing forth Christ's love.
℟. Amen.

May almighty God,
the Father, and the Son,   ✠   and the Holy Spirit,
bless all of you who have taken part in these
    sacred celebrations.
℟. Amen.

B

Introductory Rites   I will offer sacrifice in your temple; I will
    fulfill the vows my lips have promised (Psalm 66:13-14).

OPENING PRAYER

Lord, holy Father,
confirm the resolve of your servants (N. and N.).
Grant that the grace of baptism,
which they wish to strengthen with new bonds,
may work its full effect in them,
so that they may offer you their praise
and spread Christ's kingdom with apostolic zeal.

We ask this through our Lord Jesus Christ, your Son,
who lives and reigns with you and the Holy Spirit,
one God, for ever and ever.

See **Lectionary for Mass**, nos. 784-788.

PRAYER OVER THE GIFTS
Pray, brethren . . .

Lord,
accept the offering of your servants
and make them a sign of salvation.
Fill with the gifts of your Holy Spirit
those whom you have called by your fatherly providence
to follow your Son more closely.

We ask this through Christ our Lord.

Preface of Religious Profession, page 294; intercessions of the eucharistic prayers, as in the preceding Mass.
Communion Rite   Taste and see the goodness of the Lord;
blessed is he who hopes in God (Psalm 34:9).

PRAYER AFTER COMMUNION

Let us pray.

Pause for silent prayer, if this has not preceded.

Lord,
may the reception of this sacrament
and the solemnizing of this profession bring us joy.
Let this twofold act of devotion
help your servants to serve the Church and humankind
in the spirit of your love.

We ask this through Christ our Lord.

SOLEMN BLESSING

God inspires all holy desires and brings them
to fulfillment.
May he protect you always by his grace
so that you may fulfill the duties of your vocation
with a faithful heart.
℟. Amen.

May he make each of you a witness
and sign of his love for all people.
℟. Amen.

May he make those bonds
with which he has bound you to Christ on earth
endure for ever in heavenly love.
℟. Amen.

May almighty God,
the Father, and the Son, ✠ and the Holy Spirit,
bless all of you who have taken part in this celebration.
℟. Amen.

3. RENEWAL OF VOWS

The entrance and communion antiphons, if used, may be taken
from one of the three preceding Masses.

OPENING PRAYER

**God our Father,
guide of humankind and ruler of creation,
look upon these your servants
who wish to confirm their offering of themselves to you.
As the years pass by,
help them to enter more deeply into the mystery
   of the Church
and to dedicate themselves more generously
to the good of humankind.**

**We ask this through our Lord Jesus Christ, your Son,
who lives and reigns with you and the Holy Spirit,
one God, for ever and ever.**

See **Lectionary for Mass,** nos. 784-788.

PRAYER OVER THE GIFTS

Pray, brethren . . .

**Lord,
look mercifully upon the gifts of your people
and upon the renewed offering by our brothers (sisters)
of their chastity, poverty, and obedience.
Change these temporal gifts into a sign of eternal life
and conform the minds of those who offer them
to the likeness of your Son
who is Lord for ever and ever.**

Preface of Religious Profession; intercessions of the eucharistic prayers, as in the preceding Masses.

PRAYER AFTER COMMUNION

Let us pray.

Pause for silent prayer, if this has not preceded.

**Lord,
now that we have received these heavenly sacraments,
we pray that your servants will trust only in your grace,
be strengthened by the power of Christ
and be protected with the help of the Holy Spirit.**

We ask this through Christ our Lord.

PREFACE OF RELIGIOUS PROFESSION
Priest: **The Lord be with you.**

People: **And also with you.**

Priest: **Lift up your hearts.**

People: **We lift them up to the Lord.**

Priest: **Let us give thanks to the Lord our God.**

People: **It is right to give him thanks.**
Father, all-powerful and ever-living God,
we do well always and everywhere to give you thanks
through Jesus Christ our Lord.

He came, the Son of a Virgin Mother,
named those blessed who were pure of heart,
and taught by his whole life the perfection of chastity.

He chose always to fulfill your holy will
and became obedient even to dying for us,
offering himself to you as a perfect oblation.

He consecrated more closely to your service
those who leave all things for your sake
and promised that they would find a heavenly treasure.

And so, with all the angels and saints
we proclaim your glory
and join in their unending hymn of praise:

Holy, holy, holy Lord, God of power and might,
heaven and earth are full of your glory.
Hosanna in the highest.
Blessed is he who comes in the name of the Lord.
Hosanna in the highest.

III. TWENTY-FIFTH OR FIFTIETH ANNIVERSARY
OF RELIGIOUS PROFESSION
This Mass may be celebrated, using white vestments, on all days
except the Sundays of Advent, Lent and Easter, solemnities, Ash

Wednesday and the weekdays of Holy Week. The entrance and communion antiphons may be taken from one of the preceding Masses.

OPENING PRAYER

**God of faithfulness,
enable us to give you thanks
for your goodness to N., our brother/sister.
Today he/she comes to rededicate that gift
which he/she first received from you.
Intensify within him/her your spirit of perfect love,
that he/she may devote himself/herself more fervently
to the service of your glory
and the work of salvation.**

**We ask this through our Lord Jesus Christ, your Son,
who lives and reigns with you and the Holy Spirit,
one God, for ever and ever.**

PRAYER OVER THE GIFTS

Pray, brethren . . .

**All-powerful God,
together with these gifts
accept the offering of self
which N., our brother/sister, wishes to reaffirm today.
By the power of your Spirit
conform him/her more truly
to the likeness of your beloved Son.**

We ask this through Christ our Lord.

Preface of Religious Profession.

PRAYER AFTER COMMUNION

Let us pray.

Pause for silent prayer, if this has not preceded.
**God of love,
in this joyful anniversary celebration
you have fed us**

with the body and blood of your Son.
Refreshed by heavenly food and drink
may our brother/sister, N., advance happily
   on that journey
which began in you and leads to you.
Grant this through Christ our Lord.

BLESSING OF ABBOTS AND ABBESSES

BLESSING OF ABBOTS AND ABBESSES

CHAPTER I

BLESSING OF AN ABBOT

INTRODUCTION

1. The blessing of an abbot should take place, if possible, in the presence of a gathering of religious and, if circumstances permit, of the faithful. The blessing should take place on a Sunday or major feast day; for pastoral reasons another day may be chosen.

2. The rite of blessing is usually celebrated by the bishop of the place where the monastery is situated. For a good reason, and with the consent of the bishop of the place, the abbot-elect may receive the blessing from another bishop or abbot.

3. Two religious from his monastery assist the abbot-elect.

4. It is desirable that the religious assisting the abbot-elect, the abbots, priest-religious, and other priests present concelebrate the Mass with the officiating prelate and the abbot-elect.

5. If the abbot-elect receives the blessing in his own abbey at the hands of another abbot, the officiating abbot may ask the newly blessed abbot to preside at the concelebration of the eucharistic liturgy. Otherwise the officiating prelate presides and the new abbot takes first place among the concelebrants.

6. The officiating prelate and all the concelebrants wear the vestments required for Mass, together with pectoral cross and dalmatic. If the assisting religious do not concelebrate, they wear choir dress or surplice.

7. The blessing of ring, pastoral staff, and miter normally takes place at some convenient time before the actual blessing of the abbot.

8. Besides what is needed for the concelebration of Mass and for communion under both kinds, there should also be prepared: a) the Roman Pontifical; b) the Rule; c) the pastoral

staff; d) the ring and the miter for the abbot-elect, if they are to be presented to him.

9. During the liturgy of the word, the officiating prelate should sit in the official chair; the abbot-elect should sit between the assisting religious in a suitable place within the sanctuary.

10. As a rule, the blessing takes place at the chair. To enable the faithful to participate more fully, a seat for the officiating prelate may be placed before the altar or in some other suitable place; the seats for the abbot-elect and the religious assisting him should be so arranged that the religious and the faithful may have a clear view of the ceremony.

11. When all is ready the procession moves through the church to the altar in the usual way. The minister carrying the Book of the Gospels is followed by the priests who will concelebrate, the abbot-elect with the religious assisting him on either side, and finally the officiating prelate between two deacons.

LITURGY OF THE WORD

12. The liturgy of the word is celebrated in accordance with the rubrics.

13. The readings may be taken, in whole or in part, from the Mass of the day or from the texts for the blessing of an abbot in the *Lectionary for Mass* (nos. 779-783) and listed below.

14. The officiating prelate gives a homily or an address at the appropriate time during the rite of blessing.

15. The profession of faith is not said in this Mass, and the general intercessions are omitted.

BLESSING OF AN ABBOT

16. The rite of blessing begins after the gospel. The officiating prelate, wearing his miter, is seated in the chair prepared for the occasion.

PRESENTATION OF THE ABBOT-ELECT

17. The abbot-elect is escorted by his assistants to the officiating prelate, to whom he makes a sign of reverence.

18. One of the assisting religious addresses the prelate in these or similar words:

Most Reverend Father, in the name of our community we present to you the abbot-elect of our monastery of N., of the Order of N., in the diocese of N. We ask you to bless him as abbot of our monastery.

The prelate asks:
Has he been duly elected?

He replies:
We know and testify that he has.

The prelate replies:
Thanks be to God.

If, however, the abbot is one who has been given jurisdiction over a territory independent of a diocese, the prelate adds, after the question on election:

Have you a mandate from the Holy See?

The religious answers: **We have.**

Prelate: **Let it be read.**

All sit while the mandate is being read. Afterward, all say: **Thanks be to God.**

HOMILY

19. All sit while the prelate gives a brief homily to the abbot-elect, the religious and the faithful.

EXAMINATION

20. After the address the abbot-elect rises and stands in front of the prelate, who questions him in these words:

My dear brother, when a man is chosen to stand in the place of Christ and to guide others in the way of the Spirit, it is right that he should be questioned on matters concerning his office and on the qualities he brings

to it. This is the age-old teaching and requirement of our fathers in the spiritual life. Following their wise guidance, I now ask:

Will you persevere in your determination to observe the Rule of Saint N. and will you be diligent in teaching your brothers to do the same, and so encourage them in the love of God, in the life of the Gospel, and in fraternal charity?

The abbot-elect answers: **I will.**

Prelate:

Will you teach your brothers by your constant dedication to monastic life, by sound doctrine, and by the good example of your own deeds rather than by mere words?

Abbot-elect: **I will.**

Prelate:

Will you always be concerned for the spiritual good of those entrusted to your care, and seek to lead your brothers to God?

Abbot-elect: **I will.**

Prelate:

Will you be faithful in watching over the goods of your monastery and prudent in using them for the benefit of your brothers, of the poor, and of the strangers at your gate?

Abbot-elect: **I will.**

Prelate:

Will you always and in all matters be loyal, obedient, and reverent to holy Church and to our Holy Father the Pope and his successors?

Abbot-elect: **I will.**

If the abbot is one who has jurisdiction over a territory, the prelate adds:

Will, you, in cooperation with the priests and deacons who share in your ministry, be a loving father to God's holy people, cherish them, and guide them into the way of salvation?

Abbot-elect: **I will.**

Prelate:
Will you, as a good shepherd, seek out the straying sheep and gather them into the sheepfold of Christ?
Abbot-elect: **I will.**

Prelate:
Will you pray without ceasing for God's holy people, and be blameless in carrying out your duties as a shepherd of souls?
Abbot-elect: **I will.**

Prelate:
May the Lord strengthen your resolve, give you every grace, and keep you always and everywhere in his protection.
All: **Amen.**

INVITATION TO PRAYER

21. Then all stand, and the prelate, without his miter, invites the people to pray:

Dearly beloved, God has chosen N., his servant, to be the leader of his brothers. Let us pray that the Lord will sustain him with his grace.

Deacon (except during the Easter season):
Let us kneel.

LITANY OF THE SAINTS

The abbot-elect kneels at his place and, except during the Easter season, the rest kneel at their places.

Then the cantors sing the litany; they may add, at the proper place, names of other saints (for example, the patron saint, the titular of the church, the founder of the church, the patron saint of the abbess-elect) or petitions suitable to the occasion.

22. After the litany the deacon says:
Let us stand.

PRAYER OF BLESSING

23. All stand. The abbot-elect comes before the prelate and kneels. The prelate, with hands extended, says one of the following prayers:

Almighty God and Father,
you sent your only Son into the world
to be the servant of all,
the Good Shepherd who lays down his life for his
   sheep.

Listen to our prayer:
bless ✠ and strengthen N., your servant,
chosen to be abbot of this monastery.
May his manner of life show clearly
that he is what he is called, a father,
so that his teaching will, as a leaven of goodness,
grow in the hearts of his spiritual family.

Let him realize, Lord,
how demanding is the task
to which he now sets his hand,
how heavy the responsibility
of guiding the souls of others,
and of ministering
to the many and various needs of a community.

Let him seek to help his brothers
rather than to preside over them.
Give him a heart full of compassion, wisdom, and zeal,
so that he may not lose even one
of the flock entrusted to his charge.

May he dispose all things with understanding,
so that the members of the monastic family
will steadily make progress
in the love of Christ and of each other,
and run with eager hearts
in the way of your commandments.

Give him the gifts of your Spirit.
Set him on fire with love for your glory
and for the service of your Church,
and may he in turn inflame with zeal
the hearts of his brothers.

In his life and in his teaching
may he set Christ above all things,
and when the day of judgment dawns,

receive him, in the company of his brothers,
into your kingdom.

We ask this through Christ our Lord.
℞. Amen.

Or:
Lord, hear our prayers for your servant N.
He has been chosen to guide this monastic community,
and to stand in the place of Christ your Son
as shepherd of your flock.

Look on him with love,
and strengthen him with every blessing.
Open to him the storehouse of your wisdom,
that he may bring out from it
treasures both old and new.

Guide him in the way of grace and peace,
in the footsteps of your Son,
and reward him at last with the joy of everlasting life.

We ask this through Christ our Lord.
℞. Amen.

Or:
Lord, look with love on your servant N.,
chosen under your providence
to be abbot of this monastery.

Bless ✠ him and make him holy,
so that in every thought and deed
he may seek to please you.
By word and example
may he encourage his brothers
to grow in love of you and of their neighbor.
Though a stranger to the ways of this world,
may he take to heart the needs of all your children,
both of body and of soul.

May he always teach his community
to hold in high esteem
the divine office and sacred reading.
Together with his brothers
may he live the life of the Gospel,

and so enter with them
into the unending joy of heaven.

We ask this through Christ our Lord.
℟. Amen.

Or:
Almighty God and Father,
you sent your Son into the world
to minister to your flock
and to lay down his life for them.

Bless ✠ your servant N.,
chosen to be abbot of this monastery,
and make him holy.

Strengthen him by your grace
for his heavy burden of guiding souls
and of adapting himself to the various needs of those
    he serves.
Give him a heart full of compassion
for the brothers entrusted to his care,
so that he may not lose even one.
And may the Lord, when he comes in glory on the last
    day,
give him the reward of his stewardship.

We ask this through Christ our Lord.
℟. Amen.

PRESENTATION OF THE RULE

24. After the prayer of blessing, the prelate, wearing his miter, sits. The new abbot comes before him and the prelate
gives him the Rule, saying:

Take this Rule
which contains the tradition of holiness
received from our spiritual fathers.
As God gives you strength
and human frailty allows,
use it to guide and sustain your brothers
whom God has placed in your care.

PRESENTATION OF THE PONTIFICAL INSIGNIA

25. The prelate may place the ring on the ring finger of the new abbot's right hand, saying:

Take this ring, the seal of fidelity.
Wear it as the symbol of constancy
and maintain this community (monastic family)
in the bond of brotherly love.

26. Then, in silence, the prelate may put the miter on the new abbot's head.

27. Next he hands the pastoral staff, saying:

Take this shepherd's staff
and show loving care for the brothers
whom the Lord has entrusted to you;
for he will demand an account of your stewardship.

28. All stand. If the blessing has been given by a bishop or outside the new abbot's monastery by another abbot, the new abbot takes the first place among the concelebrants. If the blessing has been given by another abbot in the abbey church of the newly blessed abbot, the latter sits in the chair, and the abbot who has conferred the blessing sits at his right.

If the new abbot has jurisdiction over a territory and has received the blessing in his own church, the prelate invites him to sit in the chair while he sits at his right.

29. Lastly the new abbot puts aside his staff and receives the sign of peace from the prelate who has conferred the blessing and from all the abbots. If circumstances permit, the religious and the priests also exchange the sign of peace with the abbot.

LITURGY OF THE EUCHARIST

30. The rite for the concelebration of Mass is followed.

31. At the end of Mass the blessing is given by the celebrant. If the new abbot is the celebrant, he gives it according to the pontifical rite.

32. After the blessing the **Te Deum** or another appropriate song may be sung. During the singing all return in procession to the sacristy and go their way in peace.

If the new abbot has jurisdiction over a territory, the **Te Deum** or another appropriate song is sung at the end of the prayer after communion. Meanwhile, the new abbot is led by his assistants through the church and he blesses all present.

After the hymn, the new abbot, wearing his miter and holding his staff, may stand at the altar or at his chair and address the people briefly. The Mass concludes in the usual manner.

CHAPTER II

BLESSING OF AN ABBESS

INTRODUCTION

1. The blessing of an abbess should take place, if possible, in the presence of a gathering of women religious and of the faithful. The blessing should take place on a Sunday or major feast day; for pastoral reasons another day may be chosen.

2. The blessing is performed as a rule by the bishop of the place where the monastery is situated. For a good reason, and with the consent of the bishop of the place, the abbess-elect may receive the blessing from another bishop or an abbot.

3. The abbess-elect, assisted by two religious from her monastery, is given a place in the sanctuary, outside the enclosure, so that she may be near the bishop or prelate who gives the blessing and so that all present, nuns and faithful, may see the ceremony and take part in it.

4. Besides what is needed for the celebration of Mass, there should also be prepared: a) the Roman Pontifical; b) the Rule and, if it is to be presented, the ring; c) a chalice or chalices sufficiently large for communion under both kinds.

5. The blessing usually takes place at the chair. To enable the faithful to participate more fully, a seat for the bishop or prelate who gives the blessing may be placed before the altar or in some other suitable place; the seats for the abbess-elect and the religious assisting her should be so arranged that the nuns and faithful may have a clear view of the ceremony.

6. Before the celebration begins the prelate, accompanied by the ministers and clergy, goes to the entrance of the enclosure. The abbess-elect, with the two nuns assisting her, leaves the enclosure and takes her place in the procession to the church immediately in front of the prelate.

LITURGY OF THE WORD

7. The introductory rites and the liturgy of the word are celebrated in accordance with the rubrics.

8. The readings may be taken, in whole or in part, from the Mass of the day or from the texts for the blessing of an abbess in the *Lectionary for Mass* (nos. 779-783) and listed below.

9. The officiating prelate gives a homily or an address at the appropriate time during the rite of blessing.

10. The profession of faith is not said in this Mass, and the general intercessions are omitted.

BLESSING OF AN ABBESS

11. The rite of blessing begins after the gospel. The officiating prelate, wearing his miter, is seated in the chair prepared for the occasion.

PRESENTATION OF THE ABBESS-ELECT

12. The abbess-elect is escorted by her assistants to the officiating prelate, to whom she makes a sign of reverence.

13. One of the nuns assisting her addresses the prelate in these or similar words:

Most Reverend Father, in the name of our community we present to you the abbess-elect of our monastery of N., of the Order of N., in the diocese of N. We ask you to bless her as abbess of our monastery.

The prelate asks:
Has she been duly elected?

She replies:
We know and testify that she has.

The prelate replies:
Thanks be to God.

HOMILY

14. All sit while the prelate gives a brief homily to the abbess-elect, the nuns, and the faithful.

EXAMINATION

15. After the address the abbess-elect rises and stands in front of the prelate, who questions her in these words:

Will you persevere in your determination to observe the Rule of Saint N. and will you be diligent in teaching your sisters to do the same, and so encourage them in the love of God, in the life of the Gospel, and in mutual charity?

The abbess-elect replies: **I will.**

Prelate:

Will you always and in all matters be loyal, obedient, and reverent to holy Church and to our Holy Father the Pope and his successors?

Abbess-elect: **I will.**

Prelate:

Will you be obedient to your bishop in the governing of your monastery, in accordance with canon law and the constitutions of your Order?

Abbess-elect: **I will.**

Prelate:

Will you teach your sisters by your constant dedication to the monastic life and by the good example of your own deeds rather than by mere words?

Abbess-elect: **I will.**

Prelate:

Will you encourage your sisters to be faithful to the traditions of the religious life and to extend God's kingdom by the hidden apostolate of the life of contemplation?

Abbess-elect: **I will.**

Prelate:

May the Lord strengthen your resolve, give you every

grace, and keep you always and everywhere in his protection.
All: **Amen.**

INVITATION TO PRAYER

16. Then all stand, and the prelate, without his miter, invites the people to pray:

Dearly beloved, God has chosen N. to serve him as the leader of this monastic community. Let us pray that the Lord will sustain her with his grace.

Deacon (except during the Easter season):
Let us kneel.

LITANY OF THE SAINTS

The prelate kneels at his chair; the abbess-elect and all the others kneel in their places.

Then the cantors sing the litany; they may add, at the proper place, names of other saints (for example, the patron saint, the titular of the church, the founder of the church, the patron saint of the abbess-elect) or petitions suitable to the occasion.

17. After the litany the deacon says:
Let us stand.

PRAYER OF BLESSING

18. All stand. The abbess-elect comes before the prelate and kneels. The prelate, with hands extended, says one of the following prayers:

Almighty God and Father,
you sent your only Son into the world
to be the servant of all,
the Good Shepherd who lays down his life for his
  sheep.

Listen to our prayer:
bless ✠ and sustain N., your servant,
chosen to be abbess of this community.
May her manner of life show clearly
that she is what she is called, a mother.

Let her seek to help her sisters
rather than to preside over them.

May she dispose all things with understanding,
so that the members of her monastic family
will steadily make progress
in the love of Christ and of each other,
and run with eager hearts
in the way of your commandments.

Give her the gifts of your Spirit.
Set her on fire with love for your glory
and for the service of your Church,
and may she in turn inflame with zeal
the hearts of her sisters.

May she set Christ above all things,
and when the day of judgment dawns,
receive her, in the company of her sisters,
into your kingdom.

We ask this through Christ our Lord.
℟. Amen.

Or:
Lord, hear our prayers for your servant N.,
who has been chosen to guide this monastic community.
Look on her with love,
and strengthen her with every blessing.
Guide her in the way of grace and peace,
in the footsteps of your Son,
and reward her at last with the joy of everlasting life.

We ask this through Christ our Lord.
℟. Amen.

Or:
Lord, look with love on your servant N.,
chosen under your providence
to be abbess of this community.

Bless ✠ her and make her holy,
so that in every thought and deed
she may seek to please you.

By word and example
may she encourage her sisters
to grow in love of you and of their neighbor.

Though a stranger to the ways of this world,
may she take to heart
the needs of all your children,
both of body and of soul.

May she always teach her community
to hold in high esteem
the divine office and sacred reading.
Together with her sisters
may she live the life of the Gospel,
and so enter with them
into the unending joy of heaven.

We ask this through Christ our Lord.
℟. Amen.

Or:
Almighty God and Father,
you sent your Son into the world
to minister to your flock
and to lay down his life for them.

Bless ✚ your servant N.,
chosen to be abbess of this monastery,
and make her holy.
Give her a heart full of compassion
for the sisters entrusted to her care.
And may the Lord, when he comes in glory on the last
    day,
give her the reward of her stewardship.

We ask this through Christ our Lord.
℟. Amen.

PRESENTATION OF THE RULE

19. After the prayer of blessing, the prelate, wearing his miter, sits. The new abbess comes before him and the prelate
gives her the Rule, saying:

**Take this Rule
which contains the traditions of holiness
received from our spiritual fathers.
As God gives you strength
and human frailty allows,
use it to guide and sustain your sisters
whom God has placed in your care.**

PRESENTATION OF THE RING

20. The ring is not presented if the abbess has already received it on the day of her profession and consecration.

If the abbess has not previously received the ring, the prelate may place it on the ring finger of her right hand, saying:

**Take this ring, the seal of fidelity.
Wear it as the symbol of constancy
and maintain this community (monastic family)
in the bond of sisterly love.**

21. Then the abbess gives a sign of peace to the prelate and returns to her place with her two assistants.

CONCLUDING RITE

INSTALLATION

22. After the Mass the **Te Deum** or another appropriate song may be sung. During the singing the prelate leads the abbess to the enclosure. If the prelate is the Ordinary of the place and has immediate jurisdiction over the nuns, he leads her to her place in choir and seats her there, unless the abbess has already been given this sign of her authority immediately after her election.

BIBLICAL READINGS

BLESSING OF AN ABBOT OR ABBESS

The readings are taken in whole or in part from the Mass of the day or from the texts listed below.

READING FROM THE OLD TESTAMENT (L 806)

1. Proverbs 2:1-9
Inclining your heart to understanding.

2. Proverbs 4:7-13
Go the way of wisdom I direct you.

READING FROM THE NEW TESTAMENT (L 807)

1. Acts 2:42-47
All those who believed were together and had everything in common.

2. Ephesians 4:1-6
Striving to preserve the unity of the Spirit through the bond of peace.

3. Colossians 3:12-17
Over all these put on love, that is, the bond of perfection.

4. Hebrews 13:1-2, 7-8, 17-18
Obey your leaders. Pray for us.

5. 1 Peter 5:1-4
Be examples to the flock.

RESPONSORIAL PSALM (L 808)

1. Psalm 1:1-2, 3, 4 and 6
℞. (Psalm 40:5a) **Blessed are they who hope in the Lord.**

2. Psalm 34:2-3, 4-5, 10-11, 12-13
℞. (12) **Come, children, hear me: I will teach you the fear of the Lord.**

3. Psalm 92:2-3, 5-6, 13-14, 15-16
℞. (see 2a) **Lord, it is good to give thanks to you.**

ALLELUIA VERSE AND VERSE BEFORE THE GOSPEL
(L 809)

1. Matthew 23:9b, 10b
You have but one Father in heaven;
you have but one master, the Christ.

2. Colossians 3:15
Let the peace of Christ control your hearts,
the peace to which you were called in one Body.

GOSPEL (L 810)

1. Matthew 23:8-12
The greatest among you must be your servant.

2. Luke 12:35-44
The master will put him in charge of his servants.

3. Luke 22:24-27
I am among you as one who serves.

LITANY OF THE SAINTS

BLESSING OF AN ABBOT OR ABBESS

The cantors begin the litany; they may add, at the proper place, names of other saints (for example, the patron saint, the titular of the church, the founder of the church, the patron saint of the abbot-elect or abbess-elect) or petitions suitable to the occasion.

Lord, have mercy   Lord, have mercy
Christ, have mercy   Christ, have mercy
Lord, have mercy   Lord, have mercy

Holy Mary, Mother of God   pray for us
Saint Michael   pray for us
Holy angels of God   pray for us
Saint John the Baptist   pray for us
Saint Joseph   pray for us
Saint Peter and Saint Paul   pray for us
Saint Andrew   pray for us
Saint John   pray for us
Saint Mary Magdalene   pray for us
Saint Stephen   pray for us
Saint Ignatius   pray for us
Saint Lawrence   pray for us
Saint Perpetua and Saint Felicity   pray for us
Saint Agnes   pray for us
Saint Gregory   pray for us
Saint Augustine   pray for us
Saint Athanasius   pray for us
Saint Basil   pray for us
Saint Martin   pray for us
Saint Anthony   pray for us
Saint Benedict   pray for us
Saint Columban   pray for us
Saint Bede   pray for us
Saint Romuald   pray for us
Saint Bruno   pray for us

Saint Bernard   pray for us
Saint Francis   pray for us
Saint Dominic   pray for us
Saint Scholastica   pray for us
Saint Clare   pray for us
Saint Teresa   pray for us
All holy men and women   pray for us

Lord, be merciful   Lord, save your people
From all evil   Lord, save your people
From every sin   Lord, save your people
From everlasting death   Lord, save your people
By your coming as man   Lord, save your people
By your death and rising to a new life   Lord, save your
    people
By your gift of the Holy Spirit   Lord, save your people
Be merciful to us sinners   Lord, hear our prayer
Guide and protect your holy Church   Lord, hear our
    prayer
Keep the pope and all the clergy in faithful service
    to your Church   Lord, hear our prayer
Bring all peoples together in trust and peace
    Lord, hear our prayer
Give all who profess the counsels of the Gospel a
    deeper share in the work of redemption   Lord,
    hear our prayer
Grant that all religious communities may live and grow
    in the love of Christ and the spirit of their found-
    ers   Lord, hear our prayer
Strengthen us in your service   Lord, hear our prayer
Bless and sustain your servant, chosen to be abbot (ab-
    bess)   Lord, hear our prayer
Jesus, Son of the living God   Lord, hear our prayer
Christ, hear us   Christ hear us
Lord Jesus, hear our prayer   Lord Jesus, hear our
    prayer

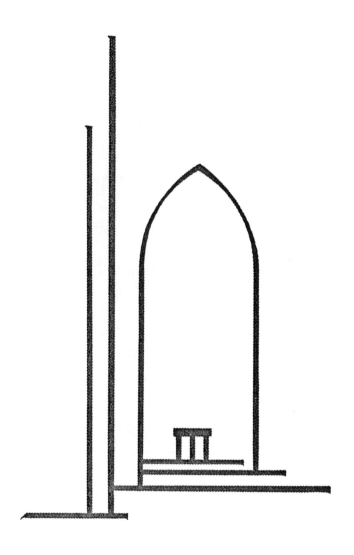

BLESSING OF
OBJECTS AND PLACES

RITE OF THE BLESSING OF OILS
RITE OF CONSECRATING THE CHRISM

Decree
Introduction (1–12)

BLESSING OF OILS AND CONSECRATION
OF THE CHRISM (13–28)

Preparations (13)
Liturgy of the Word
Renewal of Priestly Commitment

Rite of Blessing (14–18)
Procession with the Oils and the Gifts (16)
Hymn (17)
Presentation of the Oils and the Gifts (18)

Liturgy of the Eucharist (19–20)
Preparation of the Altar and the Gifts
Eucharistic Prayer
Blessing of the Oil of the Sick (20)
Communion Rite
Lord's Prayer
Prayer After Communion

Blessing of the Oil of Catechumens (21–22)

Consecration of the Chrism (23–26)
Invitation (24)
Consecratory Prayer (25)

Concluding Rite (27–28)
Blessing
Dismissal

SACRED CONGREGATION FOR DIVINE WORSHIP

Prot. n. 3133/70

DECREE

After the rites for Holy Week in the Roman Missal had been revised as required, it seemed appropriate that the rite used in the chrism Mass for the blessing of the oil of catechumens and of the sick and for the consecration of the chrism as it now stands in the Roman Pontifical should also be changed.

The Congregation for Divine Worship has therefore revised this rite and upon its approval by authority of Pope Paul VI promulgates it. The Congregation decrees its use from now on in place of the present rite in the Roman Pontifical.

The conferences of bishops have the responsibility of preparing vernacular editions and submitting them for confirmation by this Congregation.

All things to the contrary notwithstanding.

From the Sacred Congregation for Divine Worship, December 3, 1970.

Benno Cardinal Gut
prefect

A. Bugnini
secretary

INTRODUCTION

1. The bishop is to be looked on as the high priest of his flock. The life in Christ of his faithful is in some way derived from and dependent upon the bishop.[1]

He concelebrates the chrism Mass with priests from the different parts of his diocese and during it consecrates the chrism and blesses the other holy oils. This Mass is therefore one of the chief expressions of the fullness of the bishop's priesthood and is looked on as a symbol of the close bond between the bishop and his priests. For the chrism the bishop consecrates is used to anoint the newly baptized and to trace the sign of Christ on those to be confirmed; the oil of catechumens is used to prepare and dispose them for baptism; the oil of the sick, to strengthen them amid their infirmities.

2. The Christian liturgy has adopted the Old Testament usage of anointing kings, priests, and prophets with consecratory oil because they prefigured Christ, whose name means "the anointed of the Lord."

Similarly, the chrism is a sign that Christians, incorporated by baptism into the paschal mystery of Christ, dying, buried, and rising with him,[2] are sharers in his kingly and prophetic priesthood and that by confirmation they receive the spiritual anointing of the Spirit who is given to them.

The oil of catechumens extends the effects of the baptismal exorcisms: it strengthens the candidates with the power to renounce the devil and sin before they go to the font of life for rebirth.

The oil of the sick, for the use of which James is the witness,[3] provides the sick with a remedy for both spiritual and bodily illness, so that they may have strength to bear up under evil and obtain pardon for their sins.

I. THE OILS

3. The matter suitable for sacrament is olive oil, or according to local conditions, another oil extracted from plants.

---

[1] See SC art. 41 [DOL 1 no. 41].
[2] See SC art. 6 [DOL 1 no. 6]
[3] See Jas 5:14.

4. The chrism is made of oil and some aromatic substance.

5. The chrism may be mixed either in private prior to the consecration or by the bishop during the liturgical rite itself.

II. THE MINISTER

6. Consecration of the chrism belongs exclusively to a bishop.

7. If the conference of bishops decides to retain its use, the oil of catechumens is blessed by the bishop together with the other oils at the chrism Mass.

However, in the case of the baptism of adults, priests have the faculty to bless the oil of catechumens before the anointing at the designated stage in the catechumenate.

8. The oil to be used in the anointing of the sick must be blessed for this purpose by the bishop or by a priest who has the faculty in virtue of the law itself or of its special concession to him by the Holy See.

In virtue of the law itself the following may bless the oil for use in the anointing of the sick:

a. those who are the equivalents in law to a diocesan bishop;

b. in the case of necessity, any priest, but only within the celebration of the sacrament.

III. TIME OF THE BLESSING

9. The blessing of the oil of the sick and of catechumens and the consecration of the chrism are carried out by the bishop as a rule on Holy Thursday at the proper Mass to be celebrated in the morning.

10. If it is difficult for the clergy and people to gather on that day, the blessing may be advanced to an earlier day, but still close to Easter. The proper chrism Mass is always used.

IV. PLACE OF THE BLESSING WITHIN THE MASS

11. In keeping with longstanding practice in the Latin liturgy, the blessing of the oil of the sick takes place before the end of the eucharistic prayer; the blessing of the oil of catechumens and the consecration of the chrism, after communion.

12. For pastoral reasons, however, it is permissible for the entire rite of blessing to take place after the liturgy of the word, according to the rite described below.

BLESSING OF OILS AND CONSECRATION OF THE CHRISM

PREPARATIONS

13. For the blessing of oils the following preparations are made in addition to what is needed for Mass:

In the sacristy or other appropriate place:
—vessels of oils;
—balsam or perfume for the preparation of the chrism if the bishop wishes to mix the chrism during the liturgical service;
—bread, wine, and water for Mass, which are carried with the oils before the preparation of the gifts.

In the sanctuary:
—table for the vessels of oil, placed so that the people may see the entire rite easily and take part in it;
—chair for the bishop, if the blessing takes place in front of the altar.

RITE OF BLESSING

14. The chrism Mass is always concelebrated. It is desirable that there be some priests from the various sections of the diocese among the priests who concelebrate with the bishop and are his witnesses and the co-workers in the ministry of the holy chrism.

15. The preparation of the bishop, the concelebrants, and other ministers, their entrance into the church, and everything from the beginning of Mass until the end of the liturgy of the word take place as indicated in the rite of concelebration. The deacons who take part in the blessing of oils walk ahead of the concelebrating priests to the altar.

PROCESSION WITH THE OILS AND THE GIFTS

16. After the renewal of commitment to priestly service the deacons and ministers appointed to carry the oils or, in their absence, some priests and ministers together with the faithful who will carry the bread, wine, and water, go in procession to the sacristy or other place where the oils and other offerings have been prepared. Returning to the altar, they follow this order: first the minister carrying the vessel of balsam, if the bishop wishes to prepare the chrism, then the minister with the vessel for the oil of the catechumens, if it is to be blessed, the minister with the vessel for the oil of the sick, lastly a deacon or priest carrying the oil for the chrism. The ministers who carry the bread, wine, and water for the celebration of the eucharist follow them.

HYMN

17. During the procession through the church, the choir leads the singing of the hymn "O Redeemer" or some other appropriate song, in place of the offertory song.

PRESENTATION OF THE OILS AND THE GIFTS

18. When the procession comes to the altar or the chair, the bishop receives the gifts. The deacon who carries the vessel of oil for the chrism shows it to the bishop, saying in a loud voice: **The oil for the holy chrism.** The bishop takes the vessel and gives it to one of the assisting deacons to place on the table. The same is done by those who carry the vessels for the oil of the sick and the oil of the catechumens. The first says: **The oil of the sick;** the second says: **The oil of catechumens.** The bishop takes the vessels in the same way, and the ministers place them on the table.

LITURGY OF THE EUCHARIST

19. Then the Mass continues, as in the rite of concelebration, until the end of the eucharistic prayer, unless the entire rite of blessing takes place immediately (see no. 12). In this case everything is done as described below (no. 26).

BLESSING OF THE OIL OF THE SICK

20. Before the bishop says **Through Christ our Lord/you give us all these gifts** in Eucharistic Prayer I, or the doxology **Through him** in the other eucharistic prayers, the one who carried the vessel for oil of the sick brings it to the altar and holds it in front of the bishop while he blesses the oil. The bishop says or sings this prayer:

Lord God, loving Father,
you bring healing to the sick
through your Son Jesus Christ.

Hear us as we pray to you in faith,
and send the Holy Spirit, man's Helper and Friend,
upon this oil, which nature has provided
to serve the needs of men.
May your blessing ✝
come upon all who are anointed with this oil,
that they may be freed from pain and illness
and made well again in body, mind, and soul.
Father, may this oil be blessed for our use
in the name of our Lord Jesus Christ
(who lives and reigns with you for ever and ever.
℟. Amen.)

The conclusion **Who lives and reigns with you** is said only when this blessing takes place outside the eucharistic prayer.

When Eucharistic Prayer I is used, the beginning of the prayer **Through Christ our Lord/you give us all these gifts** is changed to: **Through whom you give us all these gifts.**

After the blessing, the vessel with the oil of the sick is returned to its place, and the Mass continues until the communion rite is completed.

BLESSING OF THE OIL OF CATECHUMENS

21. After the prayer after communion, the ministers place the oils to be blessed on a table suitably located in the center of the sanctuary. The concelebrating priests stand around the bishop on either side, in a semicircle, and the other ministers stand behind him. The bishop then blesses the oil of catechumens, if it is to be blessed, and consecrates the chrism.

22. When everything is ready, the bishop faces the people and, with his hands extended, sings or says the following prayer:

Lord God, protector of all who believe in you,
bless ✝ this oil
and give wisdom and strength
to all who are anointed with it

in preparation for their baptism.
**Bring them to a deeper understanding of the gospel,
help them to accept the challenge of Christian living,
and lead them to the joy of new birth
in the family of your Church.
We ask this through Christ our Lord.
R̸. Amen.**

CONSECRATION OF THE CHRISM

23. Then the bishop pours the balsam or perfume in the oil
and mixes the chrism in silence, unless this was done
beforehand.

INVITATION

24. After this he sings or says the invitation:

**Let us pray
that God our almighty Father
will bless this oil
so that all who are anointed with it
may be inwardly transformed
and come to share in eternal salvation.**

CONSECRATORY PRAYER

25. Then the bishop may breathe over the opening of the
vessel of chrism. With his hands extended, he sings or says
one of the following consecratory prayers.

**God our maker,
source of all growth in holiness,
accept the joyful thanks and praise
we offer in the name of your Church.**

**In the beginning, at your command,
the earth produced fruit-bearing trees.
From the fruit of the olive tree
you have provided us with oil for holy chrism.
The prophet David sang of the life and joy
that the oil would bring us in the sacraments of your
love.**

After the avenging flood,
the dove returning to Noah with an olive branch
announced your gift of peace.
This was a sign of a greater gift to come.
Now the waters of baptism wash away the sins of
    men,
and by the anointing with olive oil
you make us radiant with your joy.

At your command,
Aaron was washed with water,
and your servant Moses, his brother,
anointed him priest.
This too foreshadowed greater things to come.
After your Son, Jesus Christ our Lord,
asked John for baptism in the waters of Jordan,
you sent the Spirit upon him
in the form of a dove
and by the witness of your own voice
you declared him to be your only, well-beloved Son.
In this you clearly fulfilled the prophecy of David,
that Christ would be anointed with the oil of gladness
beyond his fellow men.

All the celebrants extend their right hands toward the
chrism, without saying anything, until the end of the
prayer.

And so, Father, we ask you to bless ✛ this oil you
    have created.
Fill it with the power of your Holy Spirit
through Christ your Son.
It is from him that chrism takes its name
and with chrism you have anointed
for yourself priests and kings,
prophets and martyrs.

Make this chrism a sign of life and salvation
for those who are to be born again in the waters of
    baptism.
Wash away the evil they have inherited from sinful
    Adam,

and when they are anointed with this holy oil
make them temples of your glory,
radiant with the goodness of life
that has its source in you.

Through this sign of chrism
grant them royal, priestly, and prophetic honor,
and clothe them with incorruption.
Let this be indeed the chrism of salvation
for those who will be born again of water and the
     Holy Spirit.
May they come to share eternal life
in the glory of your kingdom.
We ask this through Christ our Lord.
℟. Amen.

Or:
Father, we thank you for the gifts
you have given us in your love:
we thank you for life itself and for the sacraments
that strengthen it and give it fuller meaning.

In the Old Covenant you gave your people
a glimpse of the power of this holy oil
and when the fullness of time had come
you brought that mystery to perfection
in the life of our Lord Jesus Christ, your Son.

By his suffering, dying, and rising to life
he saved the human race.
He sent your Spirit to fill the Church
with every gift needed to complete your saving work.

From that time forward,
through the sign of holy chrism,
you dispense your life and love to men.
By anointing them with the Spirit,
you strengthen all who have been reborn in baptism.
Through that anointing
you transform them into the likeness of Christ your
     Son
and give them a share

in his royal, priestly, and prophetic work.

All the concelebrants extend their right hands toward the chrism without saying anything, until the end of the prayer.

And so, Father, by the power of your love,
make this mixture of oil and perfume
a sign and source ✛ of your blessing.
Pour out the gifts of your Holy Spirit
on our brothers and sisters who will be anointed with
 it.
Let the splendor of holiness shine on the world
from every place and thing
signed with this oil.

Above all, Father, we pray
that through this sign of your anointing
you will grant increase to your Church
until it reaches the eternal glory
where you, Father, will be the all in all,
together with Christ your Son,
in the unity of the Holy Spirit,
for ever and ever.
℞. Amen.

26. When the entire rite of blessing of oils is to be celebrated after the liturgy of the word, at the end of the renewal of commitment to priestly service the bishop goes with the concelebrants to the table where the blessing of the oil of the sick and of the oil of the chrism are to take place, and everything is done as described above (nos. 20-25).

27. After the final blessing of the Mass, the bishop puts incense in the censer, and the procession to the sacristy is arranged.

The blessed oils are carried by the ministers immediately after the cross, and the choir and people sing some verses of the hymn "O Redeemer" or some other appropriate song.

28. In the sacristy the bishop may instruct the priests about the reverent use and safe custody of the holy oils.

DEDICATION OF A CHURCH
AND AN ALTAR

DEDICATION OF A CHURCH AND AN ALTAR

CHAPTER III
DEDICATION OF A CHURCH ALREADY IN GENERAL USE FOR SACRED CELEBRATIONS

Introduction (1-2)

Rite of Dedication (3-40)

Introductory Rites (3-12)
Entrance into the Church (3-7)
Blessing and Sprinkling of Water (8-10)
Hymn (11)
Opening Prayer (12)

Liturgy of the Word (13-16)

Prayer of Dedication and the Anointings (17-31)
Invitation to Prayer (17)
Litany of the Saints (18-20)
Depositing of the Relics (21)
Prayer of Dedication (22)
Anointing of the Altar and Walls of the Church (23-25)
Incensation of the Altar and the Church (26-28)
Lighting of the Altar and the Church (29-31)

Liturgy of the Eucharist (32-40)
Prayer over the Gifts (34)
Eucharistic Prayer (35-36)
[Inauguration of the Blessed Sacrament Chapel (36)]
Prayer after Communion (38)
Blessing and Dismissal (39-40)

CHAPTER IV
DEDICATION OF AN ALTAR

Introduction (1-30)

Nature and Dignity of the Altar (1-5)

Building of an Altar (6-11)

Celebration of the Dedication (12-23)
Minister of the Rite (12)
Choice of Day (13-14)
Mass of Dedication (15-16)
Parts of the Rite (17-23)

Adaptation of the Rite (24-25)
Adaptation within the Competence of the Conferences of Bishops (24)
Decisions within the Competence of the Ministers (25)

Pastoral Preparation (26)

Requisites for the Dedication of an Altar (27-30)

Rite of Dedication (31-64)

Introductory Rites (31-39)
Entrance into the Church (31-34)
Blessing and Sprinkling of Water (35-37)
Hymn (38)
Opening Prayer (39)

Liturgy of the Word (40-42)

Prayer of Dedication and the Anointings (43-56)
Invitation to Prayer (43)
Litany of the Saints (44-46)
Depositing of the Relics (47)
Prayer of Dedication (48)
Anointing of the Altar (49-52)
Incensation of the Altar (53)
Lighting of the Altar (54-56)

Liturgy of the Eucharist (57-64)
Prayer over the Gifts (59)
Eucharistic Prayer (60-61)
Prayer after Communion (62)
Blessing and Dismissal (63-64)

CHAPTER V
BLESSING OF A CHURCH

Introduction (1-7)

Rite of Blessing (8-28)

Introductory Rites (8-15)
Entrance into the Church (8-9)
Blessing and Sprinkling of Water (10-13)
Hymn (14)
Opening Prayer (15)

Liturgy of the Word (16-19)

Blessing of the Altar (20-22)

Liturgy of the Eucharist (23-26)
Blessing and Dismissal (27-28)

CHAPTER VI
BLESSING OF AN ALTAR

Introduction (1-7)

Rite of Blessing (8-13)

CHAPTER VII
BLESSING OF A CHALICE AND PATEN

Introduction (1-4)

Rite of Blessing within Mass (5-14)

Rite of Blessing outside Mass (15-23)

CHAPTER VIII
LITANY OF THE SAINTS

SACRED CONGREGATION FOR THE SACRAMENTS AND DIVINE WORSHIP

Prot. no. CD 300/77

DECREE

The rite for the dedication of a church and an altar is rightly considered to be among the most solemn of liturgical services. A church is the place where the Christian community is gathered to hear the word of God, to offer intercession and praise to him, and above all to celebrate the holy mysteries, and it is the place where the holy sacrament of the eucharist is kept. Thus it stands as a special kind of image of the Church itself, which is God's temple built from living stones. And the altar of a church, around which the holy people gather to take part in the Lord's sacrifice and to be refreshed at the heavenly meal, stands as a sign of Christ himself, who is the priest, the victim, and the altar of his own sacrifice.

These rites, found in the second book of the Roman Pontifical, were revised and simplified in 1961. Nevertheless it was judged necessary to revise the rites again and to adapt them to contemporary conditions in view of the purpose and the norms of the liturgical reform that Vatican Council II set in motion and fostered.

Pope Paul VI by his authority has approved the new *Ordo dedicationis ecclesiae et altaris* prepared by the Congregation for the Sacraments and Divine Worship. He has ordered it published and prescribed that it replace the rites now in the second book of the Roman Pontifical.

This Congregation, by mandate of the Pope, therefore publishes this *Ordo dedicationis ecclesiae et altaris*. In the Latin text it will be in effect as soon as it appears; in the vernacular, it will take effect, after the translations have been confirmed and approved by the Apostolic See, on the day determined by the conferences of bishops.

Anything to the contrary notwithstanding.

From the office of the Congregation for the Sacraments and Divine Worship, 29 May 1977, Pentecost.

James R. Cardinal Knox
Prefect

✠ Antonio Innocenti
Titular Archbishop of Eclano
Secretary

CHAPTER I

RITE OF LAYING THE FOUNDATION STONE OR BEGINNING WORK ON THE BUILDING OF A CHURCH

INTRODUCTION

1. When the building of a new church begins, it is desirable to celebrate a rite to ask God's blessing for the success of the work and to remind the people that the structure built of stone will be a visible sign of the living Church, God's building that is formed of the people themselves.[1]

In accordance with liturgical tradition, this rite consists of the blessing of the site of the new church and the blessing and laying of the foundation stone. When there is to be no foundation stone because of the particular architecture of the building, the rite of the blessing of the site of the new church should still be celebrated in order to dedicate the beginning of the work to God.

2. The rite for the laying of a foundation stone or for beginning a new church may be celebrated on any day except during the Easter triduum. But the preference should be for a day when the people can be present in large numbers.

3. The bishop of the diocese is rightly the one to celebrate the rite. If he cannot do so himself, he shall entrust the function to another bishop or a priest, especially to one who is his associate and assistant in the pastoral care of the diocese or of the community for which the new church is to be built.

4. Notice of the date and hour of the celebration should be given to the people in good time. The parish priest (pastor) or others concerned should instruct them in the meaning of the rite and the reverence to be shown toward the church that is to be built for them.

[1]See 1 Cor 3:9. LG no. 6 [DOL 4 no. 138].

It is also desirable that the people be asked to give their generous and willing support in the building of the church.

5. Insofar as possible, the area for the erection of the church should be marked out clearly. It should be possible to walk about without difficulty.

6. In the place where the altar will be located, a wooden cross of suitable height is fixed in the ground.

7. For the celebration of the rite the following should be prepared:
—The Roman Pontifical and Lectionary;
—chair for the bishop;
—depending on the circumstances, the foundation stone, which by tradition is a rectangular cornerstone, together with cement and the tools for setting the stone in the foundation;
—container of holy water with sprinkler;
—censer, incense boat and spoon;
—processional cross and torches for the servers.

Sound equipment should be set up so that the assembly can clearly hear the readings, prayers, and instructions.

8. For the celebration of the rite the vestments are white or some festive color. The following should be prepared:
—for the bishop: alb, stole, cope, miter, and pastoral staff;
—for the priest, when one presides over the celebration: alb, stole, and cope;
—for the deacons: albs, stoles, and, if opportune, dalmatics;
—for other ministers: albs or other lawfully approved dress.

RITE OF BLESSING

APPROACH TO THE CONSTRUCTION SITE
9. The assembly of the people and the approach to the construction site take place, according to circumstances of time and place, in one of the two ways described below.

A. First Form: Procession

10. At a convenient hour the people assemble in a suitable place, from which they will go in procession to the site.

11. The bishop, in his vestments and with the miter and pastoral staff, proceeds with the ministers to the place where the people are assembled. Putting aside the pastoral staff and miter he greets the people, saying:

The grace of our Lord Jesus Christ
and the love of God
and the fellowship of the Holy Spirit
be with you all.
℟. And also with you.

Other suitable words taken preferably from sacred Scripture may be used.

12. Then the bishop briefly instructs the people on their participation in the celebration and explains to them the meaning of the rite.

13. When the bishop has finished the instruction, he says:

Let us pray.

All pray in silence for a brief period. The bishop then continues:

Lord,
you built a holy Church,
founded upon the apostles
with Jesus Christ its cornerstone.

Grant that your people,
gathered in your name,
may fear and love you
and grow as the temple of your glory.

May they always follow you,
until, with you at their head,
they arrive at last in your heavenly city.

We ask this through Christ our Lord.
℟. Amen.

14. When the bishop has finished the prayer, he receives the miter and pastoral staff, and, should the occasion demand, the deacon says:

Let us go forth in peace.

The procession takes place in the usual way: the crossbearer leads between two servers with lighted torches; the clergy follow, then the bishop with the assisting deacons and other ministers, and lastly, the congregation. As the procession proceeds the following anthiphon is sung with Psalm 84.

My soul is yearning for the courts of the Lord (alleluia).

Another appropriate song may be sung.

Then the reading of the word of God takes place as described below in nos. 18-22.

B. Second Form: Station at the Construction Site of the New Church

15. If the procession cannot take place or seems inappropriate, the people assemble at the construction site of the new church. When the people are assembled the following acclamation is sung.

Eternal peace be yours.
Let the Father's peace unite you in his love.

Abiding peace be yours.
Let the Word be peace to those who bear his name.

Lasting peace be yours.
Let the Spirit's peace comfort all the world.

Another appropriate song may be sung.

Meanwhile, the bishop, in his vestments and with miter and pastoral staff, approaches the people. Putting aside the pastoral staff and miter, he greets the people, saying:

The grace of our Lord Jesus Christ
and the love of God
and the fellowship of the Holy Spirit
be with you all.
℟. And also with you.

Other suitable words taken preferably from sacred Scripture may be used.

16. Then the bishop briefly instructs the people on their participation in the celebration and explains to them the meaning of the rite.

17. When the bishop has finished the instruction, he says:

Let us pray.

All pray in silence for a brief period. The bishop then continues:

Lord,
you built a holy Church,
founded upon the apostles
with Jesus Christ its cornerstone.

Grant that your people,
gathered in your name,
may fear and love you
and grow as the temple of your glory.

May they always follow you,
until, with you at their head,
they arrive at last in your heavenly city.

We ask this through Christ our Lord.
℟. Amen.

READING OF THE WORD OF GOD

18. Then one or more relevant passages of sacred Scripture are read, chosen especially from those in *The Lectionary* (nos. 704 and 706) for the rite of the dedication of a church, with an appropriate intervening responsorial psalm or another appropriate song. However, it is in keeping with the occasion, especially if a foundation stone is used in the rite, to read one of the following passages.

19. READINGS FROM SACRED SCRIPTURE

1. 1 Kings 5:2-18
At the king's orders they quarried huge stones, special stones, for the laying of the temple foundations.

2. Isaiah 28:16-17
See how I lay in Zion a stone of witness, a precious cornerstone, a foundation stone.

3. Acts 4:8-12
Jesus, the one you crucified, has proved to be the keystone.

4. 1 Corinthians 10:1-6
And that rock was Christ.

20. RESPONSORIAL PSALMS

1. Psalm 24:1-2, 3-4ab, 5-6
℟. (2 Chronicles 7:16a) **I have chosen and sanctified this place.**

2. Psalm 42:3, 5bcd; Psalm 43:3-4
℟. (See Psalm 43:3) **Lord, may your truth lead me to your holy mountain.**

3. Psalm 87:1-3, 4-6, 6-7
℟. (See 1) **The city of God is founded on the holy mountains.**

4. Psalm 100:2, 3, 5
℟. (See Ezechiel 37:27) **I will make my dwelling place among the people.**

5. Psalm 118:1-2, 16ab-17, 22-23
℟. (See 1 Corinthians 3:11) **There is no other foundation than Christ Jesus.**

21. GOSPEL

1. Matthew 7:21-29
A house built on rock and a house built on sand.

2. Matthew 16:13-18
On this rock I will build my Church.

3. Mark 12:1-12
It was the stone rejected by the builders that became the keystone.

4. Luke 6:46-49
He laid the foundation on rock.

22. When the readings are finished the homily is given, in which the biblical readings are elucidated and the significance of the rite explained: Christ is the cornerstone of the Church, and the temple that is going to be built by the living Church of the community of believers will be at once the house of God and the house of God's people.

23. After the homily, according to the custom of the place, the document of the blessing of the foundation stone and of the beginning of the building of the church may be read; it is signed by the bishop and by representatives of those who are going to work on the building of the church, and together with the stone, is enclosed in the foundations.

BLESSING OF THE SITE OF THE NEW CHURCH

24. When the homily is finished, the bishop takes off the miter, rises, and blesses the site of the new church, saying:

Let us pray.

Lord,
you fill the entire world with your presence
that your name may be hallowed through all the earth.

Bless all those
who have worked or contributed
to provide this site (property, land)
on which a church will be built.

Today may they rejoice in a work just begun,
soon may they celebrate the sacraments in your temple,
and in time to come may they praise you for ever in
    heaven.

We ask this through Christ our Lord.
℟. Amen.

25. Then the bishop puts on the miter and sprinkles the site of the new church with holy water. To do this he may stand in the middle of the site or go in procession around the foundations with the ministers; in the latter case the following antiphon is sung with Psalm 48.

The walls of Jerusalem will be made of precious stones, and its towers built with gems (alleluia).

Another appropriate song may be sung.

BLESSING AND LAYING OF THE FOUNDATION STONE

26. When the site has been blessed, if a foundation stone is to be laid, it is blessed and placed in position as described below in nos. 27-29; otherwise the conclusion of the rite takes place immediately as indicated in nos. 30-31.

27. The bishop goes to the place where the foundation stone is to be laid and, taking off the miter, blesses the stone, saying:

Let us pray.

Father,
the prophet Daniel spoke of your Son,
as a stone wondrously hewn from a mountain.

The apostle Paul spoke of him,
as a stone firmly founded.

Bless ✠ this foundation stone
to be laid in Christ's name.

You appointed him
the beginning and the end of all things.

May this work begin, continue,
and be brought to fulfillment in him,
for he is Lord for ever and ever.
℟. Amen.

Then the bishop may sprinkle the stone with holy water and incense it. Afterward he receives the miter again.

28. When he has finished, the bishop lays the stone on the foundations in silence or, if he wishes, saying these or similar words:

With faith in Jesus Christ
we lay this stone
on which a church will rise.

May it be a place of sacrament
and a source of grace
to the glory of the Father
who with the Son and Holy Spirit
lives and reigns for ever and ever.
℟. Amen.

29. A stone mason then fixes the stone in with mortar. Meanwhile, if the occasion demands, the following antiphon is sung.

The house of the Lord is firmly built on solid rock (alleluia).

Another appropriate song may be sung.

CONCLUDING RITE

30. When the singing is finished, the bishop takes off the miter, and invites the people to pray the general intercessions, in these or similar words:

Brothers and sisters, now that we have laid the cornerstone of our new church, let us pray to God, our Father.

All pray in silence for a brief period.

That he may transform into a living temple of his glory all whom he has gathered here and who look upon Christ as the cornerstone of their faith, let us pray to the Lord:
℟. **Bless and watch over your Church, O Lord.**

That God in his power may overcome the division and sin which separate his people so that they may ultimately worship as one, let us pray to the Lord: ℟.

That he may ground upon the bedrock of his Church the faith of all those who have undertaken the work on this building, let us pray to the Lord: ℟.

That those who are prevented from building places of worship may bear witness to the Lord by conducting themselves as living temples of glory and faith, let us pray to the Lord: ℟.

That all here present may be cleansed by his divine power and come to share in the celebration of his holy mysteries, let us pray to the Lord: ℟.

Then the bishop may introduce the Lord's Prayer in these or similar words:

Let us join the voice of the Church with that of Christ in praying to the Father using those words which the Son has given us. And so, with one voice, let us say:

Our Father . . .

The bishop continues immediately:

God of love,
we praise your holy name,
for you have made us your temple by baptism
and inspire us to build on earth
churches dedicated to your worship.

Look favorably upon your children,
for they have come with joy
to begin work on this new church.

Enable them to grow into the temple of your glory,
until, shaped anew by your grace,
they are gathered by your hand into your heavenly city.

We ask this through Christ our Lord.
℞. Amen.

31. When the bishop has received the miter and pastoral staff, he blesses the people in the usual way.

The deacon dismisses them, saying:
Go in peace.
℞. Thanks be to God.

CHAPTER II

DEDICATION OF A CHURCH

INTRODUCTION

NATURE AND DIGNITY OF CHURCHES

1. Through his death and resurrection, Christ became the true and perfect temple[1] of the New Covenant and gathered together a people to be his own.

This holy people, made one as the Father, Son, and Holy Spirit are one, is the Church,[2] that is, the temple of God built of living stones, where the Father is worshiped in spirit and in truth.[3]

Rightly, then, from early times "church" has also been the name given to the building in which the Christian community gathers to hear the word of God, to pray together, to receive the sacraments, and to celebrate the eucharist.

2. Because the church is a visible building, it stands as a special sign of the pilgrim Church on earth and reflects the Church dwelling in heaven.

When a church is erected as a building destined solely and permanently for assembling the people of God and for carrying out sacred functions, it is fitting that it be dedicated to God with a solemn rite, in accordance with the ancient custom of the Church.

3. The very nature of a church demands that it be suited to sacred celebrations, dignified, evincing a noble beauty, not mere costly display, and it should stand as a sign and symbol of heavenly realities. "The general plan of the sacred edifice should be such that in some way it conveys the image of the gathered assembly. It should also allow the participants to take the place most appropriate to them and assist all to

---

[1]See Jn 2:21.
[2]See Cyprian, *De oratione dominica* 23: PL 4, 553. LG no. 4: AAS 57 (1965) 7; ConstDecrDecl 96.
[3]See Jn 4:23.

carry out their individual functions properly." Moreover, in what concerns the sanctuary, the altar, the chair, the lectern, and the place for the reservation of the blessed sacrament, the norms of the General Instruction of the Roman Missal are to be followed.[4]

Also, the norms must be observed that concern things and places destined for the celebration of other sacraments, especially baptism and penance.[5]

TITULAR OF A CHURCH AND THE RELICS OF THE SAINTS TO BE PLACED IN IT

4. Every church to be dedicated must have a titular. This may be: the Blessed Trinity; our Lord Jesus Christ invoked according to a mystery of his life or a title already accepted in the liturgy; the Holy Spirit; the Blessed Virgin Mary, likewise invoked according to some appellation already accepted in the liturgy; one of the angels; or, finally, a saint inscribed in the Roman Martyrology or in a duly approved Appendix. A blessed may not be the titular without an indult of the Apostolic See. A church should have one titular only, unless it is a question of saints who are listed together in the Calendar.

5. The tradition in the Roman liturgy of placing relics of martyrs or other saints beneath the altar should be preserved, if possible.[6] But the following should be noted:
a) Such relics should be of size sufficient for them to be recognized as parts of human bodies. Hence excessively small relics of one or more saints must not be placed beneath the altar.
b) The greatest care must be taken to determine whether the relics in question are authentic. It is better for an altar to be dedicated without relics than to have relics of doubtful authenticity placed beneath it.
c) A reliquary must not be placed upon the altar or set into the table of the altar; it must be placed beneath the table of the altar, as the design of the altar permits.

[4]See GIRM nos. 253, 257, 258, 259–267, 271, 272, 276–277 [DOL 208 nos. 1643, 1647, 1648, 1649–57, 1661, 1662, 1666–67]. See also Roman Ritual, *Holy Communion and Worship of the Eucharist outside Mass* nos. 6 and 9–11 [DOL 279 nos. 2198 and 2201–03].
[5]See *Rite of Baptism for Children* no. 25 [DOL 295 no. 2309]; *Rite of Penance* no. 12 [DOL 368 no. 3077].
[6]See GIRM no. 266 [DOL 208 no. 1656].

CELEBRATION OF THE DEDICATION

MINISTER OF THE RITE

6. Since the bishop has been entrusted with the care of the particular Church, it is his responsibility to dedicate to God new churches built in his diocese.

If he cannot himself preside at the rite, he shall entrust this function to another bishop, especially to one who is his associate and assistant in the pastoral care of the community for which the church has been built or, in altogether special circumstances, to a priest, to whom he shall give a special mandate.

CHOICE OF DAY

7. A day should be chosen for the dedication of the new church when the people can be present in large numbers, especially a Sunday. Since the theme of the dedication pervades this entire rite, the dedication of a new church may not take place on days on which it is altogether improper to disregard the mystery then being commemorated: the Easter triduum, Christmas, Epiphany, Ascension, Pentecost, Ash Wednesday, the weekdays of Holy Week, and All Souls.

MASS OF THE DEDICATION

8. The celebration of the eucharist is inseparably bound up with the rite of the dedication of a church; when a church is dedicated therefore the liturgical texts of the day are omitted and texts proper to the rite are used for both the liturgy of the word and the liturgy of the eucharist.

9. It is fitting that the bishop concelebrate the Mass with the priests who take part with him in the rite of dedication and those who have been given charge over the parish or the community for which the church has been built.

OFFICE OF THE DEDICATION

10. The day on which a church is dedicated is kept as a solemnity in that church.

The office of the dedication of a church is celebrated, beginning with evening prayer I. When the rite of depositing relics takes place, it is highly recommended to keep a vigil at the relics of the martyr or saint that are to be placed beneath the altar; the best way of doing this is to have the office of readings, taken from the respective common or proper. This vigil should be properly adapted to encourage the people's participation, but the requirements of the law are respected.[7]

PARTS OF THE RITE

A. Entrance into the Church

11. The rite of the dedication begins with the entrance into the church; this may take place in one of the three following ways; the one best suited to the circumstances of time and place is to be used.

—*Procession* to the church to be dedicated: all assemble in a nearby church or other suitable place, from which the bishop, the ministers, and the congregation proceed to the church to be dedicated, praying and singing.

—*Solemn entrance:* if the procession cannot take place or seems inopportune, the community gathers at the entrance of the church.

—*Simple entrance:* the congregation assembles in the church itself; the bishop, the concelebrants, and the ministers enter from the sacristy in the usual way.

Two rituals are most significant in the entrance into a new church:
a) The handing over of a church: representatives of those who have been involved in the building of the church hand it over to the bishop.
b) The sprinkling of the church: the bishop blesses water and with it sprinkles the people, who are the spiritual temple, then the walls of the church, and finally, the altar.

B. Liturgy of the Word

12. Three readings are used in the liturgy of the word. The texts are chosen from those in the Lectionary (nos. 704 and 706) for the rite of the dedication of a church.

The first reading is always, even during the Easter season, the passage of Nehemiah that tells of the people of Jerusalem

[7]See GILH nos. 70–73 [DOL 426 nos. 3500–03].

gathered in the presence of the scribe Ezra to hear the proclamation of the law of God (Neh 8:1–4a, 5–6, 8–10).

13. After the readings the bishop gives the homily, in which
he explains the biblical readings and the meaning of the dedication of a church.

The profession of faith is always said. The general intercessions are omitted, since the Litany of the Saints is sung in
their place.

C. Prayer of Dedication and the Anointing of the Church and
the Altar
14. If it is to take place, the relics of a martyr are deposited
after the singing of the Litany of the Saints, to signify that
the sacrifice of the members has its source in the sacrifice of
the Head.[8] When relics of a martyr are not available, relics of
another saint may be deposited in the altar.

15. The celebration of the eucharist is the most important
and the one necessary for the dedication of a church. Nevertheless, in accordance with the tradition of the Church in
both East and West, a special prayer of dedication is also
said. This prayer is a sign of the intention to dedicate the
church to the Lord for all times and a petition for his blessing.

16. The rites of anointing, incensing, covering, and lighting
the altar express in visible signs several aspects of the invisible work that the Lord accomplishes through the Church in
its celebration of the divine mysteries, especially the eucharist.

a) *Anointing* of the altar and the walls of the church:
—The anointing with chrism makes the altar a symbol of
Christ, who, before all others, is and is called "The Anointed
One"; for the Father anointed him with the Holy Spirit and

---

[8]See RM, Common of Martyrs 8, prayer over the gifts. Ambrose, *Epistula*
22:13: PL 16, 1023: "Let the triumphant victims rest in the place where
Christ is victim: he, however, who suffered for all, upon the altar; they, who
have been redeemed by his sufferings, beneath the altar." See Ps. Maximus
of Turin, *Sermo* 78: PL 57, 689–690. Rv 6:9: "I saw underneath the altar the
souls of all the people who had been killed on account of the word of God,
for witnessing to it."

constituted him the High Priest so that on the altar of his body he might offer the sacrifice of his life for the salvation of all.
—The anointing of the church signifies that it is given over entirely and perpetually to Christian worship. In keeping with liturgical tradition, there are twelve anointings, or, where it is more convenient, four, as a symbol that the church is an image of the holy city of Jerusalem.

b) *Incense* is burned on the altar to signify that Christ's sacrifice, there perpetuated in mystery, ascends to God as an odor of sweetness and also to signify that the people's prayers rise up pleasing and acceptable, reaching the throne of God.[9]
The incensation of the nave of the church indicates that the dedication makes it a house of prayer, but the people of God are incensed first, because they are the living temple in which each faithful member is a spiritual altar.[10]

c) *The covering of the altar* indicates that the Christian altar is the altar of the eucharistic sacrifice and the table of the Lord; around it priests and people, by one and the same rite but with a difference of function, celebrate the memorial of Christ's death and resurrection and partake of his supper. For this reason the altar is prepared as the table of the sacrificial banquet and adorned as for a feast. Thus the dressing of the altar clearly signifies that it is the Lord's table at which all God's people joyously meet to be refreshed with divine food, namely, the body and blood of Christ sacrificed.

d) *The lighting of the altar*, which is followed by the lighting of the church, reminds us that Christ is "a light to enlighten the nations";[11] his brightness shines out in the Church and through it in the whole human family.

D. Celebration of the Eucharist
17. After the altar has been prepared, the bishop celebrates the eucharist, the principal and the most ancient part of the whole rite,[12] because the celebration of the eucharist is in the closest harmony with the rite of the dedication of a church:

[9]See Rv 8:3–4.
[10]See Rom 12:1.
[11]Lk 2:32.
[12]See Pope Vigilius, *Epistula ad Profuturum episcopum* 4: PL 84, 832.

—For the celebration of the eucharistic sacrifice achieves the end for which the church was built and the altar erected and expresses this end by particularly clear signs.

—Furthermore, the eucharist, which sanctifies the hearts of those who receive it, in a sense consecrates the altar and the place of celebration, as the ancient Fathers of the Church often assert: "This altar should be an object of awe: by nature it is stone, but it is made holy when it receives the body of Christ."[13]

—Finally, the bond closely connecting the dedication of a church with the celebration of the eucharist is likewise evident from the fact that the Mass for the dedication has its own preface, which is a central part of the rite itself.

ADAPTATION OF THE RITE

ADAPTATIONS WITHIN THE COMPETENCE OF THE CONFERENCES OF BISHOPS

18. The conferences of bishops may adapt this rite, as required, to the character of each region, but in such a way that nothing of its dignity and solemnity is lost.

However, the following are to be respected:
a) The celebration of the Mass with the proper preface and prayer for a dedication must never be omitted.
b) Rites that have a special meaning and force from liturgical tradition (see no. 16) must be retained, unless weighty reasons stand in the way, but the wording may be suitably adapted if necessary.

With regard to adaptations, the competent ecclesiastical authority is to consult the Holy See and introduce adaptations with its consent.[14]

ADAPTATIONS WITHIN THE COMPETENCE OF THE MINISTERS

19. It is for the bishop and for those in charge of the celebration of the rite:

---

[13]John Chrysostom, *Homilia 20 in 2 Cor.* 3:PG 61, 540.
[14]See SC art. 40 [DOL 1 no. 40].

—to decide the manner of entrance into the church (see no. 11);

—to determine the manner of handing over the new church to the bishop (no. 11);

—to decide whether to have the depositing of relics of the saints. The decisive consideration is the spiritual good of the community; the prescriptions in no. 5 must be followed.

It is for the rector of the church to be dedicated, helped by those who assist him in the pastoral work, to decide and prepare everything concerning the readings, singing, and other pastoral aids to foster the fruitful participation of the people and to ensure a dignified celebration.

PASTORAL PREPARATION

20. In order that the people may take part fully in the rite of dedication, the rector of the church to be dedicated and others experienced in the pastoral ministry are to instruct them on the import of the celebration and its spiritual, ecclesial, and evangelizing power.

Accordingly, the people are to be instructed about the various parts of the church and their use, the rite of dedication, and the chief liturgical symbols employed in it. Thus led by suitable pastoral resources to a full understanding of the meaning of the dedication of a church through its rites and prayers, they will take an active, intelligent, and devout part in the sacred service.

REQUISITES FOR THE DEDICATION OF A CHURCH

21. For the celebration of the rite the following should be prepared:

a. *In the place of assembly:*
—The Roman Pontifical;
—processional cross;
—if relics of the saints are to be carried in procession, the items indicated in no. 24 a.

b. *In the sacristy or in the sanctuary or in the body of the church to be dedicated,* as each situation requires:
—The Roman Missal;
—The Lectionary;
—container of water to be blessed and sprinkler;
—containers with the chrism;
—towels for wiping the table of the altar;
—if needed, a waxed linen cloth or waterproof covering of the same size as the altar;
—basin and jug of water, towels, and all that is needed for washing the bishop's hands and those of the priests after they have anointed the walls of the church;
—linen gremial;
—brazier for burning incense or aromatic spices; or grains of incense and small candles to burn on the altar;
—censer, incense boat and spoon;
—chalice, corporal, purificators, and hand towel;
—bread, wine, and water for the celebration of Mass;
—altar cross, unless there is already a cross in the sanctuary or the cross that is carried in the entrance procession is to be placed near the altar;
—altar cloth, candles, and candlesticks;
—flowers, if opportune.

22. It is praiseworthy to keep the ancient custom of hanging on the walls of the church crosses made of stone, brass, or other suitable material or of having the crosses carved on the walls. Thus twelve or four crosses should be provided, depending on the number of anointings (see no. 16), and fixed here and there at a suitable height on the walls of the church. Beneath each cross a small bracket should be fitted and in it a small candlestick is placed, with a candle to be lighted.

23. For the Mass of the dedication the vestments are white or of some festive color. The following should be prepared:
—for the bishop: alb, stole, chasuble, miter, pastoral staff, and pallium, if the bishop has the right to wear one;
—for the concelebrating priests: the vestments for concelebrating Mass;
—for the deacons: albs, stoles, and dalmatics;

—for other ministers: albs or other lawfully approved dress.

24. If relics of the saints are to be placed beneath the altar, the following should be prepared:

a. *In the place of assembly:*
—reliquary containing the relics, placed between flowers and lights. When the simple entrance is used, the reliquary may be placed in a suitable part of the sanctuary before the rite begins;
—for the deacons who will carry the relics to be deposited: albs, red stoles, if the relics are those of a martyr, or white in other cases, and, if available, dalmatics. If the relics are carried by priests, then in place of dalmatics chasubles should be prepared.

The relics may also be carried by other ministers, vested in albs or other lawfully approved dress.

b. *In the sanctuary:*
—a small table on which the reliquary is placed during the first part of the dedication rite.

c. *In the sacristy:*
—a sealant or cement to close the cover of the aperture. In addition, a stonemason should be on hand to close the depository of the relics at the proper time.

25. The record of the dedication of the church should be drawn up in duplicate, signed by the bishop, the rector of the church, and representatives of the local community; one copy is to be kept in the diocesan archives, the other in the archives of the church. Where the depositing of relics takes place, a third copy of the record should be made, to be placed at the proper time in the reliquary.

In this record mention should be made of the day, month, and year of the church's dedication, the name of the bishop who celebrated the rite, also the titular of the church and, where applicable, the names of the martyrs or saints whose relics have been deposited beneath the altar.

Moreover, in a suitable place in the church, an inscription should be placed stating the day, month, and year when the dedication took place, the titular of the church, and the name of the bishop who celebrated the rite.

ANNIVERSARY OF THE DEDICATION

A. ANNIVERSARY OF THE DEDICATION OF THE CATHEDRAL CHURCH

26. In order that the importance and dignity of the local Church may stand out with greater clarity, the anniversary of the dedication of its cathedral is to be celebrated, with the rank of a solemnity in the cathedral itself, with the rank of a feast in the other churches of the dioceses, on the date on which the dedication of the church recurs.[15] If this date is always impeded, the celebration is assigned to the nearest date open.

It is desirable that in the cathedral church on the anniversary the bishop concelebrate the eucharist with the chapter of canons or the priests' senate and with the participation of as many of the people as possible.

B. ANNIVERSARY OF THE DEDICATION OF A PARTICULAR CHURCH

27. The anniversary of a church's dedication is celebrated with the rank of a solemnity.[16]

RITE OF DEDICATION

INTRODUCTORY RITES

ENTRANCE INTO THE CHURCH

28. The entry into the church to be dedicated is made, according to circumstances of time and place, in one of the three ways described below.

A. First Form: Procession

29. The door of the church to be dedicated should be closed. At a convenient hour the people assemble in a neighboring church or other suitable place from which the

---

[15]See GNLYC, Table of Liturgical Days, I, 4 b and II, 8 b [DOL 442 no. 3825].
[16]See GNLYC, Table of Liturgical Days, I, 4 b [DOL 442 no. 3825].

procession may proceed to the church. The relics of the martyrs or saints, if they are to be placed beneath the altar, are prepared in the place where the people assemble.

30. The bishop, the concelebrating priests, the deacons, and ministers, each in appropriate vestments, proceed to the place where the people are assembled. Putting aside the pastoral staff and miter, the bishop greets the people, saying:

The grace and peace of God
be with all of you
in his holy Church.
℟. And also with you.

Other suitable words preferably from sacred Scripture may be used.

Then the bishop addresses the people in these or similar words:

Brothers and sisters in Christ, this is a day of rejoicing: we have come together to dedicate this church by offering within it the sacrifice of Christ.

May we open our hearts and minds to receive his word with faith; may our fellowship born in the one font of baptism and sustained at the one table of the Lord, become the one temple of his Spirit, as we gather round his altar in love.

31. When he has finished addressing the people, the bishop receives the miter and pastoral staff and the procession to the church to be dedicated begins. No lights are used apart from those which surround the relics of the saints, nor is incense used either in the procession or in the Mass before the rite of the incensation and the lighting of the altar and the church (see below, nos. 66-71.) The crossbearer leads the procession; the ministers follow; then the deacons or priests with the relics of the saints, ministers, or the faithful accompanying them on either side with lighted torches; then the concelebrating priests; then the bishop with two deacons; and lastly, the congregation.

32. As the procession proceeds, the following antiphon is sung with Psalm 122.

Let us go rejoicing to the house of the Lord.

Another appropriate song may be sung.

33. At the threshold of the church the procession comes to a halt. Representatives of those who have been involved in the building of the church (members of the parish or of the diocese, contributors, architects, workers) hand over the building to the bishop, offering him according to place and circumstances either the legal documents for possession of the building, or the keys, or the plan of the building, or the book in which the progress of the work is described and the names of those in charge of it and the names of the workers recorded. One of the representatives addresses the bishop and the community in a few words, pointing out, if need be, what the new church expresses in its art and in its own special design.

If the door is closed, the bishop then calls upon the priest to whom the pastoral care of the church has been entrusted to open the door.

34. When the door is unlocked, the bishop invites the people to enter the church in these or similar words:

Go within his gates giving thanks, enter his courts with songs of praise.

Then, preceded by the crossbearer, the bishop and the assembly enter the church. As the procession enters, the following antiphon is sung with Psalm 24.

Lift high the ancient portals. The King of glory enters.

Another appropriate song may be sung.

35. The bishop, without kissing the altar, goes to the chair; the concelebrants, deacons, and ministers go to the places assigned to them in the sanctuary. The relics of the saints are placed in a suitable part of the sanctuary between lighted torches. Water is then blessed with the rite described below, nos. 48-50.

B. Second Form: Solemn Entrance

36. If the procession cannot take place or seems inappropriate, the people assemble at the door of the church to be dedicated, where the relics of the saints have been placed beforehand.

37. Preceded by the crossbearer, the bishop and the concelebrating priests, the deacons, and the ministers, each in appropriate vestments, approach the church door, where the people are assembled. The door of the church should be closed, and the bishop, concelebrants, deacons, and ministers should approach it from outside.

38. Putting aside the pastoral staff and miter, the bishop greets the people, saying:

The grace and peace of God
be with all of you
in his holy Church.
℟. And also with you.

Other suitable words taken preferably from sacred Scripture may be used.

Then the bishop addresses the people in these or similar words:

Brothers and sisters in Christ, this is a day of rejoicing: we have come together to dedicate this church by offering within it the sacrifice of Christ.

May we open our hearts and minds to receive his word with faith; may our fellowship born in the one font of baptism and sustained at the one table of the Lord, become the one temple of his Spirit, as we gather round his altar in love.

39. When the bishop has finished addressing the people, he puts on the miter and, if it seems appropriate, the following antiphon is sung with Psalm 122.

Let us go rejoicing to the house of the Lord.

Another appropriate song may be sung.

40. Then representatives of those who have been involved in the building of the church (members of the parish or of the diocese, contributors, architects, workers) hand over the building to the bishop, offering him according to place and circumstances either the legal documents for possession of the building, or the keys, or the plan of the building, or the book in which the progress of the work is described and the

names of those in charge of it and the names of the workers recorded. One of the representatives addresses the bishop and the community in a few words, pointing out, if need be, what the new church expresses in its art and in its own special design.

If the door is closed, the bishop then calls upon the priest to whom the pastoral care of the church has been entrusted to open the door.

41. The bishop takes the pastoral staff and invites the people to enter the church in these or similar words:

Go within his gates giving thanks, enter his courts with songs of praise.

Then, preceded by the crossbearer, the bishop and the assembly enter the church. As the procession enters, the following antiphon is sung with Psalm 24.

Lift high the ancient portals. The King of glory enters.

Another appropriate song may be sung.

42. The bishop, without kissing the altar, goes to the chair; the concelebrants, deacons, and ministers go to the places assigned to them in the sanctuary. The relics of the saints are placed in a suitable part of the sanctuary between lighted torches. Water is then blessed with the rite described below, in nos. 48-50.

C. Third Form: Simple Entrance

43. If the solemn entrance cannot take place, the simple entrance is used. When the people are assembled, the bishop and the concelebrating priests, the deacons, and the ministers, each in appropriate vestments, preceded by the crossbearer, go from the sacristy through the main body of the church to the sanctuary.

44. If there are relics of the saints to be placed beneath the altar, these are brought in the entrance procession to the sanctuary from the sacristy or the chapel where since the vigil they have been exposed for the veneration of the people. For a just cause, before the celebration begins, the relics may be placed between lighted torches in a suitable part of the sanctuary.

45. As the procession proceeds, the entrance antiphon is sung with Psalm 122.

God in his holy dwelling, God who has gathered us together in his house: he will strengthen and console his people.

Or:

Let us go rejoicing to the house of the Lord.

Another appropriate song may be sung.

46. When the procession reaches the sanctuary, the relics of the saints are placed between lighted torches in a suitable place. The concelebrating priests, the deacons, and the ministers go to the places assigned to them; the bishop, without kissing the altar, goes to the chair. Then, putting aside the pastoral staff and miter, he greets the people, saying:

**The grace and peace of God
be with all of you
in his holy Church.
℟. And also with you.**

Other suitable words taken preferably from sacred Scripture may be used.

47. Then representatives of those who have been involved in the building of the church (members of the parish or of the diocese, contributors, architects, workers) hand over the building to the bishop, offering him according to place and circumstances either the legal documents for possession of the building, or the keys, or the plan of the building, or the book in which the progress of the work is described and the names of those in charge of it and the names of the workers recorded. One of the representatives addresses the bishop and the community in a few words, pointing out, if need be, what the new church expresses in its art and in its own special design.

BLESSING AND SPRINKLING OF WATER

48. When the entrance rite is completed, the bishop blesses water with which to sprinkle the people as a sign of repentance and as a reminder of their baptism, and to purify the walls and the altar of the new church. The ministers bring the

vessel with the water to the bishop who stands at the chair. The bishop invites all to pray, in these or similar words:

Brothers and sisters in Christ, in this solemn rite of dedication, let us ask the Lord our God to bless this water created by his hand.

It is a sign of our repentance, a reminder of our baptism, and a symbol of the cleansing of these walls and this altar.

May the grace of God help us to remain faithful members of his Church, open to the Spirit we have received.

All pray in silence for a brief period. The bishop then continues:

**God of mercy,
you call every creature to the light of life,
and surround us with such great love
that when we stray
you continually lead us back to Christ our head.**

**For you have established an inheritance of such mercy,
that those sinners, who pass through water made
   sacred,
die with Christ and rise restored
as members of his body
and heirs of his eternal covenant.**

**Bless ✠ this water;
sanctify it.**

**As it is sprinkled upon us and throughout this church
make it a sign of the saving waters of baptism,
by which we become one in Christ, the temple of your
   Spirit.**

**May all here today,
and all those in days to come,
who will celebrate your mysteries in this church,
be united at last in the holy city of your peace.**

**We ask this in the name of Jesus the Lord.
℟. Amen.**

49. The bishop, accompanied by the deacons, passes through the main body of the church, sprinkling the people and the walls with the holy water; then, when he has returned to the sanctuary, he sprinkles the altar. Meanwhile the following antiphon is sung.

I saw water flowing from the right side of the temple, alleluia. I brought God's life and his salvation, and the people sang in joyful praise: alleluia, alleluia.

Or, during Lent:
I will pour clean water over you and wash away all your defilement. A new heart will I give you, says the Lord.

Another appropriate song may be sung.

50. After the sprinkling the bishop returns to the chair and, when the singing is finished, standing with hands joined, says:

**May God, the Father of mercies,
dwell in this house of prayer.
May the grace of the Holy Spirit cleanse us,
for we are the temple of his presence.
℟. Amen.**

HYMN
51. Then the **Gloria** is sung.

OPENING PRAYER
52. When the hymn is finished, the bishop, with hands joined, says:

**Lord,
fill this place with your presence,
and extend your hand
to all those who call upon you.**

**May your word here proclaimed
and your sacraments here celebrated
strengthen the hearts of all the faithful.**

We ask this through our Lord Jesus Christ, your Son,
who lives and reigns with you and the Holy Spirit,
one God, for ever and ever.
℟. Amen.

LITURGY OF THE WORD

53. The proclamation of the word of God is fittingly carried
out in this way: two readers, one of whom carries *The Lectionary*, and the psalmist come to the bishop. The bishop,
standing with the miter on, takes *The Lectionary*, shows it to
the people, and says:

May the word of God always be heard in this place,
as it unfolds the mystery of Christ before you
and achieves your salvation within the Church.
℟. Amen

Then the bishop hands *The Lectionary* to the first reader. The
readers and the psalmist proceed to the lectern, carrying *The
Lectionary* for all to see.

54. The readings are arranged in this way:
a) The first reading is always taken from the Book of
Nehemiah 8:1-4a, 5-6, 8-10, followed by the singing of
Psalm 19B:8-9, 10, 15 with the response:

℟. Your words, Lord, are spirit and life.

b) The second reading and the gospel are taken from the texts
in *The Lectionary* (nos. 701-706) for the rite of the dedication
of a church. Neither lights nor incense are carried at the gospel.

55. After the gospel the bishop gives the homily, in which he
explains the biblical readings and the meaning of the rite.

56. The profession of faith is said. The general intercessions
are omitted since in their place the litany of the saints is sung.

PRAYER OF DEDICATION AND THE ANOINTINGS

INVITATION TO PRAYER

57. Then all stand, and the bishop, without his miter, invites the people to pray in these or similar words:

Let us ask the saints to support our prayers to God the Father almighty, who has made the hearts of his people faithful temples of his Spirit.

Deacon (except on Sundays and during the Easter season):

Let us kneel.

LITANY OF THE SAINTS

58. Then the litany of the saints is sung, with all responding. On Sundays and also during the Easter season, all stand; on other days, all kneel.

59. The cantors begin the litany (Chapter VIII); they add, at the proper place, names of other saints (the titular of the church, the patron saint of the place, and the saints whose relics are to be deposited, if this is to take place) and petitions suitable to the occasion.

60. When the litany is finished, the bishop, standing with hands extended, says:

Lord,
may the prayers of the Blessed Virgin Mary
and of all the saints
make our prayers acceptable to you.

May this building,
which we dedicate to your name,
be a house of salvation and grace
where Christians gathered in fellowship
may worship you in spirit and truth
and grow together in love.

Grant this through Christ our Lord.
℟. Amen.

If it is applicable, the deacon says:

Let us stand.

All rise. The bishop receives the miter.

When there is no depositing of the relics of the saints, the bishop immediately says the prayer of dedication as indicated in no. 62 below.

DEPOSITING OF THE RELICS

61. Then, if relics of the martyrs or other saints are to be placed beneath the altar, the bishop approaches the altar. A deacon or priest brings them to the bishop, who places them in a suitably prepared aperture. Meanwhile one of the following antiphons is sung with Psalm 15.

Saints of God, you have been enthroned at the foot of God's altar; pray for us to the Lord Jesus Christ.

Or:

The bodies of the saints lie buried in peace, but their names will live on for ever (alleluia).

Another appropriate song may be sung.

Meanwhile a stone mason closes the aperture and the bishop returns to the chair.

PRAYER OF DEDICATION

62. Then the bishop, standing without miter at the chair or near the altar, with hands extended, says:

Father in heaven,
source of holiness and true purpose,
it is right that we praise and glorify your name.

For today we come before you,
to dedicate to your lasting service
this house of prayer, this temple of worship,
this home in which we are nourished by your word and
  your sacraments.

Here is reflected the mystery of the Church.

The Church is fruitful,
made holy by the blood of Christ:
a bride made radiant with his glory,
a virgin splendid in the wholeness of her faith,
a mother blessed through the power of the Spirit.

The Church is holy,
your chosen vineyard:
its branches envelop the world,
its tendrils, carried on the tree of the cross,
reach up to the kingdom of heaven.

The Church is favored,
the dwelling place of God on earth:
a temple built of living stones,
founded on the apostles
with Jesus Christ its corner stone.

The Church is exalted,
a city set on a mountain:
a beacon to the whole world,
bright with the glory of the Lamb,
and echoing the prayers of her saints.

Lord,
send your Spirit from heaven
to make this church an ever-holy place,
and this altar a ready table for the sacrifice of Christ.

Here may the waters of baptism
overwhelm the shame of sin;
here may your people die to sin
and live again through grace as your children.

Here may your children,
gathered around your altar,
celebrate the memorial of the Paschal Lamb,
and be fed at the table
of Christ's word and Christ's body.

Here may prayer, the Church's banquet,
resound through heaven and earth
as a plea for the world's salvation.

Here may the poor find justice,
the victims of oppression, true freedom.

From here may the whole world
clothed in the dignity of the children of God,
enter with gladness your city of peace.

**We ask this through our Lord Jesus Christ, your Son,
who lives and reigns with you and the Holy Spirit,
one God, for ever and ever.
℟. Amen.**

ANOINTING OF THE ALTAR
AND THE WALLS OF THE CHURCH

63. Then the bishop, removing the chasuble if necessary and putting on a linen gremial, goes to the altar with the deacons and other ministers, one of whom carries the chrism. The bishop proceeds to anoint the altar and the walls of the church as described in no. 64 below.

If the bishop wishes to associate some of the concelebrating priests with him in the anointing of the walls, after the anointing of the altar, he hands them vessels of sacred chrism and goes with them to complete the anointings.

However, the bishop may give the task of anointing the walls to the priests alone; in that case, he hands the vessel of sacred chrism to them after he has anointed the altar.

64. The bishop, standing before the altar, says:

**We now anoint this altar and this building.
May God in his power make them holy,
visible signs of the mystery of Christ and his Church.**

Then he pours chrism on the middle of the altar and on each of its four corners, and it is recommended that he anoint the entire table of the altar with this.

When the altar has been anointed, the bishop anoints the walls of the church, signing with chrism the suitably distributed twelve or four crosses. He may have the assistance of two or four priests.

If the anointing of the walls is given to the priests, after the bishop has anointed the altar, they anoint the walls of the church signing the crosses with chrism.

Meanwhile one of the following antiphons is sung with Psalm 84.

See the place where God lives among his people; there the Spirit of God will make his home among you; the

temple of God is holy and you are that temple
(alleluia).

Or:

Holy is the temple of the Lord, it is God's handiwork,
his dwelling place.

Another appropriate song may be sung.

65. When the altar and walls have been anointed, the bishop
returns to the chair, sits, and washes his hands. Then the
bishop takes off the gremial and puts on the chasuble. The
priests also wash their hands after they have anointed the
walls.

INCENSATION OF THE ALTAR AND THE CHURCH

66. After the rite of anointing, a brazier is placed on the altar
for burning incense or aromatic gums. The bishop puts incense into the brazier, saying:

Lord,
may our prayer ascend as incense in your sight.
As this building is filled with fragrance
so may your Church fill the world
with the fragrance of Christ.

67. Then the bishop puts incense into some censers and incenses the altar; he returns to the chair, is incensed, and then
sits. Ministers, walking through the church, incense the
people and the walls.

68. Meanwhile one of the following antiphons is sung with
Psalm 138.

An angel stood by the altar of the temple, holding a
golden censer.

Or:

From the hand of the angel, clouds of incense rose in
the presence of the Lord.

Another appropriate song may be sung.

LIGHTING OF THE ALTAR AND THE CHURCH

69. After the incensation, a few ministers wipe the table of the altar with cloths, and if need be, cover it with a waterproof linen. They then cover the altar with a cloth, and, if opportune, decorate it with flowers. They arrange in a suitable manner the candles needed for the celebration of Mass, and, if need be, the cross.

70. Then the bishop gives to the deacon a lighted candle, and says:

Light of Christ,
shine forth in the Church
and bring all nations
to the fullness of truth.

Then the bishop sits. The deacon goes to the altar and lights the candles for the celebration of the eucharist.

71. Then the festive lighting takes place: all the candles, including those at the places where the anointings were made, and the other lamps are lit as a sign of rejoicing. Meanwhile the following antiphon is sung with the canticle of Tobias.

Your light will come, Jerusalem; upon you the glory of the Lord will dawn and all nations will walk in your light, alleluia.

Or, during Lent:
Jerusalem, city of God, you will shine with the light of God's splendor; all people on earth will pay you homage.

CANTICLE OF TOBIAS
(Vg. 13:10, 13-14ab; 14c-15; 17)

Bless the Lord, all you saints of the Lord.
Rejoice and give him thanks.

(Repeat antiphon)

Jerusalem, city of God,
you will shine with the light of God's splendor;

all people on earth will pay you homage.
Nations will come from afar,
bearing gifts for the King of heaven;
in you they will worship the Lord.

(Repeat antiphon)

Nations will consider your land holy,
for in you they will call upon the great name of the
   Lord.
You will exult and rejoice over the children of the
   righteous,
for they will be gathered together to praise the Lord.

(Repeat antiphon)

Another appropriate song may be sung, especially one in
honor of Christ, the light of the world.

LITURGY OF THE EUCHARIST

72. The deacons and the ministers prepare the altar in the
usual way. Then some of the congregation bring bread, wine,
and water for the celebration of the Lord's sacrifice. The
bishop receives the gifts at the chair. While the gifts are being
brought, the following antiphon may be sung:

**Lord God, in the simplicity of my heart I have joyously
offered all things to you; with great joy I have looked
upon your chosen people, Lord God, I have obeyed
your will (alleluia).**

Another appropriate song may be sung.

73. When all is ready, the bishop goes to the altar, removes
the miter, and kisses the altar. The Mass proceeds in the
usual way; however, neither the gifts nor the altar are incensed.

PRAYER OVER THE GIFTS

74. With hands extended, the bishop sings or says:

**Lord,
accept the gifts of a rejoicing Church.**

May your people,
who are gathered in this sacred place,
arrive at eternal salvation
through the mysteries in which they share.

Grant this through Christ our Lord.
℟. Amen.

EUCHARISTIC PRAYER

75. Eucharistic Prayer I or III is said, with the following preface, which is an integral part of the rite of the dedication of a church. With hands extended the bishop sings or says:

The Lord be with you.
℟. And also with you.

Lift up your hearts.
℟. We lift them up to the Lord.

Let us give thanks to the Lord our God.
℟. It is right to give him thanks and praise.

Father, all-powerful and ever-living God,
we do well always and everywhere to give you thanks.

The whole world is your temple,
shaped to resound with your name.
Yet you also allow us to dedicate to your service
places designed for your worship.

With hearts full of joy
we consecrate to your glory
this work of our hands, this house of prayer.

Here is foreshadowed the mystery of your true temple;
this church is the image on earth of your heavenly city:

For you made the body of your Son
born of the Virgin,
a temple consecrated to your glory,
the dwelling place of your godhead in all its fullness.

You have established the Church as your holy city,
founded on the apostles,
with Jesus Christ its cornerstone.

You continue to build your Church with chosen stones,
enlivened by the Spirit,
and cemented together by love.

In that holy city you will be all in all for endless ages,
and Christ will be its light for ever.

Through Christ we praise you, Lord,
with all the angels and saints in their song of joy:

Holy, holy, holy Lord, God of power and might,
heaven and earth are full of your glory.
  Hosanna in the highest.
Blessed is he who comes in the name of the Lord.
  Hosanna in the highest.

76. In Eucharistic Prayer I the special form of **Father, accept
this offering** is said:

Father,
accept this offering
from your whole family,
and from your servants
who with heart and hand
have given and built this church
as an offering to you (in honor of N.).
Grant us your peace in this life,
save us from final damnation,
and count us among those you have chosen.

77. In the intercessions of Eucharistic Prayer III, after the
words, **with . . . the entire people your Son has gained for
you,** the following is said:

Father,
accept the prayers of those who dedicate this church to
  you.

May it be a place of salvation and sacrament
where your Gospel of peace is proclaimed
and your holy mysteries celebrated.

Guided by your word and secure in your peace

may your chosen people now journeying through life
arrive safely at their eternal home.

There may all your children
now scattered abroad
be settled at last in your city of peace.

78. While the bishop is receiving the body of Christ the
communion song begins. One of the following antiphons is
sung with Psalm 128.

My house shall be called a house of prayer, says the
Lord: in it all who ask shall receive, all who seek shall
find, and all who knock shall have the door opened to
them (alleluia).

Or:
May the children of the Church be like olive branches
around the table of the Lord (alleluia).

Another appropriate song may be sung.

If there is no inauguration of the blessed sacrament chapel,
the Mass proceeds as below, no.83.

INAUGURATION OF THE
BLESSED SACRAMENT CHAPEL

79. The inauguration of a chapel where the blessed sacrament is to be reserved, is carried out appropriately in this
way: after the communion the pyx containing the blessed
sacrament is left on the table of the altar. The bishop goes to
the chair, and all pray in silence for a brief period. Then the
bishop says the following prayer after communion:

Let us pray.

Pause for silent prayer, if this has not preceded.

Lord,
through these gifts
increase the vision of your truth in our minds.

May we always worship you in your holy temple,
and rejoice in your presence with all your saints.

Grant this through Christ our Lord.
℟. Amen.

80. When the prayer is completed, the bishop returns to the altar, genuflects, and incenses the blessed sacrament. Afterward, when he has received the humeral veil, he takes the pyx, which he covers with the veil itself. Then a procession is formed in which, preceded by the crossbearer and with lighted torches and incense, the blessed sacrament is carried through the main body of the church to the chapel of reservation. As the procession proceeds, the following antiphon is sung with Psalm 147:12-20.

Praise the Lord, Jerusalem.

Another appropriate song may be sung.

81. When the procession comes to the chapel of reservation, the bishop places the pyx on the altar or in the tabernacle, the door of which remains open. Then he puts incense in the censer, kneels, and incenses the blessed sacrament. Finally, after a brief period during which all pray in silence, the deacon puts the pyx in the tabernacle or closes the door. A minister lights the lamp, which will burn perpetually before the blessed sacrament.

82. If the chapel where the blessed sacrament is reserved can be seen clearly by the congregation, the bishop immediately imparts the blessing of the Mass (see below, no. 84). Otherwise the procession returns to the sanctuary by the shorter route and the bishop imparts the blessing either at the altar or at the chair.

PRAYER AFTER COMMUNION

83. If there is no inauguration of the blessed sacrament chapel, when the communion of the congregation is finished, the bishop says:

Let us pray.

Pause for silent prayer, if this has not preceded.

Lord,
through these gifts
increase the vision of your truth in our minds.

May we always worship you in your holy temple,
and rejoice in your presence with all your saints.

Grant this through Christ our Lord.
℟. **Amen.**

BLESSING AND DISMISSAL

84. The bishop receives the miter and says:

The Lord be with you.
℟. **And also with you.**

Then the deacon, if appropriate, gives the invitation to the people in these or similar words:

Bow your heads and pray for God's blessing.

Then the bishop extends his hands over the people and blesses them, saying:

The Lord of earth and heaven
has assembled you before him this day
to dedicate this house of prayer.
May he fill you with the blessings of heaven.
℟. **Amen.**

God the Father wills that all his children
scattered through the world
become one family in his Son.
May he make you his temple,
the dwelling place of his Holy Spirit.
℟. **Amen.**

May God free you from every bond of sin,
dwell within you and give you joy.
May you live with him for ever
in the company of all his saints.
℟. **Amen.**

The bishop takes the pastoral staff and continues:

May almighty God bless you,
the Father, and the Son, ✠ and the Holy Spirit.
℟. **Amen.**

85. Finally the deacon dismisses the people in the usual way.

CHAPTER III

DEDICATION OF A CHURCH IN WHICH MASS IS ALREADY BEING CELEBRATED REGULARLY

INTRODUCTION

1. In order to bring out fully the symbolism and the significance of the rite, the opening of a new church and its dedication should take place at one and the same time. For this reason, as was said before, care should be taken that, as far as possible, Mass is not celebrated in a new church before it is dedicated (see chapter two, nos. 8, 15, 17).

Nevertheless in the case of the dedication of a church where the sacred mysteries are already being celebrated regularly, the rite set out in this chapter must be used.

Moreover, a clear distinction exists in regard to these churches. In the case of those just built the reason for a dedication is obvious. In the case of those standing for some time the following requirements must be met for them to be dedicated:
—that the altar has not already been dedicated, since it is rightly forbidden both by custom and by liturgical law to dedicate a church without dedicating the altar, for the dedication of the altar is the principal part of the whole rite;
—that there be something new or notably altered about the edifice, relative either to its structure (for example, a total restoration) or its status in law (for example, the church's being ranked as a parish church).

2. All the directions given in the Introduction to chapter two apply to this rite, unless they are clearly extraneous to the situation which this rite envisages or other directions are given.

This rite differs chiefly from that described in chapter two on these points:
a) The rite of opening the doors of the church (see chapter two, no. 34 or no. 41) is omitted, since the church is already open to the community; consequently, the entrance takes the form of the simple entrance (see chapter two, nos. 43–47).

However, in the case of dedicating a church closed for a long time and now being opened again for sacred celebrations, the rite of opening the doors may be carried out, since in this case it retains its point and significance.

b) The rite of handing over the church to the bishop (see chapter two, no. 33 or no. 40 or no. 47), depending on the situation, is either to be followed, omitted, or adapted in a way relevant to the condition of the church being dedicated (for example, it will be right to retain it in dedicating a church built recently; to omit it in dedicating an older church where nothing has been changed in the structure; to adapt it in dedicating an older church completely restored).

c) The rite of sprinkling the church walls with holy water (see chapter two, nos. 48–50), purificatory by its very nature, is omitted;

d) All the rites belonging to the first proclamation of the word of God in a church (see chapter two, no. 53) are omitted; thus the liturgy of the word takes place in the usual way. A different, pertinent reading is chosen in place of Neh 8:1–4a and its responsorial psalm, Ps 19b: 8–9, 10, 15 (see chapter two, no. 54 a).

RITE OF DEDICATION

INTRODUCTORY RITES

ENTRANCE INTO THE CHURCH

3. When the people are assembled, the bishop and the celebrating priests, the deacons, and the ministers, each in appropriate vestments, preceded by the crossbearer, go from the sacristy through the main body of the church to the sanctuary.

4. If there are relics of the saints to be placed beneath the altar, these are brought in the entrance procession to the sanctuary from the sacristy or the chapel where since the vigil they have been exposed for the veneration of the people. For a just cause, before the celebration begins, the relics may be placed between lighted torches in a suitable part of the sanctuary.

5. As the procession proceeds, the entrance antiphon is sung with Psalm 122.

God in his holy dwelling, God who has gathered us together in his house: he will strengthen and console his people.

Or:

Let us go rejoicing to the house of the Lord.

Another appropriate song may be sung.

6. When the procession reaches the sanctuary, the relics of the saints are placed between lighted torches in a suitable place. The concelebrating priests, the deacons, and the ministers go the places assigned to them; the bishop, without kissing the altar, goes to the chair. Then putting aside the pastoral staff and miter, greets the people, saying:

The grace and peace of God be with all of you in his holy Church.
℟. And also with you.

Other suitable words taken preferably from sacred Scripture may be used.

7. If circumstances dictate that the church is to be handed over to the bishop (see Introduction, no. 2b), representatives of those who have been involved in the building of the church (members of the parish or of the diocese, contributors, architects, workers) hand over the building to the bishop, offering him either the legal documents for possession of the building, or the keys, or the plan of the building, or the book in which the progress of the work is described and the names of those in charge of it and the names of the workers recorded. One of the representatives addresses the bishop and the community in a few words, pointing out, if need be, what the church expresses in its art and in its own special design.

BLESSING AND SPRINKLING OF WATER

8. When the entrance rite is completed, the bishop blesses water with which to sprinkle the people as a sign of repentance and as a reminder of their baptism. The ministers return the vessel with the water to the bishop who stands at the chair. The bishop invites all to pray, in these or similar words:

Brothers and sisters in Christ in this solemn rite of dedication let us ask the Lord our God to bless this water, created by his hand.

It is a sign of our repentance and a reminder of our baptism.

May the grace of God help us to remain faithful members of his Church, open to the Spirit we have received.

All pray in silence for a brief period. The bishop then continues:

God of mercy,
you call every creature to the light of life,
and surround us with such great love
that when we stray
you continually lead us back to Christ our head.

For you have established an inheritance of such mercy,
that those sinners, who pass through water made
sacred,
die with Christ and rise restored
as members of his body
and heirs of his eternal covenant.

Bless ✠ this water;
sanctify it.

As it is sprinkled upon us and throughout this church
make it a sign of the saving waters of baptism,
by which we become one in Christ, the temple of your
Spirit.

May all here today,
and all those in days to come,
who will celebrate your mysteries in this church
be united at last in the holy city of your peace.

We ask this in the name of Jesus the Lord.
℟. Amen.

9. The bishop, accompanied by the deacons, sprinkles the people with holy water; then if the altar is completely new he sprinkles it too. Meanwhile the following antiphon is sung.

I saw water flowing from the right side of the temple, alleluia. It brought God's life and his salvation, and the people sang in joyful praise: alleluia, alleluia.

Or, during Lent:
I will pour clean water over you and wash away all your defilement. A new heart will I give you, says the Lord.

Another appropriate song may be sung.

10. After the sprinkling the bishop returns to the chair and, when the singing is finished, standing with hands joined, says:

May God, the Father of mercies,
dwell in this house of prayer.
May the grace of the Holy Spirit cleanse us,
for we are the temple of his presence.
℟. Amen.

HYMN
11. Then the **Gloria** is sung.

OPENING PRAYER
12. When the hymn is finished, the bishop, with hands joined, says:

Let us pray.

All pray in silence for a brief period. Then the bishop, with hands extended, says:

Lord,
fill this place with your presence,
and extend your hand
to all those who call upon you.

May your word here proclaimed
and your sacraments here celebrated
strengthen the hearts of all the faithful.

We ask this through our Lord Jesus Christ, your Son,
who lives and reigns with you and the Holy Spirit,
one God, for ever and ever.
℟. Amen.

LITURGY OF THE WORD

13. The bishop sits and receives the miter; the people also are seated. Then the liturgy of the word takes place; the readings are taken from the texts in *The Lectionary* (nos. 701 and 706) for the rite of the dedication of a church.

14. Neither lights nor incense are carried at the gospel.

15. After the gospel the bishop gives the homily, in which he explains the biblical readings and the meaning of the rite.

16. The profession of faith is said. The general intercessions are omitted since in their place the litany of the saints is sung.

PRAYER OF DEDICATION AND THE ANOINTINGS

INVITATION TO PRAYER

17. Then all stand, and the bishop, without his miter, invites the people to pray in these or similar words:

Let us ask the saints to support our prayers to God the Father almighty, who has made the hearts of his people faithful temples of his Spirit.

Deacon (except on Sundays and during the Easter season):

Let us kneel.

LITANY OF THE SAINTS

18. Then the litany of the saints is sung, with all responding. On Sundays and also during the Easter season, all stand; on other days, all kneel.

19. The cantors begin the litany (see Chapter VIII); they add, at the proper place, names of other saints (the titular of the church, the patron saint of the place, and the saints whose relics are to be deposited, if this is to take place) and petitions suitable to the occasion.

20. When the litany is finished, the bishop, standing with hands extended, says:

**Lord,
may the prayers of the Blessed Virgin Mary**

and of all the saints
make our prayers acceptable to you.

May this building,
which we dedicate to your name,
be a house of salvation and grace
where Christians gathered in fellowship
may worship you in spirit and truth
and grow together in love.

Grant this through Christ our Lord.
℟. Amen.

If it is applicable, the deacon says:

Let us stand.

All rise. The bishop receives the miter.

When there is no depositing of the relics of the saints, the bishop immediately says the prayer of dedication as indicated in no. 22 below.

DEPOSITING OF THE RELICS

21. Then, if relics of the matyrs or other saints are to be placed beneath the altar, the bishop approaches the altar. A deacon or priest brings them to the bishop, who places them in a suitably prepared aperture. Meanwhile one of the following antiphons is sung with Psalm 15.

Saints of God, you have been enthroned at the foot of God's altar; pray for us to the Lord Jesus Christ.

Or:

The bodies of the saints lie buried in peace, but their names will live on forever (alleluia).

Another appropriate song may be sung.

Meanwhile a stone mason closes the aperture and the bishop returns to the chair.

PRAYER OF DEDICATION

22. Then the bishop, standing without miter at the chair or near the altar, with hands extended, says:

Father in heaven,
source of holiness and true purpose,
it is right that we praise and glorify your name.

For today we come before you,
to dedicate to your lasting service
this house of prayer, this temple of worship,
this home in which we are nourished by your word and
   your sacraments.

Here is reflected the mystery of the Church.

The Church is fruitful,
made holy by the blood of Christ:
a bride made radiant with his glory,
a virgin splendid in the wholeness of her faith,
a mother blessed through the power of the Spirit.

The Church is holy,
your chosen vineyard:
its branches envelop the world,
its tendrils, carried on the tree of the cross,
reach up to the kingdom of heaven.

The Church is favored,
the dwelling place of God on earth:
a temple built of living stones,
founded on the apostles
with Jesus Christ its corner stone.

The Church is exalted,
a city set on a mountain:
a beacon to the whole world,
bright with the glory of the Lamb,
and echoing the prayers of her saints.

Lord,
send your Spirit from heaven
to make this church an ever-holy place,
and this altar a ready table for the sacrifice of Christ.

Here may the waters of baptism
overwhelm the shame of sin;

here may your people die to sin
and live again through grace as your children.

Here may your children,
gathered around your altar,
celebrate the memorial of the Paschal Lamb,
and be fed at the table
of Christ's word and Christ's body.

Here may prayer, the Church's banquet,
resound through heaven and earth
as a plea for the world's salvation.

Here may the poor find justice,
the victims of oppression, true freedom.

From here may the whole world
clothed in the dignity of the children of God,
enter with gladness your city of peace.

We ask this through our Lord Jesus Christ, your Son,
who lives and reigns with you and the Holy Spirit,
one God, for ever and ever.
℞. Amen.

ANOINTING OF THE ALTAR
AND THE WALLS OF THE CHURCH

23. Then the bishop, removing the chasuble if necessary and putting on a linen gremial, goes to the altar with the deacons and other ministers, one of whom carries the chrism. The bishop proceeds to anoint the altar and the walls of the church as described in no. 24 below.

If the bishop wishes to associate some of the concelebrating priests with him in the anointing of the walls, after the anointing of the altar, he hands them vessels of sacred chrism and goes with them to complete the anointings.

However, the bishop may give the task of anointing the walls to the priests alone; in that case, he hands the vessels of sacred chrism to them after he has anointed the altar.

24. The bishop, standing before the altar says:

**We now anoint this altar and this building.
May God in his power make them holy,
visible signs of the mystery of Christ and his Church.**

Then he pours chrism on the middle of the altar and on each of its four corners, and it is recommended that he anoint the entire table of the altar with this.

When the altar has been anointed, the bishop anoints the walls of the church, signing with chrism the suitably distributed twelve or four crosses. He may have the assistance of two or four priests.

If the anointing of the walls is given to the priests, after the bishop has anointed the altar, they anoint the walls of the church signing the crosses with chrism.

Meanwhile one of the following antiphons is sung with Psalm 84.

See the place where God lives among his people; there the Spirit of God will make his home among you; the temple of God is holy and you are that temple (alleluia).

Or:
Holy is the temple of the Lord, it is God's handiwork, his dwelling place.

Another appropriate song may be sung.

25. When the altar and walls have been anointed, the bishop returns to the chair, sits, and washes his hands. Then the bishop takes off the gremial and puts on the chasuble. The priests also wash their hands after they have anointed the walls.

INCENSATION OF THE ALTAR AND THE CHURCH
26. After the rite of anointing, the brazier is placed on the altar for burning incense or aromatic gums. The bishop puts incense into the brazier, saying:

**Lord,
may our prayer ascend as incense in your sight.**

**As this building is filled with fragrance
so may your Church fill the world
with the fragrance of Christ.**

27. Then the bishop puts incense into some censers and incenses the altar; he returns to the chair, is incensed, and then sits. Ministers, walking through the church, incense the people and the walls.

28. Meanwhile one of the following antiphons is sung with Psalm 138.

An angel stood by the altar of the temple, holding a golden censer.

Or:

From the hand of the angel, clouds of incense rose in the presence of the Lord.

Another appropriate song may be sung.

LIGHTING OF THE ALTAR AND THE CHURCH

29. After the incensation, a few ministers wipe the table of the altar with cloths, and, if need be, cover it with a waterproof linen. They then cover the altar with a cloth, and, if opportune, decorate it with flowers. They arrange in a suitable manner the candles needed for the celebration of Mass, and, if need be, the cross.

30. Then the bishop gives to the deacon a lighted candle and says:

**Light of Christ,
shine forth in the Church
and bring all nations
to the fullness of truth.**

Then the bishop sits. The deacon goes to the altar and lights the candles for the celebration of the eucharist.

31. Then the festive lighting takes place: all the candles, including those at the places where the anointings were made, and the other lamps are lit as a sign of rejoicing. Meanwhile the following antiphon is sung with the canticle of Tobias.

Your light will come, Jerusalem; upon you the glory of the Lord will dawn and all nations will walk in your light, alleluia.

Or, during Lent:
Jerusalem, city of God, you will shine with the light of God's splendor; all people on earth will pay you homage.

CANTICLE OF TOBIAS
(Vg. 13:10; 13-14ab; 14c-15; 17)

Bless the Lord, all you saints of the Lord.
Rejoice and give him thanks.

(Repeat antiphon)

Jerusalem, city of God,
you will shine with the light of God's splendor;
all people on earth will pay you homage.
Nations will come from afar,
bearing gifts for the King of heaven;
in you they will worship the Lord.

(Repeat antiphon)

Nations will consider your land holy,
for in you they will call upon the great name of the
    Lord.
You will exult and rejoice over the children of the
    righteous,
for they will be gathered together to praise the Lord.

(Repeat antiphon)

Another appropriate song may be sung, especially one in honor of Christ, the light of the world.

LITURGY OF THE EUCHARIST

32. The deacons and the ministers prepare the altar in the usual way. Then some of the congregation bring bread, wine, and water for the celebration of the Lord's sacrifice. The bishop receives the gifts at the chair. While the gifts are being brought, the following antiphon may be sung:

Lord God, in the simplicity of my heart I have joyously
offered all things to you; with great joy I have looked
upon your chosen people; Lord God, I have obeyed
your will (alleluia).

Another appropriate song may be sung.

33. When all is ready, the bishop goes to the altar, removes
the miter, and kisses the altar. The Mass proceeds in the
usual way; however, neither the gifts nor the altar are incensed.

PRAYER OVER THE GIFTS

34. With hands extended, the bishop sings or says:

Lord,
accept the gifts of a rejoicing Church.

May your people,
who are gathered in this sacred place,
arrive at eternal salvation
through the mysteries in which they share.

Grant this through Christ our Lord.
℟. Amen.

EUCHARISTIC PRAYER

35. Eucharist Prayer I or III is said, with the following preface. With hands extended the bishop sings or says:

The Lord be with you.
℟. And also with you.

Lift up your hearts.
℟. We lift them up to the Lord.

Let us give thanks to the Lord our God.
℟. It is right to give him thanks and praise.

Father of holiness and power,
we give you thanks and praise
through Jesus Christ, your Son.
For you have blessed this work of our hands
and your presence makes it a house of prayer;

nor do you ever refuse us welcome
when we come in before you as your pilgrim people.

In this house you realize the mystery of your dwelling
  among us:
for in shaping us here as your holy temple
you enrich your whole Church,
which is the very body of Christ,
and thus bring closer to fulfillment
the vision of your peace,
the heavenly city of Jerusalem.

And so, with all your angels and saints,
who stand in your temple of glory,
we praise you and give you thanks, as we sing:

Holy, holy, holy Lord, God of power and might,
heaven and earth are full of your glory.
  Hosanna in the highest.
Blessed is he who comes in the name of the Lord.
  Hosanna in the highest.

36. While the bishop is receiving the body of Christ the
communion song begins. One of the following antiphons is
sung with Psalm 128.

My house shall be called a house of prayer, says the
Lord: in it all who ask shall receive, all who seek shall
find, and all who knock shall have the door opened to
them (alleluia).

Or:
May the children of the Church be like olive branches
around the table of the Lord (alleluia).

Another appropriate song may be sung.

37. The inauguration of the blessed sacrament chapel proceeds
as in Chapter II, nos. 79-82.

PRAYER AFTER COMMUNION
38. If there is no inauguration of the blessed sacrament
chapel, when the communion of the congregation is finished,
the bishop says:

Let us pray.

Pause for silent prayer, if this has not preceded.

Lord,
through these gifts
increase the vision of your truth in our minds.

May we always worship you in your holy temple,
and rejoice in your presence with all your saints.

Grant this through Christ our Lord.
℟. Amen.

BLESSING AND DISMISSAL

39. The bishop receives the miter and says:

The Lord be with you.
℟. And also with you.

Then the deacon, if appropriate, gives the invitation to the people in these or similar words:

Bow your heads and pray for God's blessing.

Then the bishop extends his hands over the people and blesses them, saying:

The Lord of earth and heaven
has assembled you before him this day
to dedicate this house of prayer.
May he fill you with the blessings of heaven.
℟. Amen.

God the Father wills that all his children
scattered through the world
become one family in his Son.
May he make you his temple,
the dwelling place of his Holy Spirit.
℟. Amen.

**May God free you from every bond of sin,
dwell within you and give you joy.
May you live with him for ever
in the company of all his saints.**
℟. **Amen.**

The bishop takes the pastoral staff and continues:

**May almighty God bless you,
the Father, and the Son, ✝ and the Holy Spirit.**
℟. **Amen.**

40. Finally the deacon dismisses the people in the usual way.

CHAPTER IV

DEDICATION OF AN ALTAR

INTRODUCTION

NATURE AND DIGNITY OF THE ALTAR

1. From meditating on God's word, the ancient Fathers of the Church did not hesitate to assert that Christ was the victim, priest, and altar of his own sacrifice.[1] For in the Letter to the Hebrews Christ is presented as the High Priest who is also the living altar of the heavenly temple;[2] and in the Book of Revelation our Redeemer appears as the Lamb who has been sacrificed[3] and whose offering is taken by the holy angel to the altar in heaven.[4]

THE CHRISTIAN IS ALSO A SPIRITUAL ALTAR

2. Since Christ, Head and Teacher, is the true altar, his members and disciples are also spiritual altars on which the sacrifice of a holy life is offered to God. The Fathers seem to have this in mind. St. Ignatius of Antioch asks the Romans quite plainly: "Grant me only this favor: let my blood be spilled in sacrifice to God, while there is still an altar ready."[5] St. Polycarp exhorts widows to lead a life of holiness, for "they are God's altar."[6] Among others, St. Gregory the Great echoes these words when he says: "What is God's altar if not the souls of those who lead good lives? . . . Rightly, then, the heart of the just is said to be the altar of God"[7]

In another image frequently used by the writers of the Church, Christians who give themselves to prayer, offer petitions to God, and present sacrifices of supplication, are the living stones out of which the Lord Jesus builds the Church's altar.[8]

[1]See Epiphanius, *Panarium* 2, 1, *Haeresis* 55: PG 41, 979. Cyril of Alexandria, *De adoratione in spiritu et veritate* 9: PG 68, 647.
[2]See Heb 4:14, 13:10.
[3]See Rv 5:6.
[4]See RM, Order of Mass, no. 96.
[5]Ignatius of Antioch, *Ad Romanos* 2:2: Funk PA 1:255.
[6]Polycarp, *Ad Philippenses* 4:3: Funk PA 1:301.
[7]Gregory the Great, *Homiliarum in Ezechielem* 10, 19: PL 76, 1069.
[8]See Origen, *In librum Iesu Nave*, Homilia 9, 1: SC 71, 244 and 246.

THE ALTAR, TABLE OF THE SACRIFICE AND THE PASCHAL MEAL

3. By instituting in the form of a sacrificial meal the memorial of the sacrifice he was about to offer the Father on the altar of the cross, Christ made holy the table where the community would come to celebrate their Passover. Therefore the altar is the table for a sacrifice and for a banquet. At this table the priest, representing Christ the Lord, accomplishes what the Lord himself did and what he handed on to his disciples to do in his memory. The Apostle clearly intimates this: "The blessing cup that we bless is a communion with the blood of Christ and the bread that we break is a communion with the body of Christ. The fact that there is only one loaf means that though there are many of us, we form a single Body because we all have a share in this one loaf."[9]

THE ALTAR, SIGN OF CHRIST

4. The Church's children have the power to celebrate the memorial of Christ and take their place at the Lord's table anywhere that circumstances might require. But it is in keeping with the eucharistic mystery that the Christian people erect a permanent altar for the celebration of the Lord's Supper and they have done so from the earliest times.

The Christian altar is by its very nature properly the table of sacrifice and of the paschal banquet. It is:
—a unique altar on which the sacrifice of the cross is perpetuated in mystery throughout the ages until Christ comes;
—a table at which the Church's children gather to give thanks to God and receive the body and blood of Christ.

In every church, then, the altar "is the center of the thanksgiving that the eucharist accomplishes"[10] and around which the Church's other rites are, in a certain manner, arrayed.[11]

At the altar the memorial of the Lord is celebrated and his body and blood given to the people. Therefore the Church's writers have seen in the altar a sign of Christ himself. This is the basis for saying, "The altar is Christ."

[9]See 1 Cor 10:16–17.
[10]GIRM no. 259 [DOL 208 no. 1649].
[11]See Pius XII, Encycl. *Mediator Dei*: AAS 39 (1947) 529.

THE ALTAR AS HONORING MARTYRS

5. All the dignity of the altar rests on its being the Lord's table. Thus the martyr's body does not bring honor to the altar; rather the altar does honor to the martyr's tomb. For it is altogether proper to erect altars over the burial place of martyrs and other saints or to deposit their relics beneath altars as a mark of respect and as a symbol of the truth that the sacrifice of its members has its source in the sacrifice of the Head.[12] Thus "the triumphant victims come to their rest in the place where Christ is victim: he, however, who suffered for all is on the altar; they who have been redeemed by his sufferings are beneath the altar."[13] This arrangement would seem to recall in a certain manner the spiritual vision of the Apostle John in the Book of Revelation: "I saw underneath the altar the souls of all the people who have been killed on account of the word of God, for witnessing to it."[14] His meaning is that although all the saints are rightly called Christ's witnesses, the witness of blood has a special significance that only the relics of martyrs beneath the altar express in its entirety.

ERECTING AN ALTAR

6. It is desirable that in every church there be a fixed altar and that in other places set apart for sacred celebrations there be either a fixed or a movable altar.

A fixed altar is one so constructed that it is attached to the floor so that it cannot be moved; a movable altar can be transferred from place to place.[15]

7. In new churches it is better to erect only one altar so that in the one assembly of the people of God the single altar signifies the one Savior Jesus Christ and the one eucharist of the Church.

But an altar may also be erected in a chapel (somewhat separated, if possible, from the body of the church) where the tabernacle for the reservation of the blessed sacrament is sit-

---

[12]See RM, Common of Martyrs 8, prayer over the gifts.
[13]Ambrose, *Epistula* 22, 13: PL 16, 1023. See Ps. Maximus of Turin, *Sermo* 78: PL 57, 689–690.
[14]Rv 6:9.
[15]See GIRM nos. 265, 261 [DOL 208 nos. 1655, 1651].

uated. On weekdays when there is a small gathering of people Mass may be celebrated at this altar.

The merely decorative erection of several altars in a church must be entirely avoided.

8. The altar should be freestanding so that the priest can easily walk around it and celebrate Mass facing the people. "It should be so placed as to be a focal point on which the attention of the whole congregation centers naturally."[16]

9. In accordance with received custom in the Church and the biblical symbolism connected with an altar, the table of a fixed altar should be of stone, indeed of natural stone. But, at the discretion of the conference of bishops, any becoming, solid, and finely wrought material may be used in erecting an altar.

The pedestal or base of the table may be of any sort of material, provided it is becoming and solid.[17]

10. The altar is of its very nature dedicated to the one God, for the eucharistic sacrifice is offered to the one God. This is the sense in which the Church's practice of dedicating altars to God in honor of the saints must be understood. St. Augustine expresses it well: "It is not to any of the martyrs, but to the God of the martyrs, though in memory of the martyrs, that we raise our altars."[18]

This should be made clear to the people. In new churches statues and pictures of saints may not be placed above the altar.

Likewise, when relics of saints are exposed for veneration, they should not be placed on the table of the altar.

11. It is fitting to continue the tradition in the Roman liturgy of placing relics of martyrs or other saints beneath the altar.[19] But the following should be noted.
a. Such relics should be of a size sufficient for them to be recognizable as parts of human bodies. Hence excessively

[16]GIRM no. 262 [DOL 208 no. 1652].
[17]See GIRM no. 263 [DOL 208 no. 1653].
[18]Augustine, *Contra Faustum* 20, 21: PL 42, 384.
[19]See GIRM no. 266 [DOL 208 no. 1656].

small relics of one or more saints must not be placed beneath an altar.

b. The greatest care must be taken to determine whether the relics in question are authentic. It is better for an altar to be dedicated without relics than to have relics of doubtful authenticity placed beneath it.

c. A reliquary must not be placed on the altar or set into the table of the altar, but placed beneath the table of the altar, as the design of the altar permits.

When the rite of depositing relics takes place, it is highly recommended to keep a vigil at the relics of the martyr or saint, in accordance with the provisions of chapter two, no. 10.

CELEBRATION OF THE DEDICATION

MINISTER OF THE RITE

12. Since the bishop has been entrusted with the care of the particular Church, it is his responsibility to dedicate to God new altars built in his diocese.

If he cannot himself preside at the rite, he shall entrust the function to another bishop, especially to one who is his associate and assistant in the pastoral care of the community for which the new altar has been erected or, in altogether special circumstances, to a priest, to whom he shall give a special mandate.

CHOICE OF DAY

13. Since an altar becomes sacred principally by the celebration of the eucharist, in fidelity to this truth the celebration of Mass on a new altar before it has been dedicated is to be carefully avoided, so that the Mass of dedication may also be the first eucharist celebrated on the altar.

14. A day should be chosen for the dedication of a new altar when the people can be present in large numbers, especially a Sunday, unless pastoral considerations suggest otherwise. However, the rite of dedication of an altar may not be celebrated during the Easter triduum, on Ash Wednesday, the weekdays of Holy Week, and All Souls.

MASS OF THE DEDICATION

15. The celebration of the eucharist is inseparably bound up with the rite of the dedication of an altar. The Mass is the Mass for the dedication of an altar. On Christmas, Epiphany, Ascension, Pentecost, and on the Sundays of Advent, Lent, and the Easter season, the Mass is the Mass of the day, with the exception of the prayer over the gifts and the preface, which are closely interwoven with the rite itself.

16. It is fitting that the bishop concelebrate the Mass with the priests present, especially with those who have been given charge over the parish or the community for which the altar has been erected.

PARTS OF THE RITE

A. Introductory Rites
17. The introductory rites of the Mass of the dedication of an altar take place in the usual way except that in place of the penitential rite the bishop blesses water and with it sprinkles the people and the new altar.

B. Liturgy of the Word
18. It is commendable to have three readings in the liturgy of the word, chosen according to the rubrical norm, either from the liturgy of the day (see no. 15) or from those in the Lectionary for the rite of the dedication of an altar (nos. 704 and 706).

19. After the readings, the bishop gives the homily, in which he explains the biblical readings and the meaning of the dedication of an altar.

After the homily, the profession of faith is said. The general intercessions are omitted, since the Litany of the Saints is sung in their place.

C. Prayer of the Dedication and the Anointing of the Altar
20. If it is to take place, the relics of martyrs or other saints are placed beneath the altar after the Litany of the Saints. The rite is meant to signify that all who have been baptized in the death of Christ, especially those who have shed their blood for the Lord, share in Christ's passion (see no. 5).

21. The celebration of the eucharist is the most important and the one necessary rite for the dedication of an altar. Nevertheless, in accordance with the universal tradition of the Church in both East and West, a special prayer of dedication is also said. This prayer is a sign of the intention to dedicate the altar to the Lord for all times and a petition for his blessing.

22. The rites of anointing, incensing, covering, and lighting the altar express in visible signs several aspects of the invisible work that the Lord accomplishes through the Church in its celebration of the divine mysteries, especially the eucharist.

a. *Anointing* of the altar: The anointing with chrism makes the altar a symbol of Christ, who, before all others, is and is called "The Anointed One"; for the Father anointed him with the Holy Spirit and constituted him the High Priest so that on the altar of his body he might offer the sacrifice of his life for the salvation of all.

b. *Incense* is burned on the altar to signify that Christ's sacrifice, there perpetuated in mystery, ascends to God as an odor of sweetness, and also to signify that the people's prayers rise up pleasing and acceptable, reaching the throne of God.[20]

c. The *covering* of the altar indicates that the Christian altar is the altar of the eucharistic sacrifice and the table of the Lord; around it priests and people, by one and the same rite but with a difference of function, celebrate the memorial of Christ's death and resurrection and partake of his supper. For this reason the altar is prepared as the table of the sacrificial banquet and adorned as for a feast. Thus the dressing of the altar clearly signifies that it is the Lord's table at which all God's people joyously meet to be refreshed with divine food, namely, the body and blood of Christ sacrificed.

d. The *lighting* of the altar teaches us that Christ is "a light to

---

[20]See Rv 8:3–4: An angel "who had a golden censer, came and stood at the altar. A large quantity of incense was given to him to offer with the prayers of all the saints on the golden altar that stood in front of the throne; and so from the angel's hand the smoke of the incense went up in the presence of God and with it the prayers of the saints."

enlighten the nations"; [21] his brightness shines out in the Church and through it in the whole human family.

D. Celebration of the Eucharist

23. After the altar has been prepared, the bishop celebrates the eucharist, the principal and the most ancient part of the whole rite,[22] because the celebration of the eucharist is in the closest harmony with the rite of the dedication of an altar:

—For the celebration of the eucharistic sacrifice achieves the end for which the altar was erected and expresses this end by particularly clear signs.

—Furthermore, the eucharist, which sanctifies the hearts of those who receive it, in a sense consecrates the altar, as the ancient Fathers of the Church often assert: "This altar should be an object of awe: by nature it is stone, but it is made holy when it receives the body of Christ."[23]

—Finally, the bond closely connecting the dedication of an altar with the celebration of the eucharist is likewise evident from the fact that the Mass for the dedication has its own preface, which is a central part of the rite itself.

ADAPTATION OF THE RITE

ADAPTATIONS WITHIN THE COMPETENCE OF THE CONFERENCES OF BISHOPS

24. The conferences of bishops may adapt this rite, as required, to the character of each region, but in such a way that nothing of its dignity and solemnity is lost.

However, the following are to be respected:
a. The celebration of the Mass with its proper preface and prayer of dedication must never be omitted.
b. Rites that have a special meaning and force from liturgical tradition (see no. 22) must be retained, unless weighty rea-

[21]Lk 2:32.
[22]See Pope Vigilius, *Epistula ad Profuturum Episcopum* 4: PL 84, 832.
[23]John Chrysostom, *Homilia 20 in 2 Cor.* 3: PG 61, 540.

sons stand in the way, but the wording may be suitably adapted if necessary.

With regard to adaptations, the competent ecclesiastical authority is to consult the Holy See and introduce adaptations with its consent.[24]

ADAPTATIONS WITHIN THE COMPETENCE OF THE MINISTERS

25. It is for the bishop and for those in charge of the celebration of the rite to decide whether to have the depositing of relics of the saints; in so doing, they are to follow what is laid down in no. 11 and they are to take as the decisive consideration the spiritual good of the community and a proper sense of liturgy.

It is for the rector of the church in which the altar is to be dedicated, helped by those who assist him in the pastoral work, to decide and prepare everything concerning the readings, singing, and other pastoral aids to foster the fruitful participation of the people and to ensure a dignified celebration.

PASTORAL PREPARATION

26. The people are to be informed in good time about the dedication of a new altar and they are to be properly prepared to take an active part in the rite. Accordingly, they should be taught what each rite means and how it is carried out. For the purpose of giving this instruction, use may be made of what has been said earlier about the nature and dignity of an altar and the meaning and import of the rites. In this way the people will be imbued with the rightful love that is owed to the altar.

REQUISITES FOR THE DEDICATION OF AN ALTAR

27. For the celebration of the rite the following should be prepared:
—The Roman Missal;
—The Lectionary;

[24]See SC art. 40 [DOL 1 no. 40].

—The Roman Pontifical;
—the cross and the Book of the Gospels to be carried in the procession;
—container with the water to be blessed and sprinkler;
—container with the holy chrism;
—towels for wiping the table of the altar
—if needed, a waxed linen cloth or other waterproof covering of the same size as the altar;
—basin and jug of water, towels, and all that is needed for washing the bishop's hands;
—linen gremial;
—brazier for burning incense or aromatic spices; or grains of incense and small candles to burn on the altar;
—censer, incense boat and spoon;
—chalice, corporal, purificators, and hand towel;
—bread, wine, and water for the celebration of Mass;
—altar cross, unless there is already a cross in the sanctuary, or the cross that is carried in the entrance procession is to be placed near the altar;
—altar cloth, candles, and candlesticks;
—flowers, if opportune.

28. For the Mass of the dedication the vestments are white or of some festive color. The following should be prepared:
—for the bishop: alb, stole, chasuble, miter, pastoral staff, and pallium, if the bishop has the right to wear one;
—for the concelebrating priests: the vestments for concelebrating Mass;
—for the deacons: albs, stoles, and, if opportune, dalmatics;
—for other ministers: albs or other lawfully approved dress.

29. If relics of the saints are to be placed beneath the altar, the following should be prepared:
a. *In the place from which the procession begins:*
—a reliquary containing the relics, placed between flowers and lights. But as circumstances dictate, the reliquary may be placed in a suitable part of the sanctuary before the rite begins;
—for the deacons who will carry the relics to be deposited: albs, red stoles, if the relics are those of a martyr, or white in other cases, and, if available, dalmatics. If the relics are carried by priests, then, in place of dalmatics, chasubles should

be prepared. Relics may also be carried by other ministers, vested in albs or other lawfully approved dress.

b. *In the sanctuary:*
—a small table on which the reliquary is placed during the first part of the dedication rite.

c. *In the sacristy:*
—a sealant or cement to close the cover of the aperture. In addition, a stonemason should be on hand to close the depository of the relics at the proper time.

30. It is fitting to observe the custom of enclosing in the reliquary a parchment on which is recorded the day, month, and year of the dedication of the altar, the name of the bishop who celebrated the rite, the titular of the church, and the names of the martyrs or saints whose relics are deposited beneath the altar.

A record of the dedication is to be drawn up in duplicate and signed by the bishop, the rector of the church, and representatives of the local community; one copy is to be kept in the diocesan archives, the other in the archives of the church.

RITE OF DEDICATION

INTRODUCTORY RITES

ENTRANCE INTO THE CHURCH

31. When the people are assembled, the bishop and the concelebrating priests, the deacons, and the ministers, each in appropriate vestments, preceded by the crossbearer, go from the sacristy through the main body of the church to the sanctuary.

32. If there are relics of the saints to be placed beneath the altar, these are brought in the entrance procession to the sanctuary from the sacristy or the chapel where since the vigil they have been exposed for the veneration of the people. For a just cause, before the celebration begins, the relics may be

placed between lighted torches in a suitable part of the
sanctuary.

33. As the procession proceeds, the entrance antiphon is
sung with Psalm 43.

**O God, our shield, look with favor on the face of your
anointed; one day within your courts is better than a
thousand elsewhere (alleluia).**

Or:

I will go to the altar of God, the God of my joy.

Another appropriate song may be sung.

34. When the procession reaches the sanctuary, the relics of
the saints are placed between lighted torches in a suitable
place. The concelebrating priests, the deacons, and the ministers go to the places assigned to them; the bishop, without
kissing the altar, goes to the chair. Then, putting aside the
pastoral staff and miter, he greets the people, saying:

**The grace and peace of God
be with all of you
in his holy Church.
℟. And also with you.**

Other suitable words taken preferably from sacred Scripture
may be used.

BLESSING AND SPRINKLING OF WATER

35. When the entrance rite is completed, the bishop blesses
water with which to sprinkle the people as a sign of repentance and as a reminder of their baptism, and to purify the
altar. The ministers bring the vessel with the water to the
bishop who stands at the chair. The bishop invites all to pray,
in these or similar words:

**Brothers and sisters in Christ, this is a day of rejoicing:
we have come together to dedicate this altar by offering
the sacrifice of Christ.**

**May we respond to these holy rites, receive God's word
with faith, share at the Lord's table with joy, and raise
our hearts in hope.**

Gathered around this one altar we draw nearer to Christ, the living stone, in whom we become God's holy temple.

But first let us ask God to bless this gift of water. As it is sprinkled upon us and upon this altar, may it be a sign of our repentance and a reminder of our baptism.

All pray in silence for a brief period. The bishop then continues:

God of mercy,
you call every creature to the light of life,
and surround us with such great love
that when we stray
you continually lead us back to Christ our head.

For you have established an inheritance of such mercy,
that those sinners, who pass through water made
sacred,
die with Christ to rise restored
as members of his body
and heirs of his eternal covenant.

Bless ✠ this water;
sanctify it.

As it is sprinkled upon us and upon this altar
make it a sign of the saving waters of baptism,
by which we become one in Christ, the temple of your
Spirit.

May all here today,
and all those in days to come,
who will celebrate your mysteries on this altar,
be united at last in the holy city of your peace.

We ask this in the name of Jesus the Lord.
℟. Amen.

36. When the invocation over the water is finished, the bishop, accompanied by the deacons, passes through the main body of the church, sprinkling the people with the holy water; then, when he has returned to the sanctuary, he sprinkles the altar. Meanwhile the following antiphon is sung.

I saw water flowing from the right side of the temple, alleluia. It brought God's life and his salvation, and the people sang in joyful praise: alleluia, alleluia.

Or, during Lent:
I will pour clean water over you and wash away all your defilement. A new heart will I give you, says the Lord.

Another appropriate song may be sung.

37. After the sprinkling the bishop returns to the chair and, when the singing is finished, standing with hands joined says:

May God, the Father of mercies,
to whom we dedicate this altar on earth,
forgive us our sins
and enable us to offer
an unending sacrifice of praise
on his altar in heaven.
℟. Amen.

HYMN
38. Then the **Gloria** is sung.

OPENING PRAYER
39. When the hymn is finished, the bishop, with hands joined, says:

Let us pray.

All pray in silence for a brief period. Then the bishop, with hands extended, says:

Lord,
you willed that all things be drawn to your Son,
mounted on the altar of the cross.
Bless those who dedicate this altar to your service.

May it be the table of our unity,
a banquet of plenty,
and a source of the Spirit,
in whom we grow daily as your faithful people.

**We ask this through our Lord Jesus Christ, your Son,
who lives and reigns with you and the Holy Spirit,
one God, for ever and ever.
℟. Amen.**

LITURGY OF THE WORD

40. In the liturgy of the word everything takes place in the usual way. The readings and the gospel are taken, in accordance with the rubrics, either from the text in *The Lectionary* (nos. 704 and 706) for the rite of dedication of an altar or from the Mass of the day.

41. After the gospel the bishop gives the homily, in which he explains the biblical readings and the meaning of the rite.

42. The profession of faith is said. The general intercessions are omitted since in their place the litany of the saints is sung.

PRAYER OF DEDICATION AND THE ANOINTINGS

INVITATION TO PRAYER
43. Then all stand, and the bishop, without his miter, invites the people to pray in these or similar words:

**Let our prayers go forth to God the Father through
Jesus Christ, his Son, with whom are joined all the
saints who have shared in his suffering and now sit at
his table of glory.**

Deacon (except on Sundays and during the Easter season):

Let us kneel.

LITANY OF THE SAINTS
44. Then the litany of the saints is sung, with all responding. On Sundays and also during the Easter season, all stand; on other days, all kneel.

45. The cantors begin the litany (Chapter VIII); they add, at the proper place, names of other saints (the titular of the church, the patron saint of the place, and the saints whose relics are to be deposited, if this is to take place) and petitions suitable to the occasion.

46. When the litany is finished, the bishop, standing with hands extended, says:

Lord,
may the prayers of the Blessed Virgin Mary
and of all the saints
make our prayers acceptable to you.

May this altar be the place
where the great mysteries of redemption are accomplished:
a place where your people offer their gifts,
unfold their good intentions,
pour out their prayers,
and echo every meaning of their faith and devotion.

Grant this through Christ our Lord.
℟. Amen.

If it is applicable, the deacon says:

Let us stand.

All rise. The bishop receives the miter.

When there is no depositing of the relics of the saints, the bishop immediately says the prayer of dedication as indicated in no. 48 below.

DEPOSITING OF THE RELICS

47. Then, if relics of the martyrs or other saints are to be placed beneath the altar, the bishop approaches the altar. A deacon or priest brings them to the bishop, who places them in a suitably prepared aperture. Meanwhile one of the following antiphons is sung with Psalm 15.

Saints of God, you have been enthroned at the foot of God's altar; pray for us to the Lord Jesus Christ.

Or:

The bodies of the saints lie buried in peace, but their names will live on for ever (alleluia).

Another appropriate song may be sung.

Meanwhile a stone mason closes the aperture and the bishop returns to the chair.

PRAYER OF DEDICATION

48. Then the bishop, standing without miter at the chair or near the altar, with hands extended, says:

Father,
we praise you and give you thanks,
for you have established the sacrament of true worship
by bringing to perfection in Christ
the mystery of the one true altar
prefigured in those many altars of old.

Noah,
the second father of the human race,
once the waters fell and the mountains peaked again,
built an altar in your name.
You, Lord, were appeased by his fragrant offering
and your rainbow bore witness
to a covenant refounded in love.

Abraham,
our father in faith,
wholeheartedly accepted your word
and constructed an altar on which to slay
Isaac, his only son.
But you, Lord, stayed his hand
and provided a ram for his offering.

Moses,
mediator of the old law,
built an altar
on which was cast the blood of a lamb:
so prefiguring the altar of the cross.

All this Christ has fulfilled in the paschal mystery:
as priest and victim he freely mounted the tree of the
     cross
and gave himself to you, Father, as the one perfect
     oblation.

In his sacrifice the new covenant is sealed,
in his blood sin is engulfed.

Lord, we therefore stand before you in prayer.

Bless this altar built in the house of the Church,
that it may ever be reserved for the sacrifice of Christ,
and stand for ever as the Lord's table,
where your people will find nourishment and strength.

Make this altar a sign of Christ
from whose pierced side flowed blood and water,
which ushered in the sacraments of the Church.

Make it a table of joy,
where the friends of Christ may hasten
to cast upon you their burdens and cares
and take up their journey restored.

Make it a place of communion and peace,
so that those who share the body and blood of your Son
may be filled with his Spirit
and grow in your life of love.

Make it a source of unity and friendship,
where your people may gather as one
to share your spirit of mutual love.

Make it the center of our praise and thanksgiving
until we arrive at the eternal tabernacle,
where, together with Christ,
high priest and living altar,
we will offer you an everlasting sacrifice of praise.

We ask this thorugh our Lord Jesus Christ, your Son,
who lives and reigns with you and the Holy Spirit,
one God, for ever and ever.
℟. Amen.

ANOINTING OF THE ALTAR

49. When the above is finished, the bishop, removing the
chasuble if necessary and putting on a linen gremial, goes to

the altar with the deacon or another minister, one of whom carries the chrism. Standing before the altar, the bishop says:

We now anoint this altar.
May God in his power make it holy,
a visible sign of the mystery of Christ,
who offered himself for the life of the world.

Then he pours chrism on the middle of the altar and on each of its four corners, and it is recommended that he anoint the entire table of the altar with this.

50. During the anointing, outside the Easter Season, the following antiphon is sung (see below, no. 51) with Psalm 45.

God, your God, has anointed you with the oil of gladness.

Another appropriate song may be sung.

51. During the Easter Season the following antiphon is sung with Psalm 118.

The stone which the builders rejected has become the keystone of the building, alleluia.

Another appropriate song may be sung.

52. When the altar has been anointed, the bishop returns to the chair, sits, and washes his hands. Then the bishop takes off the gremial and puts on the chasuble.

INCENSATION OF THE ALTAR

53. After the rite of anointing, a brazier is placed on the altar for burning incense or aromatic gums. The bishop puts incense into the brazier, saying:

Lord,
may our prayer ascend as incense in your sight.
As this building is filled with fragrance
so may your Church fill the world
with the fragrance of Christ.

Then the bishop puts incense into the censer and incenses the altar; he returns to the chair, is incensed, and then sits. A minister incenses the people. Meanwhile one of the following antiphons is sung with Psalm 138.

An angel stood by the altar of the temple, holding a golden censer.

Or:

From the hand of the angel, clouds of incense rose in the presence of the Lord.

Another appropriate song may be sung.

LIGHTING OF THE ALTAR

54. After the incensation, a few ministers wipe the table of the altar with cloths, and, if need be, cover it with a waterproof linen. They then cover the altar with a cloth, and, if opportune, decorate it with flowers. They arrange in a suitable manner the candles needed for the celebration of Mass, and, if need be, the cross.

55. Then the bishop gives to the deacon a lighted candle, and says:

Light of Christ,
shine on this altar
and be reflected by those
who share at this table.

Then the bishop sits. The deacon goes to the altar and lights the candles for the celebration of the eucharist.

56. Then the festive lighting takes place: as a sign of rejoicing all the lamps around the altar are lit. Meanwhile the following antiphon is sung.

In you, O Lord, is the fountain of life; in your light we shall see light.

Another appropriate song may be sung, especially one in honor of Christ, the light of the world.

LITURGY OF THE EUCHARIST

57. The deacons and the ministers prepare the altar in the usual way. Then some of the congregation bring bread, wine, and water for the celebration of the Lord's sacrifice. The bishop receives the gifts at the chair. While the gifts are being brought, one of the following antiphons may be sung.

If you are bringing your gift to the altar, and there you remember that your neighbor has something against you, leave your gift in front of the altar; go at once and make peace with your neighbor, and then come back and offer your gift, alleluia.

Or:
Moses consecrated the altar to the Lord and offered sacrifices and burnt offerings; he made an evening sacrifice of sweet fragrance to the Lord God in the sight of the children of Israel.

Another appropriate song may be sung.

58. When all is ready, the bishop goes to the altar, removes the miter, and kisses the altar. The Mass proceeds in the usual way; however, neither the gifts nor the altar are incensed.

PRAYER OVER THE GIFTS
59. With hands extended, the bishop sings or says:

Lord,
send your Spirit upon this altar
to sanctify these gifts;
may he prepare our hearts
to receive them worthily.

Grant this through Christ our Lord.
℟. Amen.

EUCHARISTIC PRAYER
60. Eucharistic Prayer I or III is said, with the following preface, which is an integral part of the rite of the dedication of an altar:

The Lord be with you
℟. And also with you.

Lift up your hearts.
℟. We lift them up to the Lord.

Let us give thanks to the Lord our God.
℟. It is right to give him thanks and praise.

Father, all-powerful and ever-living God,
we do well always and everywhere to give you thanks
through Jesus Christ our Lord.

True priest and true victim,
he offered himself to you
on the altar of the cross
and commanded us to celebrate
that same sacrifice,
until he comes again.

Therefore your people have built this altar
and have dedicated it to your name
with grateful hearts.

This is truly a sacred place.

Here the sacrifice of Christ is offered in mystery,
perfect praise is given to you,
and our redemption is made continually present.

Here is prepared the Lord's table,
at which your children,
nourished by the body of Christ,
are gathered into a Church, one and holy.

Here your people drink of the Spirit,
the stream of living water,
flowing from the rock of Christ.
They will become, in him,
a worthy offering and a living altar.

We praise you, Lord,
with all the angels and saints in their song of joy:

Holy, holy, holy Lord, God of power and might,
heaven and earth are full of your glory.
  Hosanna in the highest.
Blessed is he who comes in the name of the Lord.
  Hosanna in the highest.

61. While the bishop is receiving the body of Christ the
communion song begins. One of the following antiphons is
sung with Psalm 128.

Even the sparrow finds a home and the swallow a nest
wherein she places her young: near to your altars, O
Lord of Hosts, my King and my God.

Or:

May the children of the Church be like olive branches
around the table of the Lord (alleluia).

Another appropriate song may be sung.

PRAYER AFTER COMMUNION

62. Then, standing at the chair or at the altar, the bishop
sings or says:

Let us pray.

Pause for silent prayer, if this has not preceded.

Lord,
may we always be drawn
to this altar of sacrifice.

United in faith and love,
may we be nourished by the body of Christ
and transformed into his likeness,
who lives and reigns with you and the Holy Spirit,
one God, for ever and ever.
℟. Amen.

BLESSING AND DISMISSAL

63. The bishop receives the miter and says:

The Lord be with you.
℟. And also with you.

Then the deacon, if appropriate, gives the invitation to the
people in these or similar words:

Bow your heads and pray for God's blessing.

Then the bishop extends his hands over the people and
blesses them, saying:

May God, who has given you the dignity
of a royal priesthood,
strengthen you in your holy service
and make you worthy to share in his sacrifice.
℟. Amen.

May he, who invites you to the one table
and feeds you with the one bread,
make you one in heart and mind.
℟. Amen.

May all to whom you proclaim Christ
be drawn to him
by the example of your love.
℟. Amen.

The bishop takes the pastoral staff and continues:

May almighty God bless you,
the Father, and the Son, ✛ and the Holy Spirit.
℟. Amen.

64. Finally the deacon dismisses the people in the usual way.

CHAPTER V

BLESSING OF A CHURCH

INTRODUCTION

1. Since sacred edifices, that is, churches, are permanently set aside for the celebration of the divine mysteries, it is right for them to receive a dedication to God. This is done according to the rite in chapters two and three for dedicating a church, a rite impressive for its striking ceremonies and symbols.

Private oratories, chapels, or other sacred edifices set aside only temporarily for divine worship because of special conditions, more properly receive a blessing, according to the rite described below.

2. As to the structure of the liturgy, the choice of a titular, and the pastoral preparation of the people, what is said in the Introduction to chapter two, nos. 4–5, 7, 20, is to be followed, with the necessary modifications.

A church or an oratory is blessed by the bishop of the diocese or by a priest delegated by him.

3. A church or an oratory may be blessed on any day, apart from the Easter triduum. As far as possible a day should be chosen when the people can be present in large numbers, especially a Sunday, unless pastoral considerations suggest otherwise.

4. On days mentioned in the Table of Liturgical Days, nos. 1–4, the Mass is the Mass of the day; but on other days the Mass is either the Mass of the day or the Mass of the titular of the church or oratory.

5. For the rite of the blessing of a church or an oratory all things needed for the celebration of Mass are prepared. But even though it may have already been blessed or dedicated, the altar should be left bare until the beginning of the liturgy of the eucharist. In a suitable place in the sanctuary the following also should be prepared:

—container of water to be blessed and sprinkler;
—censer, incense boat and spoon;
—The Roman Pontifical;
—altar cross, unless there is already a cross in the sanctuary, or the cross that is carried in the entrance procession is to be placed near the altar;
—altar cloth, candles, candlesticks, and flowers, if opportune.

6. When at the same time as the church is blessed the altar is to be consecrated, all those things should be prepared that are listed in chapter four, no. 27 and no. 29, if relics of the saints are to be deposited beneath the altar.

7. For the Mass of the blessing of a church the vestments are white or of some festive color. The following should be prepared:
—for the bishop: alb, stole, chasuble, miter, pastoral staff;
—for a priest: the vestments for celebrating Mass;
—for the concelebrating priests: the vestments for concelebrating Mass;
—for the deacons: albs, stoles, and dalmatics;
—for other ministers: albs or other lawfully approved dress.

RITE OF BLESSING

INTRODUCTORY RITES

ENTRANCE INTO THE CHURCH

8. When the people are assembled, while the entrance song is being sung, the bishop and the concelebrating priests, the deacons, and the ministers, each in appropriate vestments, preceded by the crossbearer, go from the sacristy through the main body of the church to the sanctuary.

When the procession arrives at the sanctuary, the bishop without kissing or incensing the altar, goes immediately to the chair; the others go to the places assigned to them.

9. The bishop puts aside the pastoral staff and miter, and when the singing is finished, he greets the people, saying:

The grace and peace of God
be with all of you
in his holy Church.
℟. And also with you.

Other suitable words taken preferably from sacred Scripture
may be used.

BLESSING AND SPRINKLING OF WATER

10. Then the bishop blesses water with which to sprinkle the
people as a sign of repentance and as a reminder of their
baptism, and to purify the walls of the new church or oratory.
The ministers bring the vessel with the water to the bishop
who stands at the chair. The bishop invites all to pray, in
these or similar words:

Brothers and sisters in Christ, this is a day of rejoicing.
For we have come together to offer this new church to
God.

We ask that he bless us with his grace and, by his
power, bless this gift of water.

As it is sprinkled upon us and throughout this new
church, may it become a sign of our repentance, a reminder of our baptism, and a symbol of the cleansing
of these walls.

But first let us call to mind that we ourselves, who are
bound here in faith and love, are the living Church, set
in the world, as a sign and witness of God's love for
all.

11. All pray in silence for a brief period. The bishop then
continues:

God of mercy,
you call every creature to the light of life,
and surround us with such great love
that when we stray
you continually lead us back to Christ our head.

For you have established an inheritance of such mercy,
that those sinners, who pass through water made
 sacred,
die with Christ and rise restored
as members of his body
and heirs of his eternal covenant.

Bless ✠ this water;
sanctify it.

As it is sprinkled upon us and throughout this church
make it a sign of the saving waters of baptism,
by which we become one in Christ, the temple of your
 Spirit.

May all here today
and all those in days to come,
who will celebrate your mysteries in this church,
be united at last in the holy city of your peace.

We ask this in the name of Jesus the Lord.
℟. Amen.

12. When the invocation over the water is finished, the
bishop, accompanied by the deacons, passes through the
main body of the church, sprinkling the people and the walls
with the holy water; then, when he has returned to the
sanctuary, he sprinkles the altar, unless it is already blessed
or dedicated (see above, no. 5). Meanwhile the following
antiphon is sung.

I saw water flowing from the right side of the temple,
alleluia. It brought God's life and his salvation, and
the people sang in joyful praise: alleluia, alleluia.

Or, during Lent:
I will pour clean water over you and wash away all
your defilement. A new heart will I give you, says the
Lord.

Another appropriate song may be sung.

13. After the sprinkling the bishop returns to the chair and, when the singing is finished, standing with hands joined, says:

May God, the Father of mercies,
dwell in this house of prayer.
May the grace of the Holy Spirit cleanse us,
for we are the temple of his presence.
℟. **Amen.**

HYMN
14. Then, except on Sundays or weekdays of Advent and Lent, the **Gloria** is sung.

OPENING PRAYER
15. When the hymn is finished, the following prayer is said except on the days listed in the Table of Liturgical Days, nos. 1-4, when the prayer of the day is used. The bishop, with hands joined, says:

Let us pray.

All pray in silence for a brief period. Then the bishop, with hands extended, says:

Lord,
bless this church,
which we have been privileged to build with your
   help.

May all who gather here in faith
to listen to your word
and celebrate your sacraments,
experience the presence of Christ,
who promised to be with those
gathered in his name,
for he lives and reigns with you and the Holy Spirit,
one God, for ever and ever.
℟. **Amen.**

LITURGY OF THE WORD

16. The readings are taken, in accordance with the rubrics (see above no.4), either from the texts in *The Lectionary* (nos. 704 and 706) for the rite of the dedication of a church or from the Mass of the day.

17. Neither lights nor incense are carried at the gospel.

18. After the gospel the bishop gives the homily, in which he explains the biblical readings and the meaning of the rite.

19. The profession of faith and the general intercessions are said in the usual way.

BLESSING OF THE ALTAR

20. Then the bishop goes to bless the altar. Meanwhile the following antiphon is sung.

May the children of the Church be like olive branches around the table of the Lord (alleluia).

Another appropriate song may be sung.

21. When the singing is finished, the bishop, standing without miter, speaks to the people in these or similar words:

Brothers and sisters, our community rejoices as it comes together to bless this altar. Let us ask God to look kindly on the Church's offering placed upon it and to receive his people as an everlasting gift.

All pray in silence for a brief period. Then the bishop, with hands extended, says:

Blessed are you, Lord our God,
who accepted the sacrifice of Christ,
offered on the altar of the cross
for the salvation of the world.

Now with a Father's love,
you call upon your people to celebrate his memory
by coming together at his table.

May this altar,
which we have built for your holy mysteries,
be the center of our praise and thanksgiving.

May it be the table
at which we break the bread which gives us life
and drink the cup which makes us one.

May it be the fountain
of the unfailing waters of salvation.

Here may we draw close to Christ,
the living stone,
and, in him, grow into a holy temple.

Here may our lives of holiness
become a pleasing sacrifice to your glory.
℟. Blessed be God for ever.

The bishop puts incense into some censers and incenses the altar; receiving the miter, he returns to the chair, is incensed, and then sits. Ministers, walking through the church, incense the people and the main body of the church.

22. If the altar is to be dedicated, the profession of faith is said, and the general intercessions are omitted, and what is laid down in Chapter IV, nos. 43-56, is observed.

But if the altar is to be neither blessed nor consecrated (for example, because an altar already blessed or dedicated has been transferred to the new church), after the general intercessions the Mass proceeds as in no. 23 below.

LITURGY OF THE EUCHARIST

23. Ministers cover the altar with a cloth, and, if opportune, decorate it with flowers. They arrange in a suitable manner the candles needed for the celebration of Mass, and, if need be, the cross.

24. When the altar is ready, some of the congregation bring bread, wine, and water for the celebration of the Lord's sacrifice. The bishop receives the gifts at the chair. While the gifts are being brought, one of the following antiphons may be sung.

If you are bringing your gift to the altar, and there you remember that your neighbor has something against you, leave your gift in front of the altar; go at once and make peace with your neighbor, and then come back and offer your gift, alleluia.

Or:
Moses consecrated the altar to the Lord and offered sacrifices and burnt offerings; he made an evening sacrifice of sweet fragrance to the Lord God in the sight of the children of Israel.

Another appropriate song may be sung.

25. When all is ready, the bishop goes to the altar, removes the miter, and kisses the altar. The Mass proceeds in the usual way; however, neither the gifts nor the altar are incensed. But if the altar was not blessed or dedicated in this celebration, the incensation takes place in the usual way.

26. If a chapel of the blessed sacrament is to be inaugurated, when the communion of the congregation is finished, everything takes place as described in Chapter II, nos. 79-82.

BLESSING AND DISMISSAL
27. The bishop receives the miter and says:

The Lord be with you.
℟. And also with you.

Then the deacon, if appropriate, gives the invitation to the people in these or similar words:

Bow your heads and pray for God's blessing.

Then the bishop extends his hands over the people and blesses them, saying:

The Lord of the earth and heaven
has assembled you before him this day
to bless this house of prayer.
May he fill you with the blessings of heaven.
℟. Amen.

God the Father wills that all his children
scattered through the world

become one family in his Son.
May he make you his temple,
the dwelling place of his Holy Spirit.
℞. Amen.

May God free you from every bond of sin,
dwell within you and give you joy.
May you live with him for ever
in the company of all his saints.
℞. Amen.

The bishop takes the pastoral staff and continues:

May almighty God bless you,
the Father, and the Son, ✠ and the Holy Spirit.
℞. Amen.

28. Finally the deacon dismisses the people in the usual way.

CHAPTER VI

BLESSING OF AN ALTAR

INTRODUCTION

1. "A fixed altar is one so constructed that it is attached to the floor so that it cannot be moved; a movable altar can be transferred from place to place."[1]

A fixed altar is to be dedicated according to the rite described in chapter four. A movable altar also deserves religious respect because it is a table set aside solely and permanently for the eucharistic banquet. Consequently, before a movable altar is put to use, if it is not dedicated, it should at least be blessed with the following rite.[2]

2. A movable altar may be constructed of any solid material that the traditions and culture of different regions determine to be suitable for liturgical use.[3]

3. To erect a movable altar what is laid down in the Introduction to chapter four, nos. 6–10, is to be followed, with the necessary modifications. However, it is not permissible to place the relics of saints in the base of a movable altar.

4. It is appropriate that a movable altar be blessed by the bishop of the diocese or by the priest who is rector of the church.

5. A movable altar may be blessed on any day, except Good Friday and Holy Saturday. As far as possible, a day should be chosen when the people can be present in large numbers, especially a Sunday, unless pastoral considerations suggest otherwise.

6. In the rite of blessing a movable altar the Mass is the Mass of the day.

[1]GIRM no. 261 [DOL 208 no. 1651].
[2]See GIRM no. 265 [DOL 208 no. 1655].
[3]See GIRM no. 264 [DOL 208 no. 1654].

7. The altar should be left bare until the beginning of the liturgy of the eucharist. Hence a cross (if need be), an altar cloth, candles, and everything else necessary to prepare the altar should be on hand at a convenient place in the sanctuary.

RITE OF BLESSING

8. During Mass everything takes place in the usual way. When the general intercessions are finished the bishop goes to bless the altar. Meanwhile the following antiphon is sung.

May the children of the Church be like olive branches around the table of the Lord (alleluia).

Another appropriate song may be sung.

9. When the singing is finished, the bishop, standing without miter, speaks to the people in these or similar words:

Brothers and sisters, our community rejoices as it comes together to bless this altar. Let us ask God to look kindly on the Church's offering placed upon it and to receive his people as an everlasting gift.

All pray in silence for a brief period. Then the bishop, with hands extended, says:

Blessed are you, Lord our God,
who accepted the sacrifice of Christ,
offered on the altar of the cross
for the salvation of the world.

Now with a Father's love,
you call your people to celebrate his memory
by coming together at his table.

May this altar,
which we have built for your holy mysteries,
be the center of our praise and thanksgiving.

May it be the table
at which we break the bread which gives us life
and drink the cup which makes us one.

May it be the fountain
of the unfailing waters of salvation.

Here may we draw close to Christ,
the living stone,
and, in him, grow into a holy temple.

Here may our lives of holiness
become a pleasing sacrifice to your glory.
℟. Blessed be God for ever.

10. The bishop then sprinkles the altar with holy water and incenses it. Then he returns to the chair, receives the miter, is incensed, and then sits. A minister incenses the people.

11. Ministers cover the altar with a cloth, and, if opportune, decorate it with flowers; they arrange in a suitable manner the candles needed for the celebration of Mass, and, if need be, the cross.

12. When the altar is ready, some of the congregation bring bread, wine, and water for the celebration of the Lord's sacrifice. The bishop receives the gifts at the chair. While the gifts are being brought, the following antiphon is sung.

If you are bringing your gift to the altar, and there you remember that your neighbor has something against you, leave your gift in front of the altar; go at once and make peace with your neighbor, and then come back and offer your gift, alleluia.

Another appropriate song may be sung

13. When all is ready, the bishop goes to the altar, removes the miter, and kisses the altar. The Mass proceeds in the usual way; however, neither the gifts nor the altar are incensed.

CHAPTER VII

BLESSING OF A CHALICE AND PATEN

INTRODUCTION

1. The chalice and paten for offering, consecrating, and receiving the bread and wine[1] have as their sole and permanent purpose the celebration of the eucharist and are therefore "sacred vessels."

2. The intention to devote these vessels entirely to the celebration of the eucharist is expressed in the presence of the community through a special blessing, which is preferably to be imparted within Mass.

3. Any priest may bless a chalice and paten, provided they have been made in conformity with the norms given in the General Instruction of the Roman Missal nos. 290–295.

4. If only a chalice or only a paten is to be blessed, the text should be modified accordingly.

RITE OF BLESSING WITHIN MASS

5. In the liturgy of the word, apart from the days listed on the Table of Liturgical Days, nos. 1-9, one or two readings may be taken from those given below in nos. 6-8.

6. READINGS FROM SACRED SCRIPTURE
1. 1 Corinthians 10:14-22a (Gr. 10-22)
Our blessing-cup is a communion with the blood of Christ.

2. 1 Corinthians 11:23-26
This cup is the new covenant in my blood.

7. RESPONSORIAL PSALMS
1. Psalm 16:5 and 8, 9-10, 11
℟. (5a) **The Lord is my inheritance and my cup.**

---

[1]See GIRM no. 289 [DOL 208 no. 1679].

2. Psalm 23:1-3a, 3b-4, 5, 6

℟. (5a, d) **You prepared a banquet before me; my cup overflows.**

8. GOSPELS

1. Matthew 20:20-28
You shall indeed drink my cup.

2. Mark 14:12-16, 22-26
This is my body. This is my blood.

9. After the reading of the word of God the homily is given in which the celebrant explains the biblical readings and the meaning of the blessing of a chalice and paten that are used in the celebration of the Lord's Supper.

10. When the general intercessions are finished, ministers or representatives of the community that are presenting the chalice and paten place them on the altar. The celebrant then approaches the altar. Meanwhile the following antiphon is sung.

I will take the cup of salvation and call on the name of the Lord.

Another appropriate song may be sung.

11. When the singing if finished, the celebrant says:

Let us pray.

All pray in silence for a brief period. The celebrant then continues:

**Lord,
with joy we place on your altar
this cup and this paten,
vessels with which we will celebrate
the sacrifice of Christ's new covenant.**

**May they be sanctified,
for in them the body and blood of Christ
will be offered, consecrated, and received.**

**Lord,
when we celebrate Christ's faultless sacrifice on earth,**

may we be renewed in strength
and filled with your Spirit,
until we join with your saints
at your table in heaven.

Glory and honor be yours for ever and ever.
℟. **Blessed be God for ever.**

12. Afterward the ministers place a corporal on the altar.
Some of the congregation bring bread, wine, and water for
the celebration of the Lord's sacrifice. The celebrant puts the
gifts in the newly blessed paten and chalice and offers them
in the usual way. Meanwhile the following antiphon may be
sung with Psalm 116:10-19.

**I will take the cup of salvation and offer a sacrifice of
praise (alleluia).**

Another appropriate song may be sung.

13. When he has said the prayer **Lord God, we ask you to
receive us,** the celebrant may incense the gifts and the altar.

14. If the circumstances of the celebration permit, it is appropriate that the congregation should receive the blood of
Christ from the newly blessed chalice.

RITE OF BLESSING OUTSIDE MASS

15. After the people have assembled, the celebrant, with alb
or surplice and stole, goes to the chair. Meanwhile, an antiphon with Psalm 116:10-19 (see above, no. 12) may be sung
or another appropriate song.

16. The celebrant greets the people saying:

**The grace of our Lord Jesus Christ,
who offered for us his body and blood,
the love of God,
and the fellowship of the Holy Spirit
be with you all.**
℟. **And also with you.**

Other suitable words taken preferably from sacred Scripture may be used.

17. Then the celebrant briefly addresses the people, preparing them to take part in the celebration and explaining to them the meaning of the rite.

18. Afterward one or more texts from sacred Scripture are read, especially from those proposed above, with a suitable intervening responsorial psalm (see above, nos. 6-8) or a period of silence.

19. After the reading of the word of God the homily is given, in which the celebrant explains the biblical readings and the meaning of the blessing of a chalice and paten that are used in the celebration of the Lord's Supper.

20. After the homily the ministers or representatives of the community that are presenting the chalice and paten place them on the altar. The celebrant then approaches the altar. Meanwhile the following antiphon may be sung.

I will take the cup of salvation and call on the name of the Lord.

Another appropriate song may be sung.

21. Then the celebrant says:

Let us pray.

All pray in silence for a brief period. The celebrant then continues:

**Father,
look kindly upon your children,
who have placed on your altar
this cup and this paten.**

**May these vessels be sanctified ✠ by your blessing,
for with them we will celebrate
the sacrifice of Christ's new covenant.**

**And may we who celebrate these mysteries on earth
be renewed in strength**

and filled with your Spirit
until we join with your saints
at your table in heaven.

Glory and honor be yours for ever and ever.
℞. Blessed be God for ever.

22. Afterward the general intercessions take place either in
the usual way or as indicated below:

Let us pray to the Lord Jesus who continuously offers
himself for the Church, as the bread of life and the cup
of salvation. With confidence we make our prayer:
℞. Christ Jesus, bread of heaven, grant us eternal life.

Savior of all, in obedience to the Father's will, you
drank the cup of suffering,
grant that we may share in the mystery of your death
and thus win the promise of eternal life.

Priest of the most high, hidden yet present in the sacrament of the altar,
grant that we may discern by faith what is concealed
from our eyes.

Good shepherd, you give yourself to your disciples as
food and drink,
grant that, fed by this mystery, we may be transformed
into your likeness.

Lamb of God, you commanded your Church to celebrate the paschal mystery under the signs of bread and
wine,
grant that this memorial may be the summit and source
of holiness for all who believe.

Son of God, you wondrously satisfy the hunger and
thirst of all who eat and drink at your table,
grant that through the mystery of the eucharist we may
learn to live your command of love.

Then the celebrant may introduce the Lord's Prayer in these or similar words:

Fastened to the cross, Christ was the way of salvation; in fulfilling the will of the Father he is acclaimed the master of prayer; let his prayer be the source of ours as we say:
All: **Our Father . . .**

The celebrant immediately continues:
Lord,
by the death and resurrection of your Son
you have brought redemption to the entire world.

Continue in us the work of your grace,
so that, ever recalling the mystery of Christ,
we may finally rejoice at your table in heaven.

Grant this through Christ our Lord.
℟. **Amen.**

23. Then the celebrant blesses the people in the usual way and dismisses them saying:

Go in peace.
℟. **Thanks be to God.**

CHAPTER VIII

LITANY OF THE SAINTS

The cantors begin the litany; they add, at the proper place, names of other saints (the titular of the church, the patron saint of the place, and the saints whose relics are to be deposited, if this is to take place) and petitions suitable to the occasion.

Lord, have mercy   Lord, have mercy
Christ, have mercy   Christ, have mercy
Lord, have mercy   Lord, have mercy

Holy Mary, Mother of God   pray for us
Saint Michael   pray for us
Holy angels of God   pray for us
Saint John the Baptist   pray for us
Saint Joseph   pray for us
Saint Peter and Saint Paul   pray for us
Saint Andrew   pray for us
Saint John   pray for us
Saint Mary Magdalene   pray for us
Saint Stephen   pray for us
Saint Ignatius of Antioch   pray for us
Saint Lawrence   pray for us
Saint Perpetua and Saint Felicity   pray for us
Saint Agnes   pray for us
Saint Gregory   pray for us
Saint Augustine   pray for us
Saint Athanasius   pray for us
Saint Basil   pray for us
Saint Martin   pray for us
Saint Benedict   pray for us
Saint Francis and Saint Dominic   pray for us
Saint Francis Xavier   pray for us
Saint John Vianney   pray for us
Saint Catherine   pray for us
Saint Teresa   pray for us
All holy men and women   pray for us

Lord, be merciful Lord, save your people
From all evil Lord, save your people
From every sin Lord, save your people
From everlasting death Lord, save your people
By your coming as man Lord, save your people
By your death and rising to new life Lord, save your
    people
By your gift of the Holy Spirit Lord, save your people

Be merciful to us sinners Lord, hear our prayer
Guide and protect your holy Church
    Lord, hear our prayer
Keep the pope and all the clergy in faithful service
    to your Church Lord, hear our prayer
Bring all peoples together in trust and peace
    Lord, hear our prayer
Strengthen us in your service
    Lord, hear our prayer
Make this church (altar) holy and consecrate it
    to your worship Lord, hear our prayer
Jesus, Son of the living God Lord, hear our prayer
Christ, hear us Christ, hear us
Lord Jesus, hear our prayer Lord Jesus, hear our
    prayer

ORDER OF
CROWNING AN IMAGE OF THE
BLESSED VIRGIN MARY

ORDER OF CROWNING AN IMAGE OF THE BLESSED VIRGIN MARY

Entrance Song (32)
Greeting (33)
Brief Instruction (34)
Opening Prayer (35)

Reading of the Word of God
Readings (36)
Homily (37)

Rite of Crowning
Thanksgiving and Invocation (38)
Crowning (39-40)
Litany (41)

Concluding Rites
Blessing and Dismissal (42)
Antiphon or Song (43)

CONGREGATION FOR THE SACRAMENTS AND DIVINE WORSHIP

Prot. CD 600/81

DECREE

The Church under the guidance of the Holy Spirit honors the Blessed Virgin Mary, in whom the King of Ages took human flesh, as our Lady and our Queen. Out of reverence for her great dignity, one of the signs of honor that has become customary is the placing of a regal crown on images of Mary that are the objects of special veneration by the faithful.

After the new liturgical books had been published, the Congregation for the Sacraments and Divine Worship decided that it was opportune to revise the rite for this crowning, in order that it would be in keeping with the spirit and the norms of the reformed liturgy and would more completely express the meaning and point of the coronation of Marian images.

Pope John Paul II has approved the new *Order of Crowning an Image of the Blessed Virgin Mary* prepared by the Congregation for the Sacraments and Divine Worship and has ordered its issuance.

By mandate of the Pope, therefore, this Congregation now publishes the *Order of Crowning an Image of the Blessed Virgin Mary.* The Latin version of the rite will be in force as soon as it is issued; once the translation have been confirmed by the Apostolic See, the vernacular editions will be in force from the date decreed by the conference of bishops.

All things to the contrary notwithstanding.

Offices of the Congregation for the Sacraments and Divine Worship, 25 March 1981, solemnity of the Annunciation.

James R. Cardinal Knox
Prefect

Virgilio Noe
Adjunct Secretary

INTRODUCTION

1. Holy Mother the Church has on many occasions asserted that it is lawful to venerate images of Christ, his Mother, and the saints and has often instructed the faithful on the proper understanding of such veneration.[1]

2. Coronation is one form of reverence frequently shown to images of the Blessed Virgin Mary. But in the case of images depicting the Mother of God holding her Son in her arms, there is a crowning of both figures: in the rite the crown is placed on the Son's head first, then on the Mother's.

3. Both in the East and in the West the practice of depicting the Blessed Virgin Mary wearing a regal crown came into use in the era of the Council of Ephesus (A.D. 431). Since then Christian artists have often portrayed the glorified Mother of the Lord seated on a throne, dressed in royal robes, and surrounded by a court of angels and saints. In many such images Christ is shown placing a crown on his Mother's head.[2]

4. It is especially from the end of the 16th century that in the West the practice became widespread for the faithful, both religious and laity, to crown images of the Blessed Virgin. The popes not only endorsed this devout custom but "on many occasions, either personally or through bishop-delegates, carried out the coronation of Marian images."[3]

The growth of the custom led to the composition of a special rite for crowning images of Mary, and in the 19th century this was incorporated into the Roman liturgy.[4]

5. By means of this rite the Church proclaims that the Blessed Virgin Mary is rightly regarded and invoked as queen for the following reasons.

She is the Mother of the Son of God, who is the messianic King. Mary is the Mother of Christ, the Word incarnate, in whom "all things were created, in heaven and on earth, visible and invisible, whether thrones or dominations or principalities or authorities."[5] She is the Mother of the Son of David, and of him the angels said in prophecy: "He will be great and will be called the Son of the Most High; and the Lord God will give him the throne of his father David; and he will reign over the house of Jacob for ever; and of his kingdom there will be no end."[6] Thus, filled with the Holy Spirit, Elizabeth greeted Mary, pregnant with Jesus, as "the Mother of my Lord."[7]

She is the chosen companion of the Redeemer. By God's eternal plan, the Blessed Virgin Mary, the new Eve, had an altogether special part in the work of the redemption, by which Christ, the new Adam, redeemed us and made us his own, not with perishable things such as silver and gold, but with his precious blood,[8] and has made us a kingdom to our God.[9]

She is the perfect follower of Christ. The maid of Nazareth consented to God's plan; she journeyed on the pilgrimage of faith; she listened to God's word and kept it in her heart; she remained steadfastly in close union with her Son, all the way to the foot of the cross; she persevered in prayer with the Church. Thus in an eminent way she won the "crown of righteousness,"[10] the "crown of life,"[11] the "crown of glory"[12] that is promised to those who follow Christ. And "upon the completion of her earthly sojourn, she was taken up body and soul into heavenly glory and was exalted by the Lord as Queen of all, in order that she might be more completely conformed to her Son, the Lord of lords and the victor over death."[13]

She is the foremost member of the Church. The handmaid of the Lord, in whom ancient Israel had its culmination and the new people of God its holy beginning,[14] is "the greatest, best, principal, and finest part" of the Church.[15] Because of the singular charge entrusted to her with respect to Christ and the members of his mystical Body and because of her richness in virtue and fullness of grace, she who is blessed among women is preeminent in the Church, this chosen race, this royal priesthood, this holy nation.[16] She is therefore rightly invoked as Queen of angels and of saints, as our Lady and our Queen. The glory of Mary, who is a daughter of Adam and sister to us all, not only does honor to the people of God, but ennobles the entire human family.[17]

6. It is the responsibility of the diocesan bishop, together with the local community, to decide on the opportuneness of crowning an image of the Blessed Virgin Mary. But it should be noted that it is proper to crown only those images to which the faithful come with a confidence in the Mother of the Lord so strong that the images are of great renown and their sites centers of a genu-

ine liturgical cultus and of religious vitality.
For a sufficient period before the celebration of the rite, the faithful should be instructed on its meaning and purely religious nature, so that they will take part in the rite to good effect and with a correct understanding.

7. The crown that will be placed on the image should be fashioned out of material of a kind that will symbolize the singular dignity of Mary. But opulence and lavish display are to be avoided, or any excess in the value and number of jewels in the crown that would ill-suit the soberness of Christian worship or be in shocking contrast with the standard of living of the faithful in the region.

MINISTER OF THE RITE

8. It is fitting that the diocesan bishop carry out the rite; if he is unable to do so, he should entrust this responsibility to another bishop or to a priest, particularly one associated with him in the pastoral care of the faithful in whose church the image to be crowned is venerated.
But if an image is crowned in the name of the pope, the directives of the authorizing papal brief are to be followed.

OCCASION FOR THE CROWNING: THE DAY AND THE LITURGICAL CELEBRATION

9. The rite of crowning is fittingly held on solemnities and feasts of the Blessed Virgin Mary or on other festive days. But the rite is not to be held on the principal solemnities of the Lord or on days having a penitential character.

10. Depending on circumstances, the crowning of an image of the Blessed Virgin Mary may take place within Mass, within the liturgy of the hours at evening prayer, or within a celebration of the word of God suited to the occasion.

REQUISITES

11. In addition to the articles necessary for the liturgical celebration with which the crowning is joined, the following are to be prepared for the rite of crowning itself:
the Order of Crowning an Image of the Blessed Virgin Mary;
Lectionary for Mass;
crown or crowns ready in a convenient place;

container of holy water with a sprinkler;
censer with boat and spoon.

12. The color of the vestments for the rite is white or another festive color, except when a Mass requiring another color is celebrated (see no. 9).
When Mass is celebrated, the following are to be prepared:
for a bishop: alb, stole, chasuble, miter, pastoral staff;
for priests: alb, stole, and, if desired, chasuble;
for deacons: alb, stole, and, if desired, dalmatic;
for the reader and other ministers: alb or other lawfully
approved liturgical vesture.

NOTES

[1] See Council of Nicaea II, A.D. 787: Mansi 13, 378-379. Council of Trent,
sess. 25: Mansi 33, 171-172. Vatican Council II, Constitution on the Liturgy *Sacrosanctum Concilium*, art. 111: AAS 56 (1964) 127; Dogmatic Constitution on the Church *Lumen gentium*, no. 67: AAS 57 (1965) 65-66.
Paul VI, Apostolic Exhortation *Marialis Cultus*, 2 Feb. 1974: *AAS* 66
(1974) 113-168.
[2] See Pius XII, Encyclical *Ad Caeli Reginam*, 11 Oct. 1954: AAS (1954) 632-
633.
[3] Ibid., 633.
[4] The rite, composed in the 17th century and used for the crowning of
images in the name of the Vatican Chapter, was inserted into the *Pon-
tificale Romanun* under the tile *Ritus servandus* in *coronatione imaginis B.
Mariae Virginis.*
[5] Colossians 1:16.
[6] Luke 1:32-33.
[7] Luke 1:41-43.
[8] See 1 Peter 1:18-19.
[9] See Revelation 5:10.
[10] See 2 Timothy 4:8.
[11] See James 1:12; Revelation 2:10.
[12] See 1 Peter 5:4.
[13] Vatican Council II, Dogmatic Constitution on the Church *Lumen Gentium*, no. 59: AAS 57 (1965) 62.
[14] See Gerhoh of Reichersberg, *De gloria et honore Filii hominis* 10, 1: PL
194, 1105.
[15] Paul VI, Address to the conciliar Fathers at the end of the third session of Vatican Council II, 21 Nov. 1964: *AAS* 56 (1964) 1014; see Rupert
of Deutz, *In Apocalypsim commentarium* 7, 12: PL 169, 1043.
[16] See 1 Peter 2:9
[17] See Paul VI, Apostolic Exhortation *Marialis Cultus*, 2 Feb. 1974: AAS
66 (1974) 162-163.

1. CROWNING OF AN IMAGE OF THE BLESSED VIRGIN MARY WITHIN MASS

13. Liturgical norms permitting, it is appropriate to celebrate the Mass of the Queenship of Mary (22 August) or the Mass corresponding to the title represented by the image to be crowned.

LITURGY OF THE WORD

14. In the Mass everything up to and including the gospel reading is done as usual. After the gospel reading, the bishop gives the homily, in which he explains both the biblical readings and the maternal and regal role of the Blessed Virgin Mary in the mystery of the Church.

RITE OF CROWNING

THANKSGIVING AND INVOCATION

15. After the homily, ministers bring to the bishop the crown [crowns] with which the image [images] of [Christ and] Mary is [are] to be crowned. Putting aside the miter, the bishop rises, and, while standing at the chair, says the following prayer. If images of both Christ and Mary are to be crowned, he includes in the prayer the words (printed in brackets) referring to an image of Christ.

Blessed are you, Lord, God of heaven and earth,
for in your mercy and justice
you cast down the mighty and exalt the lowly.
Your marvelous wisdom is shown above all
in the Word made flesh and in his Virgin Mother.
For he, your Son,
who freely humbled himself even unto death on the
cross,
now sits at your right hand and is radiant with unending
glory,
the King of kings and Lord of lords;
and she, the Virgin who wished to be called your
servant,
was singled out to be Mother of the Redeemer and true
Mother of all the living:
now she is exalted above the choirs of angels

and reigns in glory with her Son,
praying for all of us,
the Queen of mercy, pleading for grace.

Merciful Lord, look upon us your servants,
who by crowning this image of the Mother of your Son,
[or: who by crowning this image of Christ and his
    Mother,]
proclaim him as King of all creation
and approach her as our queen.

Give us the grace to follow them in serving you;
to do what love demands
for the sake of our brothers and sisters;
to deny ourselves and spend ourselves,
so as to win our neighbors for you;
to be lowly on earth,
so as to be exalted in heaven
where you reward your faithful servants with a crown
    of life.

We ask this through Christ our Lord.
℟. Amen.

CROWNING

16. After the prayer, the bishop sprinkles the crown [crowns] with holy water and in silence places the crown on the image of Mary. Or, as noted earlier (no. 2), if Mary is depicted with the infant Jesus, the image of the Child is crowned, then the image of his Mother.

17. After the crown [crowns] has [have] been placed on the image [images], the following antiphon or another suitable song is sung. During the singing, the bishop incenses the image [images], then returns to the chair.

Mary, Virgin for ever,
most worthy Queen of the world,
pray for our peace and salvation,
for you are the Mother of Christ,
the Lord and Savior of all. [Easter season: Alleluia]

GENERAL INTERCESSIONS

18. After the singing, the Mass continues with the general intercessions, in the following or a similar formulary.

The bishop first invites those present to pray, saying:

Now let us humbly pray to God our Father, who has done great things for the Blessed Virgin Mary and continues his marvelous works in the Church.

Assisting minister:

For the Church, that in unison with Mary it may proclaim the wonderful works of God and make his mercy known to all the nations, for he casts down the mighty from their thrones and raises up the lowly. Let us pray to the Lord.

R̶. Lord almighty, hear us.

Assisting minister:

For all the peoples of the earth, that under the impulse of the Holy Spirit they may be gathered into the one people of God under the rule of Christ the King. Let us pray to the Lord.

R̶. Lord almighty, hear us.

Assisting minister:

For harmony among nations, that through the prayers of the Queen of peace hatred may be laid to rest, wars ended, and all the earth enjoy prosperity and peace. Let us pray to the Lord.

R̶. Lord almighty, hear us.

Assisting minister:

For those who endure illness, poverty, loneliness, imprisonment, or persecution, that the blessed Virgin, the Queen of mercy, may strengthen and encourage them

with a mother's care.
Let us pray to the Lord.

℞. Lord almighty, hear us.

Assisting minister:
For all here present, that, recognizing the unique dignity
of the blessed Virgin, we may try to imitate her humility
and spirit of service and daily love her more and more.
Let us pray to the Lord.

℞. Lord almighty, hear us.

The bishop concludes the intercessions with the following prayer.
Lord God,
through the prayers of blessed Mary, ever Virgin,
whom you have given us for our mother and queen,
grant that we too may share in the fullness of your grace.

We ask this through Christ our Lord.
℞. Amen.

LITURGY OF THE EUCHARIST
19. After the incensation of the gifts, the altar, and the cross, the
bishop may also incense the image [images]. Then the minister
and the people may be incensed. The Mass continues as usual.

CONCLUDING RITE
ANTIPHON OR SONG
20. After Mass one of the following antiphons or another suitable
song in honor of Mary is sung.
1. Hail, holy Queen, Mother of Mercy,
hail, our life, our sweetness, and our hope.
To you we cry, the children of Eve;
to you we send up our sighs,
mourning and weeping in this land of exile.
Turn, then, most gracious advocate,

your eyes of mercy toward us;
lead us home at last
and show us the blessed fruit of your womb, Jesus:
O clement, O loving, O sweet Virgin Mary.

2. Salve, Regina, mater misericordiae;
vita, dulcedo et spes nostra, salve.
Ad te clamamus, exsules filii Evae.
Ad te suspiramus, gementes et flentes
in hac lacrimarum valle.

Eia ergo, advocata nostra,
illos tuos misericordes oculos
ad nos converte.
Et Iesum, benedictum fructum ventris tui,
nobis post hoc exsilium ostende.
O clemens, O pia, O dulcis Virgo Maria.

3. We turn to you for protection,
holy Mother of God.
Listen to our prayers
and help us in our needs.
Save us from every danger,
glorious and blessed Virgin.

4. Sub tuum praesidium confugimus,
sancta Dei Genetrix;
nostras deprecationes ne despicias in necessitatibus,
sed a periculis cunctis libera nos semper,
Virgo gloriosa et benedicta.

5. Ave, Regina caelorum,
ave, Domina angelorum,
salve, radix, salve, porta,
ex qua mundo lux est orta.

Gaude, Virgo gloriosa,
super omnes speciosa;
vale, O valde decora,
et pro nobis Christum exora.

6. Loving mother of the Redeemer,
gate of heaven, star of the sea,
assist your people who have fallen yet strive to rise
  again.
To the wonderment of nature you bore your Creator,
yet remained a virgin after as before.
You who received Gabriel's joyful greeting,
have pity on us poor sinners.

7. Alma Redemptoris Mater, quae pervia caeli
  porta manes, et stella maris, succurre cadenti,
surgere qui curat, populo: tu quae genuisti,
  natura mirante, tuum sanctum Genitorem,
Virgo prius ac posterius, Gabrielis ab ore
  sumens illud Ave, peccatorum miserere.

8. During the Easter season
Queen of heaven, rejoice, alleluia.
  For Christ, your Son and Son of God,
  has risen as he said, alleluia.
  Pray to God for us, alleluia.

9. During the Easter season
Regina caeli, laetare, alleluia,
  quia quem meruisti portare, alleluia,
resurrexit sicut dixit, alleluia;
  ora pro nobis Deum, alleluia.

2. CROWNING OF AN IMAGE
OF THE BLESSED VIRGIN MARY
WITHIN EVENING PRAYER

21. Liturgical norms permitting, it is appropriate to celebrate evening prayer of the Queenship of Mary (22 August) or evening prayer from the office corresponding to the title represented by the image to be crowned.

BRIEF INSTRUCTION

22. Evening prayer begins in the usual way. After the opening verse, response, and *Glory to the Father,* and before the hymn, the bishop may give a brief instruction to the people for the purpose of preparing them for the rite and explaining its significance. He may do so in the following or similar words.

We have come here at the end of the day to offer our evening sacrifice of praise and also to crown this picture/statue/sculpture of the Virgin Mother of God [the Virgin Mother and her Son].

This ceremony has a lesson to teach us about the Gospel: that the greatest in the kingdom of heaven are those who are foremost in serving and in love.

Our Lord himself came to serve, not to be served; he drew all things to himself when he was lifted up from the earth, and he reigned from the tree by the power of gentleness and love.

And our Lady, whose glory we proclaim today, was the humble servant of the Lord when she was on earth: she gave herself utterly to her Son and his work; with him, and under him, she was an instrument in our redemption.

Now, in the glory of heaven, she is still the God-bearer to Christ's brothers and sisters: she cares about their eternal salvation; she is minister of holiness and queen of love.

PSALMODY

23. After the singing of the hymn, the psalms with their antiphons are sung or recited.

READING

24. Following the psalmody, a longer reading is appropriate, chosen from those given in the Lectionary for Mass for feasts of the Blessed Virgin Mary, but preferably the reading for 22 August (Isaiah 9:1-6).

HOMILY

25. After the reading the bishop gives the homily, in which he explains both the biblical reading and the maternal and regal role of the Blessed Virgin Mary in the mystery of the Church.

RESPONSORY

26. After the reading or after the homily, all may reflect in silence on the word of God. Then the following short responsory or a song with a similar theme is sung.

Cantor:
Holy Mary is Queen of all the world.
She reigns with Christ for ever.

℟. **Holy Mary is Queen of all the world.**
    She reigns with Christ for ever.

Cantor:
She has been assumed into heaven.

℟. **She reigns with Christ for ever.**

Cantor:
Glory to the Father, and to the Son, and to
    the Holy Spirit.

℟. **Holy Mary is Queen of all the world.**
    She reigns with Christ for ever.

RITE OF CROWNING

THANKSGIVING AND INVOCATION

27 After the singing, ministers bring to the bishop the crown [crowns] with which the image [images] of [Christ and] Mary is [are] to be crowned. Putting aside the miter, the bishop rises and, while standing at the chair, says the following prayer. If images of both Christ and Mary are to be crowned, he includes in the prayer the words (printed in brackets) referring to an image of Christ.

Blessed are you, Lord, God of heaven and earth,
for in your mercy and justice
you cast down the mighty and exalt the lowly.
Your marvelous wisdom is shown above all
in the Word made flesh and in his Virgin Mother.
For he, your Son,
who freely humbled himself even unto death on the
cross,
now sits at your right hand and is radiant with unending
glory,
the King of kings and Lord of lords;
and she, the Virgin who wished to be called your
servant,
was singled out to be Mother of the Redeemer
and true Mother of all the living:
now she is exalted above the choirs of angels
and reigns in glory with her Son,
praying for all of us,
the Queen of mercy, pleading for grace.

Merciful Lord, look upon us your servants,
who by crowning this image of the Mother of your Son,
[or: who by crowning this image of Christ and his
Mother,]
proclaim him as King of all creation
and approach her as our queen.

Give us the grace to follow them in serving you;
to do what love demands
for the sake of our brothers and sisters;

to deny ourselves and spend ourselves,
so as to win our neighbors for you;
to be lowly on earth,
so as to be exalted in heaven
where you reward your faithful servants with a crown
of life.

We ask this through Christ our Lord.
℟. Amen.

CROWNING
28. After the prayer, the bishop sprinkles the crown [crowns]
with holy water and in silence places the crown on the image of
Mary. Or, as noted earlier (no. 2), if Mary is depicted with the infant Jesus, the image of the Child is crowned, then the image of
his Mother.

CANTICLE OF MARY
29. After the crown [crowns] has [have] been placed on the
image [images], all stand as the Canticle of Mary with one of the
following antiphons is sung; the antiphon is repeated in the
usual way. During the singing, the bishop first incenses the altar
and cross, then the image [images]. Then the ministers and the
people may be incensed.

Ant.
Blessed are you for your faith in the Lord; you reign for
ever with Christ.
Or:

Ant.
Queen of all mercy and hope of the world, hear your chil-
dren crying to you.
Or:

Ant.
Mother and Virgin and Queen of the world, pray for
your children to God.

Luke 1:46-55

All then make the sign of the cross as the canticle begins.

My soul proclaims the greatness of the Lord,
my spirit rejoices in God my Savior;
for he has looked with favor on his lowly servant.

From this day all generations will call me blessed:
the Almighty has done great things for me,
and holy is his Name.

He has mercy on those who fear him
in every generation.

He has shown the strength of his arm,
he has scattered the proud in their conceit.

He has cast down the mighty from their thrones,
and has lifted up the lowly.

He has filled the hungry with good things,
and the rich he has sent away empty.

He has come to the help of his servant Israel
for he has remembered his promise of mercy,
the promise he made to our fathers,
to Abraham and his children for ever.

Glory to the Father, and to the Son,
and to the Holy Spirit:
as it was in the beginning,
is now, and will be for ever. Amen.

INTERCESSIONS

30. After the canticle, evening prayer continues with the intercessions, in the following formulary or another formulary (no. 18).

My dear people, let us pray to Christ, the King of the universe, who existed before the world was created and in whom all things hold together.

℟. Reign in our hearts, O Lord!

Assisting minister:

Christ, our King, you came into the world to bear witness to the truth. Let all the world acknowledge your truth and your love.

℟. Reign in our hearts, O Lord!

Assisting minister:
Christ, Prince of Peace, foil the talk of war, and stir up thoughts of peace in our hearts.

℟. Reign in our hearts, O Lord!

Assisting minister:
Christ, heir to the universe, gather your inheritance into the holy Church, so that all nations may inherit the kingdom with you.

℟. Reign in our hearts, O Lord!

Assisting minister:
Christ, eternal Judge, when you deliver up your kingdom to God the Father, place us at your right hand and grant that we may possess the kingdom prepared for us before the creation of the world.

℟. Reign in our hearts, O Lord!

Assisting minister:
Christ, Mediator between God and humankind, you made your Mother the Queen of mercy for us. Through her pleading, give strength to the weary, comfort to the afflicted, and pardon to sinners.

℟. Reign in our hearts, O Lord!

Assisting minister:
Christ, Savior of the world, who crowned Mary as Queen of heaven, grant that those who have died may rejoice in your kingdom for ever in the company of the saints.

℟. Reign in our hearts, O Lord!

THE LORD'S PRAYER

In the following or similar words, the bishop then introduces the Lord's Prayer.

And now, as beloved children of God, rejoicing in the glory of the Blessed Virgin Mary and trusting in her prayers, let us humbly approach God the Father in the words that our Savior gave us:

All:

Our Father . . .

CONCLUDING PRAYER

The bishop then immediately says the following prayer, except when the office of the day requires a different one.

God of mercy,
listen to the prayer of your servants
who have honored your handmaid Mary as mother
 and queen.
Grant that by your grace
we may serve you and our neighbor on earth
and be welcomed into your eternal kingdom.

We ask this through Christ our Lord.
℟. Amen.

DISMISSAL

31. The bishop next blesses the people in the usual way and the deacon says the formulary of dismissal. As a conclusion, an antiphon or another suitable song in honor of Mary may be sung (see no. 20).

3. CROWNING OF AN IMAGE OF THE BLESSED VIRGIN MARY WITHIN A CELEBRATION OF THE WORD OF GOD

INTRODUCTORY RITES

ENTRANCE SONG

32. When the people have assembled in the church, the bishop vests in the sacristy or other suitable place, putting on a surplice or alb, pectoral cross, stole, and white cope, or one of another festive color, and taking the miter and pastoral staff. He enters the church during the singing of Psalm 45 or of another suitable song.

If Psalm 45 is used, the cantor sings one of the antiphons and all repeat it; the cantor then sings the stanzas of the psalm and all repeat the antiphon after each stanza.

Ant.
The queen stands beside your throne, in cloth-of-gold and rich brocade.

Or:
Ant.
A great sign appeared in heaven, a woman clothed with the sun, the moon beneath her feet, and crowned with twelve stars.

Psalm 45:2-3, 7-10, 14-18
My heart overflows with noble words.
To the king I must speak the song I have made;
my tongue as nimble as the pen of a scribe.

Ant.
You are the fairest of the children of men
and graciousness is poured upon your lips:
because God has blessed you for evermore.

Ant.
Your throne, O God, shall endure for ever.
A scepter of justice is the scepter of your kingdom.
Your love is for justice; your hatred for evil.

Therefore God, your God, has anointed you
with the oil of gladness above other kings.

Ant.

Your robes are fragrant with aloes and myrrh
and from the ivory palace you are greeted with music.
The daughters of kings are among your loved ones;
on your right hand stands the queen in gold of Ophir.

Ant.

The daughter of the king is clothed with splendor,
her robes embroidered with pearls set in gold.
She is led to the king with her maiden companions.
They are escorted amid gladness and joy;
they pass within the palace of the king.

Ant.

Sons shall be yours in place of your fathers:
you will make them princes over all the earth.
May this song make your name for ever remembered.
May the peoples praise you from age to age.

GREETING

33. When he has reached the altar, the bishop puts aside the
miter and pastoral staff and reverences the altar. Then he goes to
the chair, where after the singing he greets the people in the following or similar words, taken mainly from sacred Scripture.

The grace of our Lord Jesus Christ, who was born of the
blessed Virgin, and the love of God and the fellowship
of the Holy Spirit be with you all.

℟. And also with you.

BRIEF INSTRUCTION

34. Then the bishop may give a brief instruction to the people for
the purpose of preparing them for the rite and explaining its significance. He may do so in the following or similar words.

My dear people, we have come here to crown this pic-
ture/statue/sculpture of the Virgin Mother of God [the
Virgin Mother and her Son]. As we begin this celebra-

tion let us be attentive and listen to the word of God in faith.

This ceremony has a lesson to teach us about the Gospel: that the greatest in the kingdom of heaven are those who are foremost in serving and in love.

Our Lord himself came to serve, not to be served; he drew all things to himself when he was lifted up from the earth, and he reigned from the tree by the power of gentleness and love.

And our Lady, whose glory we proclaim today, was the humble servant of the Lord when she was on earth: she gave herself utterly to her Son and his work; with him, and under him, she was an instrument in our redemption.

Now, in the glory of heaven, she is still the God-bearer to Christ's brothers and sisters: she cares about their eternal salvation; she is minister of holiness and queen of love.

OPENING PRAYER
35. After the brief instruction the bishop says:

Let us pray.

All pray briefly in silence and the bishop continues with the prayer.

**O God,
since you have given us Mary, the Mother of your Son,
to be our mother and our queen,
grant that we, who have come here to crown her image,
may attain the glory of your children in the kingdom
of heaven.**

We ask this through Christ our Lord.
℟. Amen.

READING OF THE WORD OF GOD
READINGS
36. Appropriate texts of sacred Scripture are then read, chosen from those given in the Lectionary for Mass for feasts of the Blessed Virgin Mary, but preferably the readings for 22 August (Isaiah 9:1-6 and Luke 1:26-38). There should be suitable responsorial psalms or intervals of silence between the readings.

The gospel reading always holds the place of honor.

HOMILY
37. After the gospel reading, the bishop gives the homily, in which he explains both the biblical readings and the maternal and regal role of the Blessed Virgin Mary in the mystery of the Church.

RITE OF CROWNING
THANKSGIVING AND INVOCATION
38. After the homily, ministers bring to the bishop the crown [crowns] with which the image [images] of [Christ and] Mary is [are] to be crowned. Putting aside the miter, the bishop rises and, while standing at the chair, says the following prayer. If images of both Christ and Mary are to be crowned, he includes in the prayer the words (printed in brackets) referring to an image of Christ.

**Blessed are you, Lord, God of heaven and earth,
for in your mercy and justice
you cast down the mighty and exalt the lowly.
Your marvelous wisdom is shown above all
in the Word made flesh and in his Virgin Mother.
For he, your Son,
who freely humbled himself even unto death on the
cross,
now sits at your right hand and is radiant with unending
glory,
the King of kings and Lord of lords;
and she, the Virgin who wished to be called your
servant,
was singled out to be Mother of the Redeemer
and true Mother of all the living:**

now she is exalted above the choirs of angels
and reigns in glory with her Son,
praying for all of us,
the Queen of mercy, pleading for grace.

Merciful Lord, look upon us your servants,
who by crowning this image of the Mother of your Son,
[*or:* who by crowning this image of Christ and his
    Mother,]
proclaim him as King of all creation
and approach her as our queen.

Give us the grace to follow them in serving you;
to do what love demands
for the sake of our brothers and sisters;
to deny ourselves and spend ourselves,
so as to win our neighbors for you;
to be lowly on earth,
so as to be exalted in heaven
where you reward your faithful servants with a crown
    of life.

We ask this through Christ our Lord.
℟. Amen.

CROWNING
39. After the prayer, the bishop sprinkles the crown [crowns]
with holy water and in silence places the crown on the image of
Mary. Or, as noted earlier (no. 2), if Mary is depicted with the infant Jesus, the image of the Child is crowned, then the image of
his Mother.

40. After the crown [crowns] has [have] been placed on the
image [images], the following antiphon or another suitable song
is sung. During the singing, the bishop incenses the image [im-
ages], then returns to the chair.

Mary, Virgin for ever,
most worthy Queen of the world,
pray for our peace and salvation,

for you are the Mother of Christ,
the Lord and Savior of all.

[Easter season: **Alleluia**]

LITANY

41. After the crowning either the following Litany of the Blessed
Virgin Mary is sung or there are intercessions, in the formulary
provided in no. 18, no. 30, or in some other suitable formulary.
Lord, have mercy   Lord, have mercy
Christ, have mercy   Christ, have mercy
Lord, have mercy   Lord, have mercy

God our Father in heaven   have mercy on us
God the Son, Redeemer of the world   have mercy on us
God the Holy Spirit   have mercy on us
Holy Trinity, one God

Holy Mary   pray for us
Holy Mother of God   pray for us
Most honored of virgins   pray for us

Chosen daughter of the Father   pray for us
Mother of Christ the King   pray for us
Glory of the Holy Spirit   pray for us

Virgin daughter of Zion   pray for us
Virgin poor and humble   pray for us
Virgin gentle and obedient   pray for us

Handmaid of the Lord   pray for us
Mother of the Lord   pray for us
Helper of the Redeemer   pray for us

Full of grace   pray for us
Fountain of beauty   pray for us
Model of virtue   pray for us

Finest fruit of the redemption   pray for us
Perfect disciple of Christ   pray for us
Untarnished image of the Church   pray for us

Woman transformed pray for us
Woman clothed with the sun pray for us
Woman crowned with stars pray for us

Gentle Lady pray for us
Gracious Lady pray for us
Our Lady pray for us

Joy of Israel pray for us
Splendor of the Church pray for us
Pride of the human race pray for us

Advocate of grace pray for us
Minister of holiness pray for us
Champion of God's people pray for us

Queen of love pray for us
Queen of mercy pray for us
Queen of peace pray for us

Queen of angels pray for us
Queen of patriarchs and prophets pray for us
Queen of apostles and martyrs pray for us
Queen of confessors and virgins pray for us
Queen of all saints pray for us
Queen conceived without original sin pray for us
Queen assumed into heaven pray for us

Queen of all the earth pray for us
Queen of heaven pray for us
Queen of the universe pray for us

Lamb of God, you take away the sins of the world
spare us, O Lord
Lamb of God, you take away the sins of the world
hear us, O Lord
Lamb of God, you take away the sins of the world
have mercy on us

Pray for us, O glorious Mother of the Lord.

℟. That we may become worthy of the promises of Christ.

The bishop concludes the litany with the following prayer:
**God of mercy,
listen to the prayers of your servants
who have honored your handmaid Mary as mother and
queen.
Grant that by your grace
we may serve you and our neighbor on earth
and be welcomed into your eternal kingdom**

**We ask this through Christ our Lord.
℞. Amen.**

CONCLUDING RITES
BLESSING AND DISMISSAL
42. After the litany (or intercessions), the bishop blesses the people in the usual way and the deacon says the following formulary of dismissal.
**Go in the peace of Christ.
℞. Thanks be to God.**

ANTIPHON OR SONG
43. In conclusion, an antiphon or another suitable song in honor of Mary is sung (see no. 20).